AN EMPTY ROOM

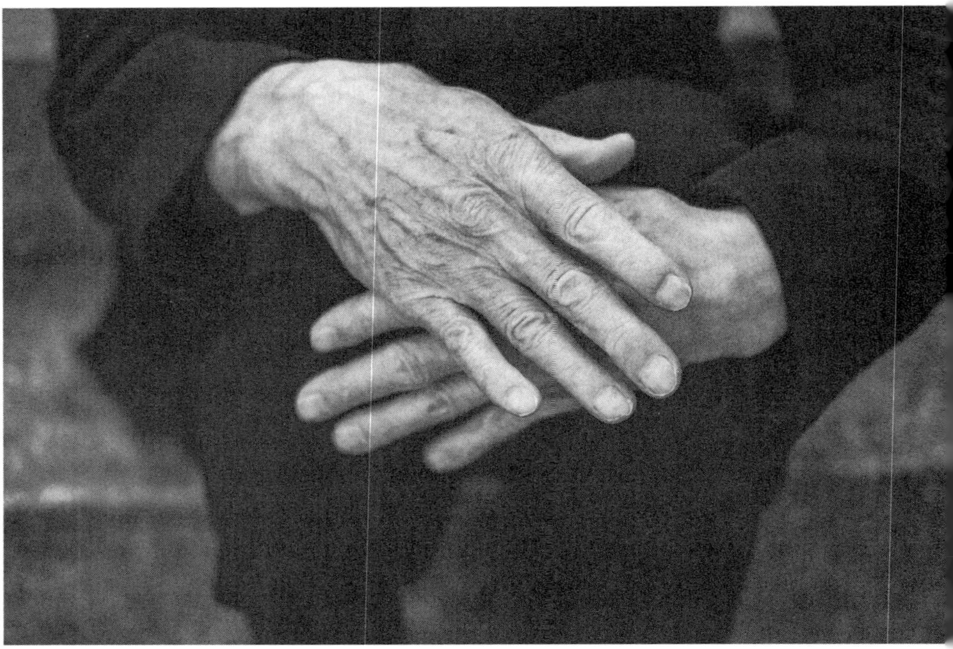

Ohno Yoshito, Yokohama, Japan, 2016.

AN EMPTY ROOM

Imagining Butoh and the Social Body in Crisis

MICHAEL SAKAMOTO

WESLEYAN UNIVERSITY PRESS

Middletown, Connecticut

Wesleyan University Press
Middletown CT 06459
www.wesleyan.edu/wespress

Manufactured in the United States of America
Designed by Richard Hendel
Typeset in Utopia by Rebecca Evans

Library of Congress Cataloging-in-Publication Data

Names: Sakamoto, Michael, 1967– author.

Title: An empty room : imagining Butoh and the social body in crisis / Michael Sakamoto.

Description: First Edition. | Middletown, Connecticut : Wesleyan University Press, 2022. | Includes bibliographical references and index. | Summary: "A creative and intellectual examination of the history, ideas, and practice of butoh performance by an experienced performer, choreographer, photographer, educator, and scholar" — Provided by publisher.

Identifiers: LCCN 2021050844 (print) | LCCN 2021050845 (ebook) | ISBN 9780819580641 (cloth) | ISBN 9780819580665 (eBook)

Subjects: LCSH: Butō.

Classification: LCC GV1783.2.B87 S25 2022 (print) | LCC GV1783.2.B87 (ebook) | DDC 792.80952—dc23/eng/20211206

LC record available at https://lccn.loc.gov/2021050844

LC ebook record available at https://lccn.loc.gov/2021050845

5 4 3 2 1

To my parents,

Tillie and Michael,

for making everything

possible, and Joy,

for lighting my way

every day

CONTENTS

PREFACE

This text began on a whim, in fall 2007 in my first grad school seminar at the University of California–Los Angeles. The class surveyed the performance studies legacy of anthropologist Victor Turner and theatre scholar-artist Richard Schechner, and was taught by Allen ("Al") F. Roberts, also an anthropologist by training, and a protégé of Turner. At age forty, after seven years in the same job, and a breakup from a decade-long relationship, I was ready for change. As a longtime contemporary artist and, especially, butoh dancer returning to school for a Dance MFA, this meant one thing in my mind: no longer defining myself as a butoh dancer, a label to which I'd held steadfastly since beginning my performance career in the 1990s. However, after spending ten weeks unpacking ritual theory, social drama, liminality, and basic forms of resistance against the hegemonic power structures of whiteness inherent in academia and Western culture that Al's lens as an Africanist cultural and religious scholar helped us to hold at arm's length, I realized one thing above all else: I *was* a butoh artist. First lesson: anything you feel the need to go out of your way to deny strongly about yourself is probably true.

Second lesson was a simple human one: follow life. Conscious of our aspirations as future academics, Al would often segue into anecdotes from his own grad training, especially with Turner at the University of Chicago, where Turner's best advice on research methods, institutional politics, and choosing a project you could live with for years on end would often come during late-night group discussions after dinner at his home. Al also taught this way in the classroom, keeping it personal with stories from his own fieldwork as student and professional; mistakes made, assumptions blown, and especially the necessary risks taken and trust earned before true secrets revealed themselves.

This book, then, is a product of that time, when I was forced to admit that butoh, or at least my version of it, would never cease to rule my life. All my artistic, intellectual, and activist work since then has been driven by my passion to work through my understanding of butoh's core vision of everyday life: *chaos*, *contradiction*, and *crisis*. Just as every paper, social media post, or essay is a potential article or book chapter, each of the latter is also the kernel of a possible artistic work. Likewise, each of my performance, visual, and media works has resulted in, or even ended up as, a scholarly text. As I state in the introduction, my art and scholarship are not only inseparable; they are the same thing. This book is an expression of that mindset, an imagining of self as scholar-artist that I hope can serve as a conceptual or strategic resource for other interdisciplinary practitioners working at the intersection of arts, culture, and discourse.

Conversely, what this book is not—but probably what a follow-up project can and should be—is a manifesto and guidebook for action. If butoh is to fulfill its potential as not only a clapback against hegemony, but a philosophy and practice of manifesting liberated modes of being, then projects such as this book are only one step in the long dance to remake this world.

Since beginning this writing many years ago, I have also moved in multiple other directions, digging deeper to complicate my artistic and intellectual practices, and also taking on a few new ones. After the 2016 U.S. presidential election, the ever-increasing struggle against anti-Blackness worldwide, and the military coup in Thailand while I was living there for eight years, I continue the lifelong path of decolonizing my mind-body. My goal is gradually and publicly to examine and dismantle my privilege as a middle-aged, cis-het, Asian American male who has benefited from the spoils of patriarchy and the white-adjacent, model minority trope, while also learning from hard and career-threatening lessons as a tenure-track academic vulnerable to the needs and whims of predominantly white institutional racism. Life happens for an academic and artist of color in the U.S.A., and for that I am both damaged and grateful.

Finally, without knowing what life will be like in American society or internationally by the time this book is published, I write in the midst of dark times. These words pour out of me months after Los Angeles County, my birthplace and home for most of my life, recorded an average 14,000 Covid-19 infections daily during Christmas week, making it the epicenter of the global crisis at the time, and later dwarfed by hundreds of thousands of infections weekly and thousands of deaths daily in India and worldwide. Millions have died from the virus, and despite vaccines that tentatively promise a long, slow climb out of the pandemic, the interpersonal, socioeconomic, political, and environmental consequences of this nightmare remain ever present for the future. Thus, in this historical moment, I offer this book to you with sadness, trust, and hope.

Michael Sakamoto
May 2021

ACKNOWLEDGMENTS

This is my first book. As such, I can only claim ignorance of the process by which it came to realization and express eternal gratitude for those who helped make it possible.

First nod to Suzanna Tamminen, director and editor-in-chief at Wesleyan University Press, without whose immediate and steadfast belief in this project over many years, it might never have been achieved.

Thank you to my graduate student colleagues and faculty in the UCLA Department of World Arts and Cultures/Dance, where this book began as my PhD dissertation. Deep gratitude to my committee members, Donald Cosentino, Peter Sellars, Carol F. Sorgenfrei, and especially my chair, Allen F. Roberts, who tirelessly supported and defended my years-long search to find my own interdisciplinary voice. Everyone contributed priceless ideas around navigating and staking one's claim through one's art and research in the academic minefield, especially plying the muddy quicksand between postmodernism's tendency to objectify and eat other cultural vernaculars for lunch and one's lived subjective truth as an aspirational agent of transformation.

A decade's worth of fieldwork and archival research from dissertation through the final writing phase was supported by many sources, but especially the Asian Cultural Council, UCLA Terasaki Center for Japanese Studies, UCLA International Institute, and the University of Iowa's Center for Asian and Pacific Studies.

For the sake of many in academia who also do cultural and race-based work and weather similar trials, I must also mention the sad reality of certain obstructionist forces at the University of Iowa that actively discounted my research and directly endangered this book's fruition. Therefore, the deepest bow of gratitude to the many colleagues who enthusiastically supported the extra long road with letters of support, feedback, resources, fieldwork and performance opportunities, and just plain camaraderie and morale boosting, including (alphabetically) Eloy Barragan, Jennifer Buckley, Peter Chanthanakone, Ananya Chatterjea, Meiver de la Cruz, George de la Peña, Thomas DeFrantz, Daniel Fine,

Rennie Harris, Kendall Heitzman, Tom Keegan, Christopher Rasheem McMillan, Tlaloc Rivas, Vince Schleitwiler, Morten Schlütter, Hannah Schwadron, Kendra Strand, Chuck Swanson, Darrell Wanzer-Serrano, Deborah Elizabeth Whaley, Jacob Yarrow, and others too numerous to name who lent a kind word, smile, or hug when I needed it.

Special thanks to my original dance teachers, Oguri and Roxanne Steinberg, and my performance mentor-mother, Rachel Rosenthal (rest in power), for taking me to my first butoh performance (Ohno Kazuo!) and then making me a performer. This project was also made possible with help from the numerous colleagues, friends, and interviewees within the butoh, photography, and arts communities and in Japan, especially (alphabetically) Bruce Baird, Tanya Calamoneri, Rosemary Candelario, Yvan Cohen, Hosoe Eikoh, Kawaguchi Takao, Alex Kerr, Jonathan Marshall, Nakajima Natsu, Megan Nicely, Waewdao Sirisook, and the Abe family in Ugo-Machi in Akita Prefecture. Special thanks to founding director Morishita Takashi and current director Ishimoto Kae of the Hijikata Tatsumi Archive at Keio University for support over many visits and years. Very special thanks to Ohno Yoshito sensei (rest in power), with his manager and director of the Dance Archive Network, Mizohata Toshio, for always welcoming me into his home and graciously consenting to the photo session that produced many of the images in this book.

At the risk of being overly sentimental, I also mention teachers from my youth: Mrs. Kulp, Mrs. Connor, Mrs. Hoff, and Mr. Lebow for recognizing and nurturing whatever intelligence and spirit to excel I possessed. A mention as well for Bob Trachinger (rest in power), who, as the first university professor to treat me as a professional, gave me the confidence to excel in "the real world." Each of you will always be my heroes.

Thanks very much. This belongs to all of you.

AN EMPTY ROOM

From the photo essay, "MuNK," Tashiro, Japan, 2016.

INTRODUCTION
(MY) BUTOH

"Ceci l'histoire d'un homme marqué par une image d'adolescence."
— from *blind spot*, Michael Sakamoto (2014), after Chris Marker

"無."

PUNCTUM: FIRST EXPOSURE

Some memories are vague. Others are sharp. This one cuts like a knife.

It happened during my undergraduate years. I don't remember exactly where or when; only that I couldn't stop staring at the photo image searing itself into my mind and body.

Stark contrasts of black, white, and barely grey, as if silver halides were still burning, dancing, in a flash of light in a pitch-black chamber.

Everything situated in a minimal space. On the street? In a room?

A studio.

On the left, a large, organic object. A worm-like or phallic sculpture?

A human body.

To the right, gnarled tree branches stood on end? Large insect legs?

Three arms and fisted hands planted on the ground.

Questions flood my brain. Are these people or creatures? Are they women, men, or aspects of self, knowable and expressible only through the body? When did this strange moment take place? Why did the photographer disembody his models in this way?

More than anything, I ask myself: Is this the kind of art I want to make?

I want to meet the photographer, to know why he took this photo; why he thought it was necessary.

Even more, I want to be one of those bodies . . .

STUDIUM: NOT SEEING

In my early to mid twenties, I repeatedly came upon an image from the photo essay, *Otoko to Onna* (Man and Woman), published in 1961, by Japanese photographer Hosoe Eikoh in collaboration with three dancers, including butoh performance founder Hijikata Tatsumi. Each time, my consciousness was pierced in the same way. My assumptions about the body, rooted in socioeconomic relations dominating American gender roles in the mid-twentieth century, felt challenged. As a young Asian American, based on scant knowledge of my great grandparents' Japanese immigrant generation, my grandparents' conservative second generation, and the modern Japanese television shows airing on UHF channels in the 1970s and 1980s that my family watched regularly, I thought that I understood Japanese people as essentially acquiescent, hardworking, and self-effacing. But rather than showing recognizable identities or whole bodies, Hosoe's image depicted parts akimbo and unruly in stark relief, revealing another Japan, one shot through with confusion, disjuncture, and a blinding *ankoku*—utter darkness. The photo is rough and sensual, a potential threat to the female entity from the male limbs, their arms and fists gazing upon and marching toward her. But the female, with the curves of her coccyx and buttocks aimed at the men's limbs, is facing them down. Everything in tension. The crisis of desire.

> "I'm interested in the human body because it
> has endless possibilities."
> — Hosoe Eikoh (2010)

Here is normally the place in a text where the reader would be shown the photo in question. But just as philosopher and literary critic Roland Barthes, in his classic photo theory book, *Camera Lucida* (1981), refused to show the Winter Garden photo of his mother at age five that haunts every page, so I cannot show Hosoe's image. It would defeat my purpose, subverting the subjective truth of my narrative by pricking each reader differently, giving them their own experience distinct from mine. They would create their own relationship with the image. It would become *their* photo.

Similarly, when Hijikata choreographed dancers through sequences of *butoh-fu*, his choreographic image-words, to stimulate movement, each performer manifested them with subtle differences according to their body's interpretation. Their resulting movement demonstrated the subjective affect dormant within the intersection of each image-word prompt and the performer's mind. Hijikata's dance, rooted in his own idiosyncratic imaginary, was thereby transposed and became their dance. Moreover, when subjectivity in such expression reaches deeper, when the dancer is, in effect, dancing themselves, but filtered by archetypal image-words referencing bodies, elements, and emotions, the performing self becomes other as well. It is here, then, in bodies vulnerable to the amorphous practice we call butoh, that I propose a calling, in the place where lines become blurred between personal space and the world at large, and the instability of the former embodies the turmoil of the latter, and where the rootless quandary of the contact zone among artists and witnesses becomes the agency of change.

MY, NOT "I"

Mass media and digital technology have overwhelmed our daily lives. Well beyond the electronic broadcast saturation and packaged audio-visual experiences proliferating since the late twentieth century, dominant ideologies now constantly invade our bodies through cultural and socioeconomic dependence on personal computers, the internet, and especially mobile devices and social media. The media-saturated, service-oriented, commodified body consumes its virtual self. We are eating our selves alive.

For these reasons, I believe that butoh performance is, in many ways, an attempt to save lives. It is a legislative bill put forward in a congress of mind, body, and spirit. It is a call to arms against our selves, the ones that we are not. What is the generative potential of butoh, a cluster of dance and performance practices that began as radical over six decades ago in Japan, but are now common enough to be stereotyped and cliché in the international art world? The first generation of butoh artists responded to the historical moment and place of post-World War Two Japan. How might artists influenced by butoh's subsequent global diaspora, however, generate strategies appropriate for social urgencies in the twenty-first century, to imagine newly radicalized and expanded butoh-based practices?[1]

I look to the conceptual roots of Hijikata's early experiments, the philosophical core of what we now label *butoh*. Tracing corporeal-intellectual subtexts from the late 1950s through the 1970s, I see *crisis* as a core concept on which butoh was formed and its lineage of practices continue to evolve. I ask how we may employ elements from butoh's range of foundational concepts, forms, and techniques to devise a method for maintaining not merely an avant-garde practice, but the power of cultural transformation over time and in multiple contexts. Hijikata propagated the idea that the body possesses inherent knowledge of its own psycho-physiological needs and innate mechanisms for escaping, negotiating, and reimagining adverse life conditions. He also situated the ambivalence of Japanese postwar identity between a late capitalist Western body and a premodern Japanese body. Hijikata expressed both in relation to social imaginaries, at first inspired by routinized materialistic behavior in the oppressive urban environment of postwar Tokyo, and in later years, exaggerated tales of his childhood in the Tohoku region of northern Japan. Decades and hundreds of butoh artists later, I posit this framework as paradigmatic, a method of activating what Hijikata called *the body in crisis*. This instrument rooted butoh in oppositional binaries, dialogic and dialectic frameworks to address and transform psycho-physical and psycho-social crisis.

My project is thus a speculative approach to butoh practice and discourse. I theorize on how to witness simultaneously beautiful and harsh aspects of one's reality and make of this understanding what is sociopolitically possible. Butoh dancers counter the surface-level positivism of images by attempting to become radical enigmas and force viewers to witness the rebirth of embodied agency in every expiration of meaning.

DESIRING DEATH, WRITING MY SELVES

When an avant-garde practice moves past innovation to convention, iconic figures often appear that symbolize its validity and ossify its authority. What is not always obvious, however, are the motivations, instigations, and avenues through which this journey occurs. These elements often remain obscure until the moment of innovation's occurrence, which is the selfsame as its passing. The figure's realization is also its death.

Hijikata was such a figure, deriving innovation from the detritus of marginalized identities left behind by the status quo, transitioning from late modern to early postmodern, and always in danger of settling into an orthodoxy of his own creation. He often approached the immolation of his own circular thinking about art-life-death, an incessant becoming of his personally imagined *ankoku*, a pitch-black well of being and nothingness from and into which any and all manner of selves arose and subsided.[2] In his mid-career essay, "From Being Jealous of a Dog's Vein" (1969), for example, he expresses a desire for closeness with death: "I cherish wet animals and the bodies of the old, withered like dead trees, precisely because I believe that through them I may be able to come close to my desire. My body longs to be cut into pieces and to hide itself somewhere cold" (2000, 56).

I take inspiration for this book from Hijikata's panoply of figurative deaths, which generated a broad lexicon of images, gestures, and identities to present, in a Barthesian, *punctum*-like mode, a cosmology rooted in life's challenges and eventual demise.[3] I am provoked also by the knife edge of certain post-structuralist poetics, such as in Jacques Derrida's eulogistic essay, "The Deaths of Roland Barthes" (1981). The author speaks of Barthes as having already attained death, even in life, through the fact of his name:

> While so many codes and rites work to take away this privilege, because it is so terrifying, the proper name alone and by itself forcefully declares the unique disappearance of the unique—I mean the singularity of an unqualifiable death. . . . Death inscribes itself right in the name, but so as immediately to disperse itself there, so as to insinuate a strange syntax—in the name of only one to answer (as) many. (2001, 34)

Derrida speaks of death as final, incomplete, and unknowable until it is upon us, and yet eternally with us in the myriad ways in which we exist, feel, and act. He demonstrates this proliferation in a typically Barthesian manner, crafting his essay as a succession of short texts, each incomplete and dependent on the others. Derrida's text is akin also to one of Barthes's key topics, the "unary photograph," replete with both the definitive objectivity of *studium* and the prickly, evocative, and unknowable subjectivity of *punctum*. Derrida's essay is fragmentary and incomplete in order that subject and reader may complete it, making it both death and possibility for life. Each incomplete statement, by writ of its *desire* for the other, is also a plea, a writhing, butoh-like grasp, begging the question of death's inevitability and the generative potential of the renewal that necessarily follows it.

Written with a similar goal, each chapter herein is one of many possible means of continuing what I believe Hijikata started, a modus operandi of dancing through the inexorability of life and death. I am inspired by Derrida witnessing rebirth in every expiration and failure of word and image, and especially Barthes's countering of *studium*, the positivist social desire to definitively know the immanent qualities underlying an image via its apparent surface details, with *punctum*, the radical enigma inherent in every viewer's perception. Likewise, I gesture unsteadily toward a tangled web of action and reflection, not the least reason for which is my intercultural identity: born to parents of Japanese and Chinese ethnicity; adopted by a Japanese American family; consistently read in American society as simply "Asian" or "Asian-American";[4] Western postmodern in artistic foundation, but rooted in an exotified, premodern-styled, Japanese dance vernacular choreographed through a social justice lens. As a butoh-based scholar-artist of unstable identity, I make sense in the way that historian Robin D. G. Kelley attributes his intellectual patience to his mother raising her children as Hegelians, teaching that "the purpose of critique is dialectical, to reach a higher synthesis, which in turn reveals new contradictions demanding new critique" (2017). As a practice that has always involved diving headlong into contradictions, butoh demands perpetual reimagining.

Given butoh's customary engagement with personal narrative, this project also demands my cyclical re-envisioning of self at each step. I take my experience of butoh—encountering a photobook in 1991, attending my first performance in 1993, student training from the mid to late 1990s, and developing an intercultural and interdisciplinary artistic practice since then—as central metaphors of my understanding. Throughout this book, I refer to these and other encounters and reflections, checking in with my past, present, and future selves; my thinking body, dancing mind, and living spirit; or, as I refer to it in the title to this introduction, *(my) butoh.*

My aim is an implicit resolution, as much through juxtaposition as integration. My voice tells its own story and makes confessions about positionality, truth, and lies. My epistemology embraces the paradox of equating authority and subjectivity with fiction and truth. The latter binary feeds my expressive mode of subjecting one's being to being one's subject. Thus, I charge my auto-ethnographic self, not as an objective participant-observer, nor a primarily intellectual artist-scholar, but rather as a nonbinary and expressive *observer-participant* and *scholar-artist.*

Moreover, this book is a performative-literary expression of self. Language is my dance as much as dance is my language, both inextricably entwined within my liminally ambivalent, Japanese American identity, making my writing indeterminate and precarious in a mode akin to African American literature as described by cultural scholar Vince Schleitwiler, "wherein the task of learning how to read is always problematized, critical, and unfinished, never reducible to formal processes of education. It troubles the privileging of either print or oral media, the visual or the aural; it is associated with mobility, as both dislocation and flight; it signifies both the possibility of freedom and the threat of its foreclosure" (2017, 4). Schleitwiler asserts that such literary texts are activated in the present, and we must learn to undertake their "historical and theoretical preparations so that their unpredictable agency might be called forth in the process of reading" (4).

In attempting such a mission, this book functions similarly to butoh, a reflexive expression that questions its own transnationally prescribed premises, redolent with competing value structures and tropes of power: Japanese and American, Asian and Western, imperialist and postcolonial. I gesture toward strategies of vulnerability, difference, and imagination as ends in themselves, inspired by such seminal butoh works as *Kinjiki* (1959), *Kamaitachi* (1968), *Hijikata Tatsumi to Nihonjin: Nikutai no Hanran* (1968), and others that laid the ground for future butohs to come. I am also inspired by auto-ethnography, wherein, as James Clifford describes, "objects and epistemological grounds are now appearing as constructs, achieved fictions, containing and domesticating heteroglossia" (1988, 95). While not purposely telling lies about my story, I hope that my heteroglossia of data achieves the persuasive sensitivity of good fiction in its ability to depict the often startling and transformative ambiguity of butoh practice. Or as Clifford states, "If this ethnographic self-fashioning presupposes lies of omission and of rhetoric, it also makes possible the telling of powerful truths" (112). Or, as scholar Bruce Baird notes in his critical biography of Hijikata, "As he progressed, he was to take more and more seriously the idea of self-fashioning, communicating with different types of people, and being instantly at home in many worlds" (2012, 73).

The butoh community underscores this point. Butoh means many things to many practitioners, begging the question of why one should even use the word. Dancer Oguri asserts that butoh was less a concrete art form than an artistic movement that essentially ended decades ago after Hijikata's passing (2010). Butoh artist Katsura Kan says butoh is whatever you need it to be to move your practice forward (2009). Ishimoto Kae, a longtime butoh dancer and director of the Hijikata Tatsumi Archive at Keio University since 2020, advocates for multiple lineages of butoh across the globe in the modern era. My only definite answer is to say that I cannot escape it. Even when I see performers whom I feel are lacking in expressive talent, depth, or rigor, I often still sense an ineffable quality of energy or gravity that binds them to my sense of life. When I see photos of Hijikata, my mind immediately questions and expands. When I see images of Ohno Kazuo—Hijikata's own dance inspiration and a prime force throughout the first half century of butoh until his death at 103 years—I want to grow old, know pain, and feel love. When I spend time with butoh artist colleagues, I feel as much myself with them as in my hometown.

My reflexive writing is, simply put, a manifestation of my butoh. Since the late 1990s, when I began creating original performances, my work has been presented in fifteen countries in main stages, festivals, alternative spaces, museums, galleries, and natural sites. I have spent over a quarter century deeply invested as an actor in the narrative that I examine. I am also devoted to questioning my artistic lineage, thus addressing my multiple identities and positions through a multilateral voice. In short, my scholarship is also my art.

IT IS WHAT IT IS

The fact remains that butoh as a term has stuck to an ever-widening lineage of movement practices, ranging from Hijikata and his cohorts to other Japanese and international dancers. As Morishita Takashi, Hijikata's former producer and the founding director of the Hijikata Tatsumi Archive, states: "Today's Butoh is diverse, and we are barely able to determine coordinate axes or a frame of reference on which to distribute it. Butoh itself has proliferated beyond logic. In these circumstances, the likelihood that Hijikata's Butoh has been faithfully passed on is close to nil" (2015, 8).

Butoh has also circulated in the presenting venues and intellectual discourses of Western postmodern and contemporary performance since the 1970s, when Japanese artists began performing in Europe and the United States, to the present day, when butoh (or, at least, a butoh-inspired aesthetic) is appropriated and referenced by artists, critics, and audiences globally. Just like jazz and modern dance transformed through numerous and sundry forms, butoh as a broader spectrum than its original impetus happened, and it continues to become whatever it can or needs to be within artistic, social, or geographic contexts, creating a potent brew of communal mythology and heated debate. From micro-gestural improvisation that comes and goes like a barely witnessed flash flood, to pale, commodified tableaux vivants designed as epic spectacles, butoh is all over the map.

This ambiguity has produced a continuous subtext of confusion and debate within butoh's global community. Discussions proliferate over whether certain performances of precisely set choreography or improvisational movement are more butoh than the other, how authentic a disciple is within a lineage depending on exactly when and how much time they spent with Hijikata Tatsumi, Ohno Kazuo, Ashikawa Yoko, Maro Akaji, or other older-generation artists, or even if certain otherwise venerated dancers should be accorded the butoh imprimatur at all.[5] I have witnessed conversations wherein one artist tarred another (including myself!)[6] with the scent of inauthenticity because the latter either only learned under someone adjacent to the commonly accepted pantheon of core lineage artists, worked with Hijikata for only a short period, or stylistically veered far afield of certain traditionalist aesthetic tropes. Such quandaries and arguments may be engrossing in the context of a panel discussion at a Euro-American festival or academic conference, or a late night, post-performance gathering at a Tokyo bar, but I'm not certain how much they actually move the practice forward.

Butoh's foundational artists were operating, if anything, in their historical moment and in the manner befitting their individual abilities, stories, and needs. I believe that we must keep the broader narrative in perspective if we are going to develop and uphold a functional standard that can keep the butoh community vibrant and relevant. Butoh artist Murobushi Ko states, "I think butoh is closer to a philosophy. Philosophy thinks about what art is, and butoh is very influenced by European thought about art. Each butoh artist has their own aspect or opinion or position" (2012).

As butoh artist Tamano Hiroko responds when asked what butoh is,

"Who are you?" this book is a dance in the mirror to delve painstakingly through that reflected image as a communal by-product of my experience and that of select other artists, and ask, "Who am I *now*?" I address this question via permutations that, while limited by my subjectivity, are also made possible by it. In light of the many creative and intellectual practitioners active in the growing field of butoh studies, I defer to others who are better equipped than I to parse through the vast sea of esoteric criteria around form, technique, history, culture, and identity. It is also beyond the scope of this project to begin adequately recognizing the long-undervalued histories of, and still growing efforts to make space for, the global spectrum of female, queer, racialized, and disabled bodies in butoh, and to theorize their futures, let alone the culturalized, nationalist, and misogynist tendencies embedded in much of butoh's legacy.[7] This book is also not intended as a primer on butoh practice, nor am I trying necessarily to prove what butoh has been, is, or should be. While I make efforts to be clear regarding my sources, to frame my subjects' and informants' words with respect, my research and decades-long artistic practice are also simply jumping-off points around a very particular idea of butoh that is both completely personal and endemically social. In a sense, I don't care what butoh is. My concern is that in this age of increasing mediatization of everyday life and globalized, socioeconomic stratification, we as hybrid artists and scholars continue to speak from the idiosyncratic truth of lived practices and examine their potential for more complex, penetrating, and discerning communication. What matters to me are the particular forces that led to butoh's inception and initial phase, how and why butoh developed along certain principles and routes, and how it might expand in the future as a mode of transdisciplinary dialogue between individuals and society. Thus, this "it" is what I hope to reveal and even, if necessary, invent.

With this approach in mind, my intellectual definition of butoh for the purposes of this book is practical, philosophical, and theoretical: *a process of subjectively engaging, embodying, and expressing chaos, contradiction, and crisis for the purpose of psycho-physiological and/or psycho-social awareness and transformation.* This is my own definition and not one that I have otherwise read or encountered. It is designed to encompass key aspects of butoh's myriad histories, practices, and values and initiate the direction of this book. The chapters herein theorize ways to comprehend, devise, and employ new and imagined bodies in crisis. Chapter 1 lays out elements of post-World War Two Japanese art and culture from which butoh arose and drew inspiration. In chapter 2, I draw on butoh's relationship with photography to reveal butoh as a recursive sociopolitical practice rooted in subjectively imagined embodiments and structured by a particularly sensual and mysterious body/image dialectic. Chapter 3 begins the work of reimagining butoh by reframing its principles beyond the confines of its historical roots and into broader discourses, laying out the core concepts of a theory I call *an empty room*. Chapters 4, 5, and 6 explore three primary elements of my theory: *desire, trickster*, and the *cultural commons*. These concepts act as touchstones and filters through which my futurizing images of butoh contact, converge, and integrate in order to move forward.

I conclude chapter 6 and the book with a critical examination of my collaborative performance, *Soil*, as a case study in imagining an application of this butoh-based theory. In this work, my collaborators and I attempted autobiographical, idiosyncratic embodiments of the cultural commons as well as *democracy* and *sustainability* in the sense, not of normative notions of majoritarian statist rule or reification of a moralizing status quo, but of multiple mutating subject positions navigating the rough seas of neoliberal globality, the early Cold War-era roots of which Hijikata and his brethren resisted. With a civic agenda for individual and collective empowerment, a butoh-based performance theory may inspire and embody strategies to address desire, potentialize being, and activate communal space and a multiplicitous social dialogue.

I argue that butoh practice may elicit, maintain, and nourish multiplicity within one's self, and thereby enable other individuals to attempt the same. I view butoh as a subjectivizing technology in resistance not only to late capitalism's corporatist lifestyle, but to any form of statist or authoritarian control. As José Esteban Muñoz describes, "The state understands the need to keep us from knowing ourselves, knowing our masses. It is ready, at the drop of the proverbial dime, to transform public transportation into policing machines, to call out thousands of cops to match thousands of activists, to wield clubs and fists" (2009, 64). In order to withstand such measures, butoh artists allow for ambiguity, illogic, and absurdity, resisting the conventional image machine of neoliberal globality with the type of customized, subject-forming, "slow learning" advocated by Gayatri Chakravorty Spivak, what she refers to as "cooking the soul" (2012). To cultivate relevance to a larger community of artists, butoh must surpass itself in order to be itself. Sooner or later, even the most iconic and accomplished of butoh artists and teachers must be transcended, with their model of multiplicitous and communal being inspiring new and unforeseen manifestations of intersectional, rhizomatic bodies in their own right. In short, I see butoh as a practice of resistant imagining dedicated to memory, power, and difference. Through translocal, transcultural, and transnational personal narratives, butoh artists imagine worlds beyond resolution that they can embody or in which they desire to live.

I should also state that I do not necessarily anticipate succeeding in my goal. I cannot say with certainty that manifesting a more democratic or sustainable body through butoh practice is achievable. If we think of such bodies as ideal states of being, they become contradictions in terms. If we approach them, however, as permutations of an ever-manifesting process tumbling through disparate, dialogic permutations, as butoh practice has always been, then there is an opportunity for activating butoh's generative nature. I view butoh in much the same way that Muñoz posits queerness as a nonexistent yet futurizing and utopic ideality, "a structuring and educated mode of desiring that allows us to see and feel beyond the quagmire of the present" (1). For me, butoh is a bodily utopia rooted in and made possible by irresolution. Butoh is a contradiction. It is the fact that it can never be. The butoh practitioner wields the outward manifestation of myriad identities and identifications; that which they desire but cannot be all at once. Performing butoh is expressing the fact that one's multitudes may never exist as a whole, yet this is what we each can and must do.

Moreover, the practical driving force of my project is a performance of my thesis based in the belief that one can only answer this inquiry through embodiment—to do in principle what other butoh artists have done before and what many artists have stated to me over the years: namely, *find your own butoh.*

Or, as I once witnessed Zen teacher Paul Genki Kahn advise to someone anxious to know how to resolve suffering, negativity, evil, and attachment, "Become the thing itself" (2007).

From the photo essay, "MuNK," Tashiro, Japan, 2016.

1 : DEVELOPING A PRACTICE

PUNCTUM: AN IMAGE IN CRISIS

Fall 1991. Kinokuniya Bookstore, Downtown Los Angeles.

All I can think is that this man is in pain. There's a large book in my hands with a cover photo that I don't understand. An old Japanese man holds a flower, twisted and bent, petals shriveled. His arms and hands curl inward to his concave chest. One shoulder droops low, withering. Twisted, asymmetrical, chaotic, his body struggles to stay upright. White makeup covers him in patches, as if lived in too long. Bright red lipstick and yellowed teeth, mouth half-open but somehow feeling agape, as if he has something to say, but without a sound, the words instead oozing, bleeding through all his pores.

On his eyelids, smears of sky blue, desperate for attention; rooted, not in attraction, but pity; a long-lost desire to be someone's queen for a day, or an hour, a minute even. An inexorable slide into decay.

And those eyes. Surrounded by thick, messy, black streaks trailing to the side, hopeful and despairing. He stares upward, longing, resigned, saintly.

It's obvious. He's dying. You're not supposed to watch this kind of thing happening. I can't keep my eyes off of him. People in the store are beginning to stare at me staring at this book.

I've never seen anything so beautiful.

That's what I felt then. Now, decades later, looking at the cover of the book, *Butoh: Dance of the Dark Soul* (1987), by photographer Ethan Hoffman and critic Mark Holborn, I notice how staged this photo is. The curve of the flower petals perfectly matching the arc of the lips, the fall of the hair, and the center point in the frame. No obvious tension in the large hands. The dancer's static pose in perfect focus seems tailored and held for the camera.

There is still, however, that expression.

Ohno Kazuo sees something. Heaven or God, perhaps, since he is a devout Christian, opening wide to take in the breath of angels. Or maybe a ghost, a lost or kindred soul that fills him with childlike awe and aged exhaustion. I still feel a visceral, potentialized space opening up every time I see this photo. Ohno seems intimidated and anxious for what comes next, engendering a sense of betweenness.

I may, however, be imposing my own predilections upon the image. In considering whether a photo is acting upon me or vice versa, I recall the competing desires among the first photographers in history, either to observe reality passively or actively to depict it. What many people assume is a conscious choice made by every photographer is, in fact, an existential question that has vexed artists and scholars to this day.

This passive/active binary is at the core of Roland Barthes's final book, *Camera Lucida* (1981), in which he describes the act of viewing photos through the binary of *studium* and *punctum*. He defines studium as the impression of a photo's generalizable qualities, the collective references within its place and time, and its cultural, political, aesthetic, scientific, or otherwise objective facts. Moreover, because studium is external, it impresses, even imposes, itself upon us: "The Photograph is violent . . . because on each occasion *it fills the sight by force*, and because in it nothing can be refused or transformed" (91). Conversely, arriving ambiguously within our being as a "wound," "prick," "little hole," or "cast of the dice," a photograph's punctum arises from imagination:

> Nothing surprising, then, if sometimes, despite its clarity, the *punctum* should be revealed only after the fact, when the photograph is no longer in front of me and I think back on it. I may know

> better a photograph I remember than a photograph I am looking at, as if direct vision oriented its language wrongly, engaging it in an effort of description which will always miss its point of effect, the *punctum*. (53)

The punctum effect incites desires, anxieties, or other emotions both to destabilize and inure memories, making every instance of punctum not only idiosyncratic and subjective, but potentially lasting. In *The Poetics of Space* (1958), Gaston Bachelard speaks of the power of such an effect—of poetry on psycho-physiological consciousness—to the point that it alters one's lifelong perception of an image: "Great images have both a history and a prehistory; they are always a blend of memory and legend, with the result that we never experience an image directly. Indeed, every great image has an unfathomable oneiric depth to which the personal past adds special color" (1994, 33). Bachelard contends that dream-like images are unfathomable because, like punctum, they are unanswerable, a fact rooted in their purely internal logic and potential for particularity: "When I receive a new poetic image, I experience its quality of inter-subjectivity. I know that I am going to repeat it in order to communicate my enthusiasm. When considered in transmission from one soul to another, it becomes evident that a poetic image eludes causality" (xxiv).

While *Camera Lucida* meditates on photography's meaning and function, the book is ultimately driven by Barthes's relentless mourning around the death of his mother, with whom he had lived most of his life. His text is an intricately reasoned yet deeply sorrowful exploration of subjective truth as a way to deal with the shock of objective reality. Similarly, the prevalence of subjective expressive forms in the post-World War Two Japanese avant-garde were largely a response to authoritarian conditions imposed under the American occupation and then the new Japanese government and oligarchs, which constituted much of the strange brew in which butoh developed. Much like many post-bebop jazz artists in the same era, the first butoh artists felt that they had a voice to reclaim and a struggle worth fighting. Like so many postwar societies reshaped by the Allied victors, theirs was an ambivalent liberty redolent with racial hierarchies undergirding capitalist superstructures of upwardly mobile consumerism. In the midst of Japan's rapid Westernization, butoh artists reimagined and retooled the performing body and the contested Japanese identity that it represented. Hijikata Tatsumi, butoh's creator and primary driving force in its formative decades, explored an imagined, premodern Japanese past, excavating the image of a broken, dying, nativist body as a myth with utility specific to the conditions of Japanese neocolonial subjects in the Cold War era.

Kinjiki (Forbidden Colors) was the first explicit step in this journey. Hijikata's sexually violent dance duet with Ohno Yoshito, the twenty-one-year-old son of butoh cofounder Ohno Kazuo, premiered in May 1959. Titled after a Mishima Yukio novel, *Kinjiki* featured Hijkata's character attempting to molest Ohno, who ostensibly smothered a chicken between his legs.[1] Now legendary in butoh history, *Kinjiki* was butoh's forbidden fruit; a first salvo and declaration of independence of the movement.

Notorious for giving contradictory accounts about himself, Hijikata spent much of his life spinning tales that fed his public persona. In the decade following *Kinjiki,* he became who he wanted or needed to be, what others wanted from him, or all of the above. Hijikata also was not the only one playing this game. Numerous subversive artists of the period, such as Jean-Luc Godard, Bob Dylan, or Andy Warhol, just to name a few, spent the same late 1950s through late 1960s period dissecting and rejecting the totalizing authority of their Modernist forebears. Eventually running out of "tricks," they were then forced to make positive statements—to actually say something—by the end of the 1960s, when, after exploding onto their respective art scenes, they each retreated within a world of their own making.

Of course, looking back to a time when I was just born, in a culture once removed and a country an ocean away, is an act of imagination, like staring into a faded magic lantern image or straining my ear into a broken harmonium, trying to commune with a beyond that yet lies always already within oneself, to find out where and how the past and future live in the here and now.

In other words, *You weren't there, Michael. How could you possibly know what you're talking about?*

I don't. That's the point.

I may know better a dance that I remember than one I am watching.

October 2, 1993, Los Angeles.

Around 3 p.m., I receive a phone call from performance artist Rachel Rosenthal. As an aspiring filmmaker who has always admired performing artists from afar, I'm helping with video documentation of her latest show.

"I have two extra tickets for you and your wife to see Kazuo Ohno tonight performing his masterpiece, Admiring la Argentina,*" she says, with a delightful gravity. "He's amazing and one of the great dance masters in Japan. You can't miss it."*[2]

The seats are tenth row center. The curtain drawn, house lights up, stage bare. The faint sound of Maria Callas singing an aria from "Manon Lescaut" sounds like a dream. An eighty-six-year-old Japanese man slowly stands up from an aisle seat, dressed like a woman in a formal cape, an old silvery party dress, wide-brimmed hat, and white makeup from head to toe. He is like a hybrid specter of a nineteenth-century opera diva and a male prostitute.

Ohno slowly makes his way toward the proscenium, hesitating, looking back at the audience and the space around him, or rather looking through those things, searching out hidden ghosts, or maybe unsure whether he is one himself. On stage, he sheds the outer layer of costume, methodically, like a snake molting its skin, laying it on the ground, a corpse-like shadow, and proceeds to perform a slow, gasping dance of death and rebirth to Bach's iconic Toccata and Fugue in D Minor.

Ohno exits and returns dressed simply in black dancer shorts and dress shoes, with his body, covered in ashen white makeup, now exposed. He performs standing in front of a grand piano in an expression of pure spirit, a muddied yet energized blank slate, first in silence and then to excerpts from Bach's Well-Tempered Clavier.

In the second half of the show, Ohno returns carrying the spirit of Antonia Merce, known as La Argentina, the early twentieth-century, Spanish-Argentinian dancer who inspired this performance. He dances a succession of tango numbers in severe, ornate costumes, overtly blending the mixed-heritage dance influences of La Argentina (tango and flamenco) as well as his own inspirations (prewar German Expressionism and postwar butoh). The evening ends with Ohno dressed in a white ruffled gown, depicting decay as well as youthful innocence, dancing to Puccini's "O Mio Babbino Caro," written from the point of view of a teenage girl but sung again in the show in a recording by Maria Callas, that most quintessentially deep-throated of woman sopranos.[3]

I can't breathe or stop smiling. I'm welled up with tears, and so is half the audience.

Adopted by my parents as a baby, I was raised an only child and never experienced the sensation of feeling that I resembled another person. But that night, for the first time, I saw myself in another human being.

> After the atomic bomb, Japan is destroyed. And after that came the most creative work in Japanese history, and it almost breaks down. I always say after the Second World War, in Europe also, after Hitler's Holocaust, they must start to think about this rupture. From zero, they must start to think about tradition, history, or whatever. In that moment, our ground became zero. And Hijikata had to start, to stand, with this condition, because he began to think about the crisis of existence, the crisis of standing.
>
> — Butoh artist Murobushi Ko (2012)

Japan's twentieth-century progression of mutating identities through imperial expansion, wartime destruction, and postwar reconstruction set the stage for butoh's initial development. The movement was influenced by broader engagements in Japanese arts and culture with, overtly, a radical and holistic *subjectivity* and, by implication, *crisis*. Subjectivity as a cultural movement, aesthetic style, and thematic concept is fundamentally dialectic, requiring an objective, positivist, or otherwise authoritarian position against which to act or feel. Beginning in 1968, the same year that Hijikata staged *Hijikata Tatsumi to Nihonjin: Nikutai no Hanran* (Hijikata Tatsumi and the Japanese: Revolt of the Flesh), a performative diatribe against Western cultural imperialism, Jacques Derrida echoed the subjective positionality of postwar Japanese artists with the development of his concept of *différance*, the "systematic play" and "spacing" of differences and traces between oppositional entities (1982, 27). Derrida asserts that the power dynamic within which differences operate determines the politico-economic nature and consequences of such positionalities:

> Subjectivity—like objectivity—is an effect of *différance*, an effect inscribed in a system of *différance*. This is why the *a* of *différance* also recalls that spacing is temporization, the detour and postponement by means of which intuition, perception, consummation—in a word, the relationship to the present, the reference to a present reality, to a *being*—are always *deferred*. Deferred by virtue of the very principle of difference which holds that an element functions and signifies, takes on or conveys meaning, only by re-

ferring to another past or future element in an economy of traces. (28–29)

In Derrida's terms, an "economy of traces" was evident in the contrast between the shards of war that littered Japan's physical and mental landscape and Westernized elements of postwar reconstruction. An expressivity rooted in "intuition, perception, consummation" that "deferred" many artists' "relationship to the present" was exactly what they adopted as their métier for recursiveness, both as subalterns in relation to centers of power and within each individual crisis body. This dialectic approach to identity in postwar Japan, and the use of subjectivity and autobiography, influenced the politico-aesthetics of many in the avant-garde milieu, from "new wave" filmmakers to theatre[4] artists to music composers and novelists.

The play of *différance* at work here might be compared with the classical Japanese terms of *omote*, the outer face or mask of a person or group, and *ura*, the mind, heart, or soul. Doi Takeo speaks of these concepts as one entity in practice in Japanese language: "We speak of the *omote-ura* of things, referring to the two sides of everything. . . . Even when we use them separately, one term implies the other: to speak of *omote* is to speak of *ura*; to speak of *ura* is to speak of *omote*" (2001, 23). Literary scholar Jane Gallop, in describing the unresolvable finality of her autobiographical writing, has called this type of textual-existential phenomenon *cohabitation*, an "irreducible doubleness" that, in Hegelian terms, defies synthesis while yet simultaneously embodying thesis and antithesis (Gallop and Blau 2003, 18). Carol F. Sorgenfrei points to Sakabe Megumi's theory that the inseparable *omote* and *ura* entity may be one end of another binary with *kage* (shadow or reflection), a concept that heightens identity as something paradoxically false and genuine (Sorgenfrei 2005, 10). Michele Marra explains these elements in Sakabe's theory as two sides of the same visualized object:

> The presence of a self as "surface" (*omote*, meaning both "mask" and "face") implies the existence of a structure of "reciprocity" (*sogosei*) and "reversibility" (*kagyakusei*) that problematizes the visual self as "something that is seen by others, that sees itself, and that sees itself as other." This latter definition applies to both the mask and the face, depriving them of the justificatory ground for positing any kind of differentiation. (2002, 231)

If each person, in other words, is composed of conjoined inner and outer selves, but without their integrated self visible, then every aspect of such an entity is only knowable via implication, allusion, or inference.

Numerous postwar artists were also inspired by the concept of *home*. After World War Two, the military and monarchy were neutralized, and the very definitions of authority and belonging became unstable. Nevertheless, Japan's operative institutional structures—suspended ambivalently between a prewar, Confucian-inspired patriarchy and the postwar revival of a matriarchal presence in daily life—remained insular and tightly controlled, thus providing ready fodder for innovative creators to subvert the lived qualities of everyday life in relation to authority and invent new modes of expression and reflection that redefined their sense of belonging.

Victor Turner's concept of *social drama* may also help to frame certain social developments in Japan. Turner observed that many societies are characterized by alternating states of identity and liminality that engender four general stages: *breach* (a break in normative social order), *crisis* (imbalance and a liminal state outside of normative order), *redress* (regaining balance and clarity), and *reintegration* (restoration of balance to a new social order, except in the case of *schism*) (1980, 141–68).

Applying this frame to twentieth-century Japan, I identify two interrelated cycles. The first, instigated by Japan's imperialist ambitions in the early years of the Showa Era (1925–1989), may be identified as: *breach*—unilateral Japanese military aggression in Asia beginning in 1931; *crisis*—World War Two, with the entry of the United States and its allies into the Pacific War in 1941; *redress*—Japanese defeat in 1945; *reintegration*—postwar occupation and restructuring. These events overlapped with and introduced a second cycle of Japanese cultural shifts characterized by: *breach*—war defeat; *crisis*—the American Occupation (1945–52); *redress*—search for identity in the 1950s to 1960s; and *reintegration*—nominal stabilization of mainstream Japanese identity since the 1970s.

D. P. Martinez speaks of the outcome of this history as myth production around modern Japanese identity, on the one hand propagated by Japanese society and on the other readily perpetuated by Westerners through the consumption of Japanese popular culture (e.g., anime, television programs, toys, and the tourist gaze), circulated in simplistic and exotic forms in a global marketplace dominated by the Western media industry (1998, 2–3). The abiding dominance of Euro-American cultural norms inside and outside Japan continues to affect not only how others see Japan, but also how many Japanese view themselves. Such cultural dynamics gave birth to much of postwar Japanese art and laid the aesthetic groundwork for later domestic and international Japanese artists. While the manner in which contemporary Japanese society coheres is a matter of debate, my concern is to see how certain persons and groups in the postwar era attempted to "redress" and "reintegrate" themselves and others through a variety of expressive strategies—mythical, realist, or otherwise—thereby influencing art and cultural history in the process.

EARLY POSTWAR PERIOD

In fall 1945, the U.S. military took up positions throughout Japan as the arbiters of a new government. With Japan's military infrastructure destroyed and its leaders excised, civilian, royalist, and industrial influences rose to fill the vacuum. Petty bureaucrats and *zaibatsu* (industrial) oligarchs secured administrative, financial, and commercial monopolies in government ministries, factory production, and services catering to both domestic markets and the foreign occupying force. With the retention of the Imperial House by U.S. authorities as a tool to maintain unquestioning social order, keep political parties in check, and serve as an additional bulwark against Soviet Communism, Japan's national power structures were set in place for decades to come by the end of the formal occupation in 1952. America had created a satellite inspired by its own example, a nation dedicated to economic prosperity and nominally to principles of personal freedom, democracy, and "openness," but also fashioned by decree and monopolistic design with the rigidness of traditional royalist, business, and government hierarchies largely intact (Dower 1999; Koschmann 1996).

Many democratic activists, left-wing radicals, and other progressives saw this new Japan as simply another colony in everything but name. In chaos and poverty, with the heretofore clearly defined, national identity now eviscerated, contemporary artists felt impelled to work out where exactly they belonged, resulting in an existential dilemma and newly severe and ascetic modes of expression. Photographer Tomatsu Shomei, just beginning his practice a few years into the Occupation, later reflected on the solitary desperation of this period: "Around that time, I first heard the word 'democracy.' As our defeat marked a turning point, traditional values were completely altered and the reality of life quickly changed. I lost my belief in everything. The only things that I believed were the things I could touch and the things that I saw with my own eyes" (2006, 30). Even old-guard artists successful before the war, such as photographer Domon Ken and film director Mizoguchi Kenji, were affected. From the 1930s to the 1960s, Domon was Japan's preeminent modern photographer and a premiere advocate of an activist humanism. While promoting a universalist aesthetic of "Realism" and rejecting subjective art and criticism focused on the individual, he nevertheless held up the independent, personal, and poetic *geijutsuka* (fine artist) as the kind of photographer who can make a difference:

> To depict a societal reality, the photographer himself is already equipped—in his very person—with the absolutely unstaged snapshot, for which the camera mechanism provides the ideal vehicle. He is not a painter, a poet, a novelist, or a performer, but a *geijutsuka*-"photographer," whose work has embedded within it the potential to be the sole creative method that can truly contribute to society. (2006, 24–25)

Likewise, Mizoguchi was one of the most successful filmmakers since the silent era, with a style tending toward gently subtle depictions of social tensions. Nevertheless, his postwar films display a haunted gravitas and anger directed against the country's demoralizing conditions. His 1948 film *Women of the Night* depicts a hellish Tokyo where even the most chaste, faithful, and well-meaning women fall easy prey to corruption, prostitution, disease, and death. Despite its critical and commercial success, Mizoguchi later swore off the film, labeling it "'barbarous' and the result 'of the overpowering sense of resentment I'd accumulated during the long years of wartime repression'" (Koresky 2008).

Writers such as Tamura Taijiro and Dazai Osamu were emblematic of the radical subjectivity of this period. Melodramatic and poignant tales of rootlessness, lust, and decadence raised the "I-novel," a genre of autobiographical fiction begun in early twentieth-century Japan, to new levels of social engagement and self-absorption (Dower 1999, 148–67). These writers and other creative iconoclasts were the denizens of *kasutori* culture, named after the cheap shochu liquor that they drank, which "flourished into the 1950s and left a gaudy legacy of escapism, titillation, and outright sleaze—a commercial world dominated by sexually oriented entertainments and a veritable cascade of pulp literature" (148). They offered a cynical, enervating sense of disillusionment and despair while thumbing their noses at authority and absorbing themselves in a solipsistic lifestyle of sex, alcohol, and free expression.

Alternatively, the writers working in and around the journal *Kindai Bungaku* (Modern Literature) also stressed realism, but in an attempt to realize a more visionary and progressive paradigm. While challenging the objectivizing tendencies of the Japanese Communist Party, to which they were partially aligned and which was pushing for democratic revolution, the *Kindai Bungaku* group "was largely responsible for focusing the attention of postwar intellectuals on the practical ideals of individual autonomy, humanism, and modernity as components of the democratic revolutionary process" (Koschmann 1996, 164). Such writers were also involved in Japanese postwar culture's move toward more reflexivity:

> Critics in the group . . . developed a dialectical style of thought and expression and an affinity for imagery related to the body, the ego, and the void that resonated with major themes in postwar fiction. They also appealed to European ideals of autonomous selfhood in their self-critical attempts to come to terms with the war responsibility and the postwar emperor system. (64)

In many respects, by giving voice to Japan's social desolation and anguish, writers like those in the *kasutori* and *Kindai bungaku* movements established a thematic and creative template for later avant-garde artists. One aspect of their approach was a *search for identity* within an environment of social ambiguity. This phenomenon arose from the core tensions and confusing paradoxical void of the culture clash between the Occupation Authority's nominally egalitarian value structure and Japan's vertically rigid social order. Neither ideology in its self-contradictory practice was satisfying for a contemporary-minded populace, especially when enforced. While paying lip service to democratic ideals of an empowered citizenry, the Occupation Authority largely misunderstood and dismissed Japanese customs of daily life and interpersonal relations.

A second element was the use of *subjectivity* as a creative reaction to crisis. Surrounded by desolation, corruption, and a foreign authority imposing its own structures of socioeconomic development as the very definition of Japan's advancement, many saw no choice but to retreat within. Artists, social critics, and philosophers wondered aloud about the sudden ambivalence of the self in relation to the collective. This public discursive position was not only given to egoism, as in the case of the *kasutori* writers, but also inspired by social justice and egalitarianism, with subject formation politicized in the context of democratic revolution (Koschmann 1996, 232).

A third thematic element was a *focus on the body*. Previous to 1945, Japanese citizens were expected to understand themselves collectively as part of the *kokutai*, the national, Emperor-centric body, to which all citizens, either explicitly or implicitly, swore allegiance in life and death (Dower 1999, 157). As J. Victor Koschmann explains, postwar Japanese efforts toward a broad civil democracy were stifled by the Occupation Authority's maintenance of the Emperor as Japanese society's figurehead and nominal head of state (1996, 11–13). Those citizens with democratic impulses were left with nowhere to turn but their private selves, a situation that often elicited a destructive solipsism. Critic and novelist Sakaguchi Ango presaged this condition with his 1942 essay "Nihon Bunka Shikan" (A Personal View of Japanese Culture), in which he established a space of collective reinscription, where devotion to tradition mattered less than a self and nation based on imagination responding to contemporary concerns: "Even though the ancient culture may be destroyed, our day-to-day lives would not come to an end, and as long as these are intact, our uniqueness is assured. It is safeguarded by the fact that we would have lost neither the needs that belong to us alone nor the desires that spring from those needs" (2011, 436). Or as James Dorsey comments on Sakaguchi's text:

> The self-realized individual is one who burrows beneath the misleading "static" of abstract thought by acting on impulse and, similarly, the "true" Japan is one unconcerned with locating or preserving its indigenous heritage as it faces the immediate challenges presented to its survival and well-being. In other words, although "emptied," the categories of the individual and the nation remain, serving as receptacles for the incessant recreation of content. (2001, 350)

From this idea, a latent cultural narcissism germinated among the denizens of Tokyo's literary subculture, leading to increasingly self-absorbed expression and behavior. Miryam Sas cites Sakaguchi's seminal 1946 essay "Darakuron" (On Decadence) as "a key site for exploring the frameworks that guided understandings of ideology and subjectivity" in the postwar era, especially in its wielding of the term *daraku* (decadence):

> *Daraku,* related to the Buddhist term for falling away, has often been translated as decadence, depravity, or degeneration. Rotting or dissipation under the guise of an amoral, banal chaos, *daraku* is the anti-hierarchical, the "topsy-turvy." Ango sees *daraku* as the chaotic state that is also in fact the "real nature" of human beings, their "human essence." (2011, 5)

Sakaguchi and other avant-garde artists depicted postwar Japan's physical, mental, and social landscape as devoid of inspiration for interpersonal relations beyond the confines of one's body and abject conditions of daily existence. Thus was cultivated a heightened consciousness of the self through the individual body, which artists glorified in terms of *nikutai* (flesh). In Tamura's case, for instance, "all that was indisputably real, honest, fundamental—was the solitary physical individual," within which "the 'gate of flesh' was the 'gate to modernity'" (Dower 1999, 157). Or as Sakaguchi asserts in his 1946 essay, "Nikutai jitai ga shiko suru" (Flesh Itself Thinks), the body is left to its own devices in the absence of a comforting and reassuring *furusato* (nostalgically imagined hometown), and approaches "a cliff that we come to in life that is without morals (or amoral), or in other words, without any possibility of any coherent belief or value system; but taking that moment itself seriously represents a kind of *moraru* (moral)" (Sas 2011, 9).

STASIS AS STABILITY: THE PERSONAL IS (NOT) THE POLITICAL

By the mid-twentieth century, the long project of the Enlightenment to deliver political, economic, technological, and cultural progress to the masses was seen by many as failed, embodied in the dehumanizing evolution of high modernism, from prewar Fordism to the planned communities of postwar suburbia (Kaminer 2011). Years before the revolutions and assassinations of the 1960s across the United States, Europe, Central America, Africa, and Asia, Japanese intelligentsia, cultural figures, and students began to feel powerless and marginalized, largely due to the failed ideals of left-wing activist and student movements. After mass protests against the Occupation Authority's soft-gloved authoritarianism and the vice grip of the right-wing oligarchs, the 1951 Japan–U.S. Treaty of Mutual Cooperation and Security and its renewal in 1960 led to increased cynicism among opposition groups. Containment and modernization by the Americans compromised political and economic reform efforts, especially given the occupiers' reinforcement of imperial state authority, single-party rule, and historical narratives obscuring war responsibility on both sides. Progressives repeatedly failed to establish an effective foothold in either the Diet, the elected core of Japan's parliamentary government, or the ongoing popular imagination (Dower 1999, Viala and Masson-Sekine 1988, Marotti 2006).

In rejecting Westernization, and especially Americanization, many leftists and artists turned inward for a kind of saving grace. As Japan's political, economic, and cultural capital, Tokyo served as the flashpoint for new modes of personal resistance. When young, avant-garde artists took up the mantle of critique, it was within a milieu framed by the defeats of the immediate past, but also creative possibilities for the near future. In speaking of the conditions that inspired rebellious artistic movements in the 1960s, Jacob Raz writes:

> Many Japanese felt inferior when confronted with American culture, which gave rise to a fervent desire to attain equal standing with America in both economic and cultural affairs. But modernization meant Americanization, and this created conflicting feelings. . . . Modernization could not be accepted, but neither could it be fought. It could only be laughed at, escaped from via nostalgia and "tradition," or dug into and reconstructed, as a nightmare image on stage. (Viala and Masson-Sekine 1988, 10–11)

Moreover, this "nightmare" of an Americanized modernity was also a racialized projection as product of the U.S.'s imperialist-colonialist agenda. Lucky Strikes, Levis, Coca-Cola, and the 1950s Japanese consumer product triumvirate of the washing machine, television, and refrigerator[5] represented the aspirational fantasy of white American homogeneity that avant-gardists reflected in their art. This materialist culture of what Vince Schleitwiler calls a "heterogenous production of whiteness" institutionalized by the Occupation in postwar Japan engendered "unforeseen varieties of nonwhiteness in its wake" (2017, 47). Many such practices, including butoh, moved alongside "new hierarchical forms of racial privilege masquerading as freedom" (47) as ambivalent reflections and psycho-physiological consequences, critiques, and alternatives.

Thus grew an avant-garde movement by the early 1960s wherein subjectivity became an all-encompassing paradigm. Reference to idiosyncratic personal experience became common, resulting in highly autobiographical approaches. Writers such as Oe Kenzaburo and Abe Kobo explored modern self-identification in increasingly surreal and absurd novels and plays.[6] Theatre artists such as Terayama Shuji and Kara Juro established the *angura* (underground) movement of small ensembles performing personal and abstract narratives in socially marginalized physical sites. Photographers such as Tomatsu Shomei, Hosoe Eikoh, Moriyama Daido, and Fukase Masahisa established the *subjective documentary* and *are-bure-bokeh* (rough, blurry, out of focus) movements of photographic visualization of interior experience.[7]

Perhaps because of cinema's ability to reach the masses, Japanese New Wave filmmakers were especially effective at expressing an ambiguous internal dialogue around identity. Directors such as Imamura Shohei, Teshigahara Hiroshi, Hani Susumu, and, most notably, Oshima Nagisa, were, like their counterparts in France, Brazil, West Africa, and other regions, pushing cinema's boundaries to express rootlessness, solipsism, and politicization of the country's youth.[8] Hani's work from the start in the 1950s combined documentary techniques (e.g., nonprofessional actors, cinema verité visual style, and improvisation) with feature film narrative structures. He made numerous socially conscious films while becoming increasingly pessimistic, eventually leaving feature filmmaking to become a nature documentarian.[9] Oshima, Japan's most famous and respected filmmaker internationally since Kurosawa Akira, created a dozen features between 1959 and 1970 mercilessly depicting an enervated, corrupt, and nihilistic Japan. He ended this prolific period, however, with a muted and introverted ambiguity in a movie about a young political artist who films his will and commits suicide with the camera running:

> The illusion I experienced, which is expressed in the title, *The War of Tokyo: Postwar Confidential* (1970), is related to the deep interest I took in the life and death struggle launched by the various sects of the student movement to prevent Prime Minister Sato from visiting

> the United States in 1969, a struggle which . . . seeing not a single death, ended the student struggles of the 1960s in a mood of defeat. I, too, wandered through the demonstrations at Haneda Airport, carrying a camera and filming what I could, but, of course, I did not die either. For me, the question of how to die in the 1970s is an answer to the question of how to live. (undated)

Of course, Japan was not the only site of national growing pains and international upheaval: there were the two wars in Vietnam, Hungarian Uprising, Chinese Cultural Revolution, and 1968 in Paris, Mexico City, Prague, Chicago, and countless other sites of protest and counterculture. By the 1970s, social progressives and their tenuous allies among the critical intelligentsia had reached a nadir in both direct action and ideological warfare. As Tahl Kaminer describes, no longer could the Left aspire to build an alternative modernist space when the very notion of the totalizing modernist project was off the rails:

> The questioning of utopia and progress were, in many ways, a sign of a more mature society, more aware of self-created myths and delusions, freeing itself from the subordination to the illusions of grand narratives. It also meant a growing awareness of the monstrosities created by modernity, the injustices and horrors of the Soviet gulags and the shanty towns of the third world. (2011, 19)

The void of late Modernism allowed Japanese subjectivity to thrive as the wider movement underlying butoh's genesis, providing it generative space to blossom, and imbuing it with an aesthetic permissiveness toward mythology and imaginaries. Many postwar artists embraced a skewed image of traditional culture, each person's own idiosyncratic Japan lost in time, situated in tension with their schizophrenic feelings toward contemporary society. This community included a young escapee from the northern backwaters of Tohoku, born Yoneyama Kunio, who arrived destitute in Tokyo, spent years shuffling through referential artist identities like cards in a deck—Hijikata Kunio, Hijikata Genet, Hijikata Nue, Hijikata Nero, and finally, in 1958, Hijikata Tatsumi (Baird 2012, 12)—and emerged to refashion himself into a neoprimitivist cultural force.[10]

Within an avant-garde community that questioned postwar Japan's economic and cultural production models, Hijikata fashioned an alternative dance form that he eventually labeled *ankoku butoh* (dance of utter darkness), and later shortened in familiar usage to simply *butoh*. He employed deconstruction, absurdity, and darkness to portray a tragic psyche, choreographing the nightmare image of a foreign and inhumane modernism overpowering his native culture into a "body in crisis," at war against itself.

The reality was also more subtle. Japanese Modernists, for example, had forged their own domestic style in design, photography, visual art, and cinema before World War Two, employing a wide range of traditional, contemporary, and international references (Silverberg 2009, Tanizaki 1977). Hijikata's narrative, nonetheless, was a convenient semi-fantasy around which to craft his new style. He looked to the past, performing a consciously primitivist and sexually deviant dance to express an essentialized mind, body, and spirit, thus challenging the mainstream, historically progressive social order represented by the Japanese dance world's appropriation of Western classical and modern dance. Butoh artist Tamano Hiroko, who studied and performed for Hijikata in the 1970s, believes Hijikata's personal challenges and insecurity as a young dancer provoked butoh's impetus:

> The naivete, I think, coming from Tohoku. A kind of European atmosphere when he came out to Tokyo, and he learned classic ballet and flamenco and western dance. It's so exotic. . . . Doing ballet, jumping and flying like a bird. Then one day he saw his own figure in the mirror. And he said, "Uh, oh, it's not right. I'm not fitting in this beautiful classic ballet form. My body's different. Short legs. Chest is skinny." . . . As much as he tried to get skilled, the body is not fitting there. Which means, Where am I? Who am I? Where do I come from? Why is my body like this? (2010)

While employing aspects of ballet technique in his training regimen, Hijikata rejected ballet's upward, gravity-defying mobility, balanced, clean linearity, and superlative aesthetics.[11] As photographer and frequent Hijikata collaborator, Hosoe Eikoh, remarked about Hijikata's legacy:

> While Western dancers or dances want to express their energies or powers toward the sky, butoh dancers look for the energies down toward the earth, as if you have the gods in heaven and also the gods in the earth. Because their energies go downward, it means they're looking for their identity in their own inner world. (1991)[12]

Hijikata likewise rejected the ostensibly liberatory lexicon, externalizing drive, and everyman heroic uplift of modern dance pioneers, feeling that it was too melodramatic for its own sake.[13] Canadian contemporary dance artist and butoh practitioner Denise Fujiwara, who worked for many years in modern and postmodern dance and still choreographs primarily for similarly trained dancers, views butoh's relationship with Western dance as fundamentally tenuous: "The Western forms of dance that I studied, and also gymnastics, value technique, athleticism, form, dynamics, filling space, action, virtuosity, sending energy out to the audience, and charisma. Butoh, as I learned it, may at times possess some of those qualities, but values none of them" (2018).

Hijikata is not known to have explicitly considered Western postmodern dance, which also rejected these values through use of lateral and horizontal space, random or quotidian movement, minimal to no costuming, and conceptual themes. His work, however, did address psycho-physiological, energetic, and social qualities of the dancing body, influenced by Japanese modern dancers trained in the lineages of Ishii Baku or Eguchi Takaya, who was a student of German Expressionist dance pioneer Mary Wigman. As Carol Brown explains, German Expressionist dance framed the body within a mechanistic paradigm, embraced stark emotional contrasts and psychoanalytic frameworks, and welcomed a sense of contradiction: "Dances which, in their content and form explored *being-outside-of-oneself* and which embodied states of rapture, delirium and intensity of projection, represented the unconscious depths of the dancing body and projected this depth into an outside where it transcended the space-time of the present" (2010, 60).

Similarly, first-generation butoh artist Kasai Akira, who danced with Hijikata in the 1960s before creating his own work up to the present day, sees one's relationship with their image of their internal self, as well as larger outside influences, such as history, society, family, or country, as fundamental to butoh. Additionally, he sees "the moment of creation" as a third core element: "For example, getting pregnant. Just the moment of the birth. . . . To just show the baby means nothing. (There's) life inside of the body, and the life is growing up, growing up, growing up. And finally they're born. . . . If the dancer has this, it's butoh" (2009).

Much butoh performance has always appeared slow and methodical, often to the point of deathly, with a lowered center of gravity and given to grotesque and transgressive imagery. Unlike many dance forms in which technique and content are designed for outward expression, Hijikata in his early period rejected superficial appearance without the sense of an underlying, subjective being present and struggling, often against a dominant ideology. In the essay, "To Prison" (1961), he railed against Western hegemony, advocated a dance of darkness inspired by criminality and death, and framed his art as an anti-capitalist credo:

> All the power of civilized morality, hand in hand with the capitalist economic system and its political institutions, is utterly opposed to using the body simply for the purpose, means, or tool of pleasure. Still more, to a production-oriented society, the aimless use of the body, which I call dance, is a deadly enemy, which must be taboo. . . . In this sense my dance, based on human self-activation, including male homosexuality, crime, and a naive battle with nature, can naturally be a protest against the "alienation of labor" in capitalist society. (2000, 44–45)

Hijikata's self-marginalization outside a capitalist paradigm marked his practice as concerned with the fraught relations among body, identity, and commerce. Tanaka Min, for example, who developed a semi-improvisational dance form in the 1970s, felt drawn to work with Hijikata, and did so with their collaboration "Foundation of Love Butoh" in 1984. Tanaka has always resisted creating work that is readily commoditized:

> Dance is collected to the theater for showing to intellectual people or dance audiences. It's a dance society. I'm really bored with this. I think dance as a fashion is finished. From this century, we really have to make it much more pure, and think more about where we came from. Where dance came from, and for what dance has to exist. That's why I'm really studying ancient things, rituals, and imaginations of ancient peoples. And most of the performers of Japan, originally they are the people not included in society. Most

physical expressions are started from them. We are the children of those who were thrown out of society. (2009)

After six decades, butoh artists in Japan remain a somewhat fringe community largely outside the mainstream, despite the fact that, according to historian Thomas R. H. Havens, in 1980, during Japan's rise to global economic powerhouse, Japan was second only to the United States in its number of professional dancers and dance teachers (1982, 13). Havens asserts that by this time there were still three enigmas facing contemporary Japanese artists: audiences' fascination with foreign spectacle events and "blockbuster" art; the emphasis on social conformity in Japanese society, which tends to marginalize the arts as unserious and existing solely as entertainment; and Japanese cultural emphasis on artistic technique over expressive quality and content (19–20). Havens also observed that Hijikata opposed what he saw as a "barren and meaningless" domestic society and maintained an ambivalence "very well tuned to the nonabsolute, concrete quality of most Japanese social thinking after the war" (225).

Butoh was thus marginal in its first decades, and still remains an object of fascination for many Japanese. Numerous books on butoh have been published and are readily available throughout Japan. In nine trips to Japan, I have always been struck that many people are surprised that I am a butoh artist and wonder aloud why I would choose a seemingly unfathomable art form. I feel that they assume my becoming a butoh dancer was a weighty decision to declare my nonconformity, as opposed to simply acting on my artistic inclinations or intellectual desire to reflect on my existence.[14]

Japanese dance critic Goda Nario describes the connection between butoh's outsider stance, in which intuitive and socialized behaviors paradoxically conflict, and the effect of performing a disabled bodily image: "Within your body consciousness, sometimes there is a subconscious rebellion you cannot explain. If you pursue these strange things, you show your confused self, and you feel the shock of your body" (Horton Fraleigh 1999, 175). This tenuous self-image was crucial to butoh's formation in Japan. In 1960, Hijikata presented an evening of new performances contextualized by his essay, "Inner Material/Material," wherein he articulated his work's darker aspects:

> Audiences pay money to enjoy evil. We must make compensation for that. Both the "rose-colored dance" and the "dance of darkness" must spout blood in the name of the experience of evil. A body that has kept the tradition of mysterious crisis is prepared for that. Sacrifice is the source of all work and every dancer is an illegitimate child set free to experience that very quality. (2000, 39)

Hijikata argues for the necessity of crisis in his dance:

> In this separation between this material and myself, bodies that have maintained the crisis of the primal experience celebrate their mutually dizzying encounter. It is most surely that which lies behind the symbolic quality of all bodies. Under a vivid sign the material and I take our first step to the treatment site for movement while anticipating various things in giving up our lives to a sweaty "engagement." This battle is the matrix of my art. (2000, 41)

In "To Prison," Hijikata describes his stance more viscerally: "I would like to be sitting, without even a passport, smack in the middle of a mistake" (2000, 45). In a 1977 interview, he states, "I am not being visited by a sense of crisis, rather I am demanding it" (Hijikata, Senda, and Suzuki 2000, 62–63).

In short, *crisis*, along with its existential struggles, became one of Hijikata's core operative metaphors from the inception of butoh. His mission was to disable dancers' connection, their psycho-physiological vulnerability, to the hegemonic order. Both inviting and resisting commodification, he engaged desire and repulsion, refusing legitimacy, yet demanding to be heard, challenging viewers' expectations for completeness. As Goda describes: "In Hijikata's Butoh, half of the self is not conceived, so it is very dynamic. It is theatrical because it is alive and unfinished. . . . Total art is totalizing (totalitarian). We can learn to be happy with what is finished and imperfect. . . . If you perform what you experience, if you show your confused self, it is total" (Horton Fraleigh 1999, 176).

As Richard Schechner observes in citing the relationship between supposedly "unliterate" cave paintings and modern drama, "Historically speaking, in the West, drama detached itself from doing; communication replaced manifestation" (1985, 22). In relation to such systems developed over centuries for inscribing key texts of dominant, "literate" cultures on their respective societies, *drama as manifestation* becomes a political act. Thus, the surreal and irrational meaning-making process of butoh's early years pushed back against hegemonic inscription. Embodiment reclaiming drama; manifestation replacing communication. Hijikata's efforts were one with the postwar avant-garde's preoccupation with the carnal body, *nikutai,* as a primary generative site for narrative and resistance. Or as Morishita Takashi states, Hijikata's solo performance, *Tatsumi Hijikata to Nihonjin: Nikutai no Hanran,* "was an anthem praising the transcendence of the body" (2015, 16).

Such an approach, however, necessitates a socializing structure since language is incorporated into the training of countless art forms and life practices. One example is the *kensho* experience in Zen Buddhism, wherein, after long study with a teacher, a student may suddenly realize the nature of the concept of "no separation" or comprehend the essential meaning of *mu* (emptiness). As kensho occurs after long, rigorous study, mostly dialectic, until the student only comprehends without direct semantic reference, this condition might be understood, not so much as nonliterate or unliterate, but as *postliterate.* Getting the mind to transcend language may require navigating, not around, but through words. This is one rationale for zen koans, which cannot be engaged logically. Koans decontextualize language by subverting its meaning-making premises.[15]

Similarly, Hijikata's *butoh-fu* training employs imagery through text to stimulate surreal movement and body imagery as well as the embodiment of contradiction. Through deconstruction, subversion, and transformation of their domesticated bodies, butoh artists may be considered *post-socialized.* Through psycho-physiological states rooted in their sensual-perceptual faculties, the dancers act as energetic focal points, windows through which an audience may view a ritual state of presence and visibility, i.e., being one's subjective being itself, framed by, and in resistance to, objectivity. As its purpose is to reify body and desire unmoored from a hegemonically imposed environment or delusion, butoh opposes the capitalist goals intrinsic to *spectacle* as defined by Guy Debord:

> The first phase of the domination of the economy over social life brought into the definition of all human realization the obvious degradation of *being* into *having.* The present phase of total oc-

> cupation of social life by the accumulated results of the economy leads to a general sliding of *having* into *appearing*, from which all actual "having" must draw its immediate prestige and ultimate function. (2006, 120)

Conversely, butoh's purposeful degradation from permanence and stasis to impermanence and fluidity is an anti-authoritarian maneuver, opposing the capitalist degradation from being to appearing. Generally speaking, butoh practitioners, even many who employ spectacle, resist ideological dominance by delving into a chaotic dark side, avoiding perfection, and seeking irresolution, asymmetry, and compromise; the beauty of incompleteness within the transient decay of life. Disabled and grotesque imagery has become butoh artists' stock-in-trade while portraying the hidden, corporeal ambivalence within everyday life. As butoh dancer Katsura Kan details, such notions may come to represent the dread of weakness and disintegration as well as their transcendence:

> The body and face were very conservative when butoh artists began, but they committed many taboos onstage, and they were shocking for many people. And then many people gradually accepted and appreciated it, because we evoke from the viewers' own dark side, which they are used to hiding. If we show our dark side, we become total existence, and then become healthy. So we are aiming to make the world healthy. And so we are still seeking. . . . Many people believe we are looking for beauty, but butoh is looking for before beauty. (2009)

Butoh artist Nakajima Natsu, having experienced many of Hijikata's initial performances as one of his first students, also believes in butoh's rebellious impulse: "Even one glance, it's something. In the mind of audiences, revolution can start. So whether the performer will experience something or whether audiences will experience something, I think that's the point" (2011).

The philosophical framework and image-oriented techniques through which butoh practice navigates its various dualities—interior/exterior, light/dark, beauty/ugliness, passivity/revolution, and the like—and the way they may overlap, conjoin, and interact makes *liminality* central to butoh. For example, butoh cofounder Ohno Kazuo taught a container-like technique focused on liminality. As Jean Viala describes:

> The dancer must separate himself from his physical and social identity. Ono says that Butoh revolves around the idea of the "dead body," into which the dancer places an emotion, which can then freely express itself. Without this technique, the "living body" would divert the emotion, drawing us into its own logic. (Viala and Masson-Sekine 1988, 22)

Due to butoh's etymology and its formation by trained dancers, the practice also paradoxically has become a standardized cultural form maintained by appropriating normative disciplinary signs and modalities. Though practitioners are often loath to define their art, they usually refer to themselves as dancers and employ costume, lighting, rehearsals, and traditionally hierarchical relationships, i.e., choreographers and directors arranging dancers, performers, and students. Yet these roles also serve as an oppositional catalyst, a virus infecting the dominant order, from which practitioners attempt to hold themselves apart by dissociating from standardized "texts" of socialization.

Ask a butoh artist three times, "Are you a butoh dancer?" and you may receive three different answers, just as each person will give different definitions from each other. For Kan, his identity as a butoh dancer is bound up with the effect of his work on audiences: "I think it's better to say I'm a butoh dancer, because if I say butoh dancer, people ask me what does that mean, 'butoh'? If I call myself something more abstract, people don't have so strong a question about me" (2009). For Nakajima, who trained for four years with Hijikata and now has practiced for well over half a century, butoh has been a matter of finding one's personal relationship to the practice and moving on: "Artists should make their own style. So in some ways I created my own style. I don't know if this is butoh or not, but it's my style. So what I'm dancing now is kind of a definition of my butoh" (2011).

By rejecting recognizable textual status—becoming, as it were, unscriptable—butoh artists place themselves in a profane territory outside of the sacred realm of legitimacy, unrelated to bourgeois tastes, and useless to the hegemonic cultural aristocracy. They transform this profane embodiment into a dialectically mediated expression and encode signs from objectified archetypes and tropes (e.g., salaryman, ghostly female, village idiot) through the simultaneously signified and embodied filter of a primitivized, "premodern" (and pre-Western) body in crisis (Klein 1988; Viala and Masson-Sekine 1988). Audiences decoding such performances are faced with seeming contradictions: sexual desire/repression; coordination/disability in socialized gestures; abstract/concrete imagery; or physical and psychic conflict/resolution. Hijikata and his progeny sought status as liminal and subversive entities secretly self-employed in the assembly line of hegemonic cultural production, constructing themselves as partially readable signs assembled from damaged codes and presented as unsettling, semi-unconsumable commodities.

Such a strategy of framing one's self outside of capitalist social relations, yet also by its terms, is not only to decommodify an ambivalent self, but also to deny the notions of self-control and the authority of the individual that lie at the heart of American culture, the very target of the aggressive expressivity of many artists of Hijikata's generation. Manifest Destiny is not simply a superior-minded claim on the lands and peoples under America's thumb, nor even about making a profit off of said narrative, but more deeply a contention that the classic heroism of the American individual is defined by their being the master of their own destiny. In American culture, to tell your story—to produce yourself—is an exercise in power. As Victoria Thoms writes of *Blood Memory*, the autobiography of American modern dance legend Martha Graham, in which Graham charts a lifetime of personally embodying a pantheon of supremely powerful female characters, even in the decay of later life: "Narrative is about mastery. It masters the problem of loss of self by insisting that through a recounting of a life, the self is coherent through time" (2008, 8). For Hijikata, however, personal narrative is about loss and embracing an incoherent, decaying self over time as the only stable quality of one's character, which produces butoh's persistent state of desire.

With Graham's highly personalized superstructure of form, technique, and style central to the lineage of American modern dance, she is, in some ways, the apotheosis of American individualism in dance, making the gradual dissolution of the loss of the body all the more potent:

> For Graham, the inability to dance was a form of death that was almost as final as death itself. The inability to dance becomes a very compelling symbol of nonidentity. Death is the very absence of selfhood. To stop dancing was more than just a great loss for

Graham; it was a self-annihilation because it forced her to acknowledge that she had lost a very powerful means of knowing and communicating herself. (6)

In the context of postwar Japan, Hijikata's anti-authoritarian corporeality denies the cross-cultural value of Graham's American-styled achievement. Hijikata's scheme embraced anxiety, with disability an empowering aspect of identity, and death the very essence of selfhood. A body in crisis was not loss for Hijikata, but, in fact, a powerful means of knowing and communicating. Like Graham, Hijikata's form and style were autobiographically inspired, but his method of movement generation and expression was only semi-prescriptive. By placing the performer's body and psyche in a tenuous state of not necessarily being able to realize his exact choreography, individual dancers' personalities determined a greater amount of the subtle aspects of their dancing. By making his dance always already personal, not only by default, but by design, Hijikata obliged himself and his dancers to remap their corporeal identity each time they moved.

From collaborations with modern and avant-garde colleagues in the Dance Experience concerts of 1960–61, to happenings and performance art events such as *Anma* (Masseur) in 1963 or *Bara-Iro* (Rose-Colored Dance) in 1965, or his magnum opus solo, *Tatsumi Hijikata to Nihonjin: Nikutai no Hanran* in 1968, each presentation evolved Hijikata's priorities and disciplinary approach. By the mid-1970s, he had invented hundreds of *butoh-fu* image-words for his students and dancers to learn, memorize, and recreate on stage. His language- and image-based method of composition required performers to utilize their physical ability and movement technique after entering into a mental-emotional process of accessing a vast realm of expressive possibilities, what Morishita Takashi describes as assimilating "Hijikata's personal dimension and spirit world" (2015, 45).

Coming out of postwar Japan, *butoh-fu* may be understood as a form of decolonizing Japanese performance art. Bruce Baird asserts that in this environment, which I believe was characterized by external control and internal obsession, "the real skill to be mastered was coping with insufficient information" (2012, 182). Hijikata defined and self-inscribed his dance and way of life within a marginal and delegitimized social milieu, where agency could be devised from any active source. He identified, for example, with street hustlers ("My friendship with the male prostitutes at Ueno Kurumazaka is what strongly inclined me toward the art of imitation. A ragged head of hair, size 11 feet, rouge, death from cold in a public lavatory—with these tools at hand any choreographer, no matter how lazy, should be able to create a dance" [2000, 41]) and imprisoned criminals ("I see my own dance in a state of joyful group bathing in prison, and I see inmates on death row in the fall of modern civilization and in the family crest of its good sense. I see the original form of my dance in their walk" [46]). By rooting his performative personae in de-valued territories, by searching for "home" in places of capture and loss, Hijikata marked his butoh as a pursuit of abjection, through which, as theorist Julia Kristeva states, desire is unending and played out in a dialectic of sublimation and perversion:

> The border between abjection and the sacred, between desire and knowledge, between death and society, can be faced squarely, uttered without sham innocence or modest self-effacement, provided one sees in it an incidence of man's particularity as *mortal and speaking*. "There is an abject" is henceforth stated as, "I am abject, that is, mortal and speaking." (1982, 88)

As Hijikata describes the existential nature of a prisoner on death row: "A person not walking but made to walk; a person not living but made to live; a person not dead but made to be dead must, in spite of such total passivity, paradoxically expose the radical vitality of human nature" (2000, 46).

While Hijikata signified this body as politically charged, he also ran counter to multiple socioeconomic ideologies of the mid-twentieth century. As described, for example, by Lester Tomé, drawing on Cuban Revolution–era media depictions and Mark Franko's observations of Depression-era American dance, both American capitalism and Soviet-Cuban Marxism objectified the dancing body through industrially mechanistic and arduous agrarian labor (Tomé 2017, 6–7). Despite being ideological opposites, both capitalist and Marxist depictions of the dancing body as a means of production frame such individuals as servants and objects of a master visionary. Whether in the bone-breaking, corporatist production assembly of the unison chorus line, or in comparison to the grueling physical tasks of manual farm work, the dancer as laborer is often a utilitarian and positivist trope of ideological systems organizing socioeconomic existence. Conversely, after experiencing both urban and rural lifestyles, Hijikata resisted such objectification and mechanization, instead positing a raw, immature, and untamed body:

> It's good to be able to pick up material from among the boys wiping up at metal-plating workshops or squatting in garages. I look at their hands. A movement of coarse particles spills over. Their backbones incline slightly forward. There is a dance that slides down that slope. Gelatin can be changed by an unfortunate glance. (2000, 40)

These are bodies incomplete and without purpose in relation to objective reality, unlike the assembly line of classic Hollywood spectacle, which objectified the dancer as an ideal of "labor efficiency in industrial capitalism" (Tomé 2017, 6), reifying them as objects of capitalist desire. Neither do Hijikata's bodies resonate with the Soviet-Cuban revolutionary narrative objectifying the dancer as a tireless, socially engaged farm worker for the sake of the nation-collective. His approach was rather to frame both the urban laborer and the farm worker as dancers through their subjectivity for the sake of being resolutely nonproductive entities. While Marxist farm workers labored under the imposing shadow of a Hegelian, dialectic endgame, and capitalist factory workers were made to march lockstep within the Western manifest destination of someday arriving and owning a piece of the American dream, both ideological bodies were framed as heroic precisely because of their homogeny. Conversely, Hijikata signed his name through abjection, refusing to be a productive member of society:

> I do not know how often I proposed the need for chopping heads with a hoe. Tragedy must be given precedence over production or it is just too frivolous. I remember how intensely lonely I felt when they all laughed at me for saying that we absolutely had to chop heads with a hoe. (2000, 38)

In this sense, butoh training decommodifies the expressive body of both socialist and, especially, capitalist standards of rigor, cultivating identities framed as valueless and unmarketable. Butoh's indeterminacy and crisis removes the self from normative modes of exchange, including that between performer and audience. Choreographing this self as performance, however, places it within a conventional system of exchange. Performing a decommodified self onstage is fundamentally an act of recommodification and points to butoh's paradoxical nature. As Maro Akaji, founder-director of Dairakudakan, one of the first and still most successful butoh companies, states, "Butoh is timeless. It is always about to be born. If it actually came into being, it would cease to exist. Butoh is eternally unborn" (Blackwood 1990).

INSIDE OUT: EMBODYING DUALITY

> Butoh training is like entering yourself. Do you know the film, *Fantastic Voyage*? I watched that film on TV when I was a small kid. I was so surprised. Something like traveling in your body.
> — Butoh artist Itoh Kim (2010)

Within butoh's corporeal and social engagement are myriad binaries at work. The imagined and projected tension between a domesticated exterior and primitive interior reflects a public/private duality focused on the material flesh, or carnal body (*nikutai*).[16] Performers are driven by hegemonic structures underlying everyday behavior. Hijikata identified this exterior persona with Western culture, framing Japan's modernization as a foreign invasion and idealizing older Japanese whom he saw as maintaining a culturalist essence, a premodern corporeality that he fetishized: "I eventually arrive at my material by carefully walking around Tokyo where the generation whose hands made eyes has not altogether died out" (2000, 40).

By heightening the tension between inner/outer and insider/outsider dualities, Hijikata promoted crisis as a space for such oppositions. This modality rejects separating public and private face, instead positing a simultaneous engagement with visible and invisible, accepted and rejected, centered and marginalized. Resistance to such seeming contradiction is the exact crisis that Hijikata spoke of exposing as a false safety net:

> This cast-off skin is our land and home . . . totally different from that other skin that our body has lost. . . . One skin is that of the body approved by society. The other skin is that which has lost its identity. So, they need to be sewn together, but this sewing together only forms a shadow. I admire our ancestors who took

good care of the feeling in the soles of their feet. (Hoffman and Holborn 1987, 121).

Hijikata embraced contradictions in order to transcend their paradox. Combining this self-integration with abject personae, his dances figuratively stared into the mirror without reason, pretension, or judgment: "If we, humans, learn to see things from the perspective of an animal, an insect, or even inanimate objects . . . the road trodden everyday is alive" (Viala and Masson-Sekine 1988, 65). Sakabe's theoretical connection between the inner-outer self of *omote-ura* and the mirror of *kage* then becomes an experience of surface and reflection seen from within and without the same dual entity of self. In many cultures, a person's persona, or mask, presented to others is considered separate from one's underlying identity. In Japanese society, which tends to view one's self-defined identity according to one's collectively perceived identity, outer mask and inner self are often viewed as one and the same. As Sakabe asserts about Japanese culture, "there is neither the category of Cartesian substance for any kind of rigid or fixed dualism between soul and body, exterior and interior, seen and unseen," and "there is nothing but grids of surfaces that are, at least in principle, strictly reversible, the one into the other" (2002, 247). Reality for Sakabe is a hall of mirrors, which "*are* reality, and reality is constantly in flux. The shadow and the reflection are not delusions, nor do they lead one astray; rather, they are intertwined, interconnected components of being, which is itself a process of continual transformation" (Sorgenfrei 2005, 57). Or, as Marra interprets Sakabe's noting of Noh master Zeami's concept of an actor's *hana* (flower) as the source of poetic truth that is more significant than one's mimetic skill: "Without losing his meaning as a subject, the persona retains it as a form upon which truth is predicated. Truth is production of meaning that cannot be meant. Rather than in a sign, truth can be recovered in the anxiety caused by the demise of meaning" (2002, 234).

In this sense, Zeami's flower is akin to Hijikata's body in crisis. Both embody Sakabe's unified dualism of mask and face and give primacy to a subjectively experienced meaning-making process enacted by the performer in a critical state of self-unknowing. Thus, I interpret Hijikata's statements to mean that if practitioners can accept their identities as perennially in flux, they can become intimately familiar with their transformative potential, thereby loosening themselves from the grip of hegemony's attempts to determine their every move. From that point onward, every movement motivated by awareness of one's existential mutability becomes a resistant act.

LIFE IN THE LOOKING GLASS

Hijikata was not alone in crafting a reflexive methodology. For many postwar Japanese artists, looking into the mirror was not just a political act, but a way of life, making autobiography an essential tool. Terayama Shuji, for example, spoke of breaking down what he saw as arbitrary barriers between fact and fiction: "I want to question the validity of . . . distinctions (the false versus the real, imaginary experience versus real-life experience). I want to ask what these distinctions imply, and I want to restore people's identification with the coexistence of opposites (making them one and the same)" (Sorgenfrei 2005, 57). Terayama advocated against any element of life superseding any other, and for all extremes and seeming contradictions in the self and society to resolve into coexistence as a unified entity.

Like Hijikata, Terayama repeatedly mined a fantastically imagined childhood in Tohoku as a data bank of images, emotions, and psychic states "in a way that generated new, mythlike narrative streams" (Ridgely 2011, xxv). Sorgenfrei states that it "was Terayama's project to transform his home prefecture (and his own childhood) into something both alien and familiar to his urban audiences. His Aomori became the object of nostalgic desire, a mythic locale that epitomized the otherness within Japan" (2005, 117). Terayama's staging of his own real and imagined duality through a world of subaltern characters and marginalized identities was a self-reflection portraying an intricate web of insider/outsider dualities that resonated with postwar Japanese audiences dealing with the same issues. Home for Terayama wasn't just a nightmare Aomori over which he was obsessed and to which he could never return; it was the very real terror of a compromised society within which his audiences were still trapped.

The danger in a postwar society characterized by a wholesale loss of traditional cultural identity, of how one defines one's home, is that such audiences are lost within the codependence of needing home, making such codependence also coterminous, leaving the ostensible child without a parent and nowhere to turn but inward. The search for identity through subjective means may then become less a willful act of defiance than a desperate search for home fraught with self-indulgence, solipsism, or narcissism. This is *kage* without a subject: a reflection without a face.

Many Japanese artists in the 1960s crossed over this line. Terayama's autobiographically inspired stage and television plays, such as *Aomori-ken no Semushi Otoko* (The Hunchback of Aomori, 1967), *Inugami* (The Dog-God, 1969), and *Den en ni Shisu* (Pastoral: To Die in the Country, 1974), are replete with images and moments of loss, hubris, and psychopathology, especially in regards to the artist's relationship with his real-life mother and how it was projected and imagined in his work (Ridgely 2011; Sorgenfrei 2005). Conversely, Abe Kobo's existentialist novel *Woman in the Dunes* (1962) leaves its readers staring at their own feet. The book portrays a man trapped in a huge sand pit, struggling against the loss of any systematic knowledge of self, and finally acceding to the isolated comfort of a nameless woman, who will provide a mother/home for him for the rest of his life. Starting in the late 1960s, influenced by Terayama's surreal frenzy and the solitary aesthetic of photographers like Tomatsu, Hosoe, and Narahara Ikko, photographer Moriyama Daido published or contributed photo essays to numerous books and magazines that posited not only the legitimacy or value of individual perspective, but took it to the point of identifying with himself: "Photographs I take while on a trip are the commemoration of the fact that *I existed* in that place or that I happened to see something there—they are not the commemoration of my visit" (Vartanian, et al. 2006, 101).

The ultimate example (and, some would argue, dead end) of such a path is photographer Araki Nobuyoshi, who revealed his foibles, prejudices, amorality, and obsessions, as well as his deep and abiding love for the world, his work, and, especially, his wife Yoko. He photographed and wrote about her, displaying her physically and emotionally naked body for all to see over the course of twenty years, from the self-publication in 1971 of "Sentimental Journey," a photo essay of their honeymoon, to her terminal illness and death in 1990, a period covered in a follow-up publication, "Sentimental Journey/Winter Journey" (1991). Araki depicts a struggle against the absolute reality of a photo-subject that one cannot fundamentally alter, causing the photographer to see oneself more clearly, warts and all; the impossible subject as mirror. Araki has said,

"To me, photography is an act in which my 'self' is pulled out via the subject" (Goldin 1995).

Ultimately, these artists represent art making as self-actualization: an imagined and visualized performance of self through the looking glass of the stage, screen, page, and camera, in order to develop one's core expressive vernacular. Peering back on Hijikata's public performance of self, we can see how his actions paralleled his Tokyo colleagues. Even more, his exploits embodied self-actualization most quintessentially through the lens of Hosoe Eikoh, and the consequences of this artistic relationship have affected the practice of butoh to this day.

MEMORY: CLIMBING THE WALL

Christmas Day, 2016. Tashiro, Akita Prefecture, Japan.

I'm with a village elder, who recalls his parents meeting Hijikata by the side of the road while on break from harvesting the rice fields. I ask if he knows where Hosoe shot the famous Kamaitachi *photo of Hijikata on a tall rice stalk drying rack. Abe Yuta, the manager of the ryokan where I'm staying, drives me to the location. The rice field is still there, but the road where they used to assemble the drying racks now contains tall metal walls designed to keep the roads clear in winter by blocking the massive snow drifts that blow through the valley.*

I climb gingerly to the top. The metal is freezing cold and slippery. I ask Yuta to snap a few images as I imagine Hijikata's state of mind. I descend and inspect the images, mannered and full of artifice. I climb back up. As my fingers go numb and I almost slip off the railing, I wonder what I'm doing here.

Yuta opens the shutter . . .

From the photo essay, "MuNK," Tashiro, Japan, 2016.

2 : IMAGINING INNOCENCE LOST

I'm not a creator of Butoh, but I know butoh from
the very beginning before it was called butoh by Hijikata.
I'm affected by him. He was affected by me.
— Hosoe Eikoh (2010)

CREATING A LANGUAGE

In the mid-1960s, two men traveled from Tokyo to the farm plains of the Tohoku region of northern Japan armed with a 35mm Nikon F camera, black-and-white Tri-X film, and a facility for invoking searing imagery rooted in childhood memories. One man was Hijikata Tatsumi, who had resigned in protest from Japan's National Dance Association after the uproar surrounding his transgressive dance work, *Kinjiki*, and staked out a career independent of mainstream legitimacy. The other was Hosoe Eikoh, a young photographer freshly minted into the upper echelon of contemporary visual arts after creating *Barakei* (Ordeal by Roses, 1963), a photobook collaboration with writer Mishima Yukio, in which the latter was enveloped and enthralled within a baroque, deathly fantasy world sprung from Hosoe's mind and Mishima's body.

Hosoe and Hijikata's images were eventually collected into a photo essay, *Kamaitachi* (Sickle-Weasel, 1969), named after an invisible beast from Tohoku folklore that hid in wind flurries and attacked passersby on lonely roads, cutting and sealing them up before bleeding, so that the injury and pain lay underneath, mysteriously agitating and eating away from within. Since the photos were first exhibited in 1968 and published in 1969, they have become seminal in art history. But how is *Kamaitachi*, in the words of Hosoe and his postwar photography contemporaries, a "subjective documentary"? How were both men's childhoods in Tohoku mined and reconstructed to create a visual-performative expression inspired by folk mythology, that resulted in a contemporary mythology around Hijikata himself? What do the photos show us? Do they possess *immanence*—do they desire something in the viewer—or does such a quality reside exclusively in the eye of the beholder?[1]

The images consist of over three dozen monochrome photos of Hijikata in various states of being.[2] Except for the first handful in urban locations in and around Tokyo, and a short foray into a photo studio, the majority are in rural landscapes in Akita Prefecture near where Hijikata's paternal family lived. In all the images, his character lies within a continuum of gazes. With villagers and city dwellers, Hijikata is watching, being watched, and competitively observing—a kind of mutual *othering*—with those around him. He is inspected, mocked, honored, embraced, mourned. He threatens, lurks, ingratiates, seduces, molests, flees, attacks, and struggles. He flares devil horns in broad daylight. He hibernates like a hidden demon or incipient plague on a shelf in an old barn. He marries an adolescent farm girl and initiates her pubescent eroticism in a field of zinnias. He chases another bride, older, fat, toothless, and drunk, who matches his maddened state, step for disjunctive step. He repeatedly leaps through the air, kimono panels flaring, as if transformed into chaos itself. In one of the final images, he careens through a rice paddy with a screaming baby in one arm, the other outstretched, as if clawing the very air that constitutes and conceals his unnamable, uncontrollable nature.

This dark dreamscape, iconic in butoh history, was Hosoe's brainchild. Born in the northern prefecture of Yamagata, Hosoe then grew up in Tokyo, but lived in the countryside briefly as a twelve-year-old evacuee during the Tokyo fire bombings of 1944–45. He recalls, "I liked the landscapes and the environment of the country, but I hated the country itself. . . . Children playing around the corner would watch me with old, cold eyes. . . . Farmers' children were plump, but we from the city were thin from hunger. Their laughing expressions were awful. The dark, snowy country seemed to be full of ghosts" (Viala and Masson-Sekine 1988, 191–92). Hosoe's impetus for *Kamaitachi* was quite personal: "I had the strange feeling . . . that I should not hate the land where my mother was born. If I hated it, I would hate my own mother. *Kamaitachi*, then, is a very personal record of my own memory from boyhood, with all the complex feelings of love and hate from those days in the countryside" (192).

In the 1950s, Hosoe and Hijikata matured as artists through the avant-garde zeitgeist of questioning Japan's new identity. Hijikata came to an upending ethos, framing as positive what was dark, grotesque, and rejected by a psychically compromised society. As Nanako Kurihara explains, Hijikata was deeply inspired by rebellious artists like French writer Jean Genet, who provided the dancer a paradoxical ethos to live and work by: "the ugly is the beautiful; death is life" (2000, 18).

Among a new breed of Japanese photographers dedicated to personal imagery, Hosoe found his voice in stark contrasts of light and dark. After witnessing *Kinjiki* in person, he became Hijikata's collaborator and lifelong friend. Both artists delved into the alienation of late capitalism, Hosoe by forging a visceral style poised between tradition, modernity, and fetishization of the body, and Hijikata by reveling, vaccine-like, in its tragic schizophrenia as a form of ritualized affliction and cure.[3]

Hijikata plied the murky waters of society's fringes to find a working method and ready source of material. Coming of age through avant-garde dance and a marginalized economic subculture, he was employed as a longshoreman, junk dealer, and other lowly occupations. Unlike Hosoe, Hijikata had only moved to Tokyo full time in 1952 at age twenty-four. His allegedly asymmetrical physique (one leg slightly shorter than the other due to an injury when he was young) and lack of high-level dance training limited his prospects for a career in mainstream modern dance, perhaps driving him inward to forge new aesthetic criteria (Kurihara 1996, 17–18). In Hijikata's early career, he did not speak of his rural background so much as a surrealist identity that was urban, anti-capitalist, and criminal:

> Eyes intervene in the current generation whose soul too is unable to live merely through the succession of property. (2000, 41)

> My dance . . . is behavior that explicitly flaunts its aimlessness in the face of a production-oriented society. (2000, 44)

> I wager reality on a nonsensical vitality that has purged the echo of logic from my body and I dream of the day when I am sent to prison. (2000, 45)

Hijikata created an imagined Tokyo representative of a clash between a premodern, intuitive, Japanese corporeality and a modern, industrialized, and domesticated Western body. From 1959 to 1968, he performed themes of sociocultural marginalization within a Tokyo imaginary redolent with subliminal, internalized conflict, full of insecurity, hatred, obsession, and desire. By the late 1960s, however, Hijikata was moving away from this approach, which, after all, was designed to crumble under the weight of its spiritual emptiness. Thus, after a decade and a half in Tokyo and the work on *Kamaitachi*, Hijikata began explicitly referencing Tohoku. He and Hosoe had returned home with distinct agendas: nostalgic excavation and filial reconciliation for Hosoe, and reimagination and repurposing of visual-corporeal memory for Hijikata. The period around *Kamaitachi* represents a shift in Hijikata's festering yet fertile hinterland of social marginality, from external, typed, and male to internal, biographical, and female. *Nikutai no Hanran* included both masculine and feminine portrayals, after which he began choreographing women, one of whom, Ashikawa Yoko, became his leading protégé. Stories of crawling through rice fields, playing with deadly farming tools, fearing mythical beasts, drunken singing by his father, and alleged sale of his sister into prostitution contributed to the formation of a loosely codified *butoh-fu* (butoh language) inspired by a highly idiosyncratic Tohoku imaginary. By the premiere in 1972 of *27 Nights for Four Seasons*, a month of Tohoku-inspired performances by his dancers, Hijikata was defining himself less by what he was not and did not have and more by what he was alleged to have experienced and become. His focus on a Tohoku cultural indigeneity continued until his death in 1986, when he had just completed a new ensemble performance, *Tohoku Kabuki*. This work combined fantastic childhood memories with the raw aesthetic of pre-Meiji kabuki, a largely working-class entertainment until appropriation as a late nineteenth-century, bourgeois reconstruction by a Japanese government selling an image of world-class sophistication to Western imperial powers.

Hijkata's gendered duality in his later career was foreshadowed by his first major photo collaboration with Hosoe, the photo essay *Otoko to Onna* (Man and Woman, 1961). High-contrast, monochrome photos of Hijikata and two female dancers primarily show body fragments, with faces, limbs, and torsos juxtaposed in a raw portrait of gender-based tension. From this work, the two men continued an intense exploration of intuitive, domesticated, and internalized subjectivities.

Hosoe also had set a precedent with *Barakei*, which both dismantled and exposed a latent homoerotic mythology around Mishima's public persona, thereby laying the artistic ground for the personalized narrative invention of *Kamaitachi*. Speaking of the *Barakei* sessions with Mishima, Hosoe has stated:

> I thought I would use whatever Mishima loved or owned to form a document on the writer. However, the interpretation and expression would be my own. At our first shoot, I had spoken of an iconoclastic act to Mishima—the destruction of myth—but in fact I was suggesting a creative process *through destruction*. (2006, 134)

Kamaitachi was thus a midpoint in Hosoe and Hijikata's mutual progression from rebellion against conventional typologies of physicality, gender, and sexuality to creation of self-styled cosmologies rooted in subjectivized corporeal vocabularies.[4] While no image explicitly references childhood trauma or its aftermath, each picture's environment directly sets the tone of Hijikata's presence. In the city, he is shown at odds with the other inhabitants and surroundings: under a magnifying glass, fleeing through concrete gardens, alone with children's toys, or a devil in the marketplace. In every image, Hijikata is in tension or opposition with the surrounding people and places, evoking a constant subtext of looking and othering.[5] In the countryside, however, he transforms into an elemental force: crawling through shadows, hurtling with the wind, melting into the mud. Villagers mock and fete him. He joins with two brides in absurd, obsessive matrimonial rituals. He dies in captivity, appears again in harvested, denuded fields, and becomes as one with the air and earth, light and darkness.

These stances, gestures, and movements are manufactured entry points, ways of performing and being in and of an imagined, post-indigenous body that transcends its urban and rural foundations into a spontaneous lexicon of memory, subjectivity, and presence. This body is imagined because semi-fictional, and post-indigenous because Hijikata posited an essentialized nativist identity off its moorings in an early postmodern world not of its own making.[6] Through Hosoe's biographical framework and aesthetic, Hijikata unveiled his potential for realizing a broader and deeper artistic vision, one that Murobushi Ko felt was a reset of Hijikata's dance form: "About *Kamaitachi*, Hijikata's starting point. I said it's a Japanese mother ground. Is it alienation? Hijikata's starting point became zero" (2012). Murobushi also asserts that the images represent the kernel of Hijikata's mature conception of corporeality:

> Hijikata, at that moment of *Kamaitachi*, he's moving a lot in the photos. Not only form or something. *Kamaitachi* is strong. Because

> it's Hijikata's movement in the photos, the poses are very natural and realistic, not so pantomine-like. Just sitting on the fence or running through the field. I say this is an edgy feeling, but he always said this is the body in crisis. (2012)

These images begin with active energy already at play in the subject rather than attempting to sculpt a predetermined idea. As photographer Joel Meyerowitz states about the essence of street photography, "Watching life, and welcoming ambiguity and the surreal, even though it's chaos. . . . It seemed to me, that's what you photographed; the instantaneous gesture, where life will become clarified" (Dunn 2013). Scouring the streets and alleys of Tokyo and the back roads and fields of Tashiro, Hosoe and Hijikata approached *Kamaitachi* with much the same attitude:

> He just sensed what I wanted too. "Come on, go there, do that," I would say. And he would go there, I'd follow him, and then we'd be finished. When we were wandering down the lane in one of the fields, we found a group of farmers taking a rest. "Just go over there," I said. "*Do it!*" He walks over, I sat back, and he just sat down before them. At first they were afraid of him. But they soon realized he was doing nothing wrong, but he did something funny, so they laughed. I told him, "You must finish very soon. Don't take more than two minutes or so, otherwise you'll lose the tension." (2010)

In his essay, "Kamaitachi: Toward a Vacuum's Nest," which introduces the book version of *Kamaitachi*, critic Takiguchi Shuzo stresses that Hosoe and Hijikata's images are a fundamentally different breed from typical staged photos. Takiguchi asserts this is because Hijikata enters into an existential state akin to the subject matter at hand whenever he performed, thus actuating Hosoe's camera into a real-life stage: "This is not even theatrical photography, but rather a rare instance in which the camera obscura becomes a theater. And it is the paradoxical existence of the camera—which can photograph a vast void when we mean to capture a concrete object—that proves to be a stroke of luck for Hijikata, the master of movement" (2009).

Kamaitachi thus provided Hijikata a legible frame for his chaotic aesthetic and the freedom to revisualize his roots and develop a more orderly creative method of working through his fantasies.[7] Over his remaining years, Hijikata would come to claim this invented Tohoku landscape as the root of his mature choreographic invention. In *The Lure of the Local* (1998), Lucy Lippard speaks of such a process as going beyond observation, occurring through one's intimate, lived-in relationship to a particular landscape, making it a *place* (1998, 7–8). Hijikata's Tohoku is a once lived-in landscape that becomes subjectively observed, intimately from within the psyche of childhood experience, and at a distance from the perspective of his adult future and imagined, redramatized memories. His mythology, as so many are, is based in a past and future present. Myths are typically synchronic in this manner because they must be available at all times for those who want to believe in them (Cosentino 2009). Lippard also emphasizes the connection between art and place:

> Of all the art that purports to be *about* place, very little can be said to be truly of place. . . . I am concerned here only with that which is directly tied to place—with examining the ways art can help us focus on existing places, how their topography and every detail reflects and generates memory and a certain kind of knowledge about nature and culture. (1998, 20)

Kamaitachi and dances based on Hijikata's Tohoku are sited between such an "about" and "of." They are neither explicitly about, that is indexically referencing, nor exactly of, that is wholly rooted in Hijikata's childhood. His Tohoku is an invention, a subjective documentary conceit, extended over time by bending the truth of his recollections or through outright lying (Kurihara 1996; Baird 2005). At root, then, *Kamaitachi* was born of a desire to resolve the authors' ambivalence around their urban cultural life and rural roots. *Kamaitachi* also largely avoids the banal reality exemplified by Moriyama Daido and Araki Nobuyoshi's headlong dives into personal universes of compulsive imagery. Through theatrical, carnal, absurd, repulsive, and disturbing images that are yet fictional and staged, as opposed to explicitly documentary and autobiographical, *Kamaitachi* evades explicitly wallowing in ego or self-absorption. The project stands as a consummate example of subjectivity resonating with sociocultural issues of time and place in postwar Japanese art.

After *Kamaitachi*, Hijikata and Hosoe went on to even greater notoriety. Hijikata choreographed regularly throughout the 1970s and 1980s, though ironically, the performances engendered by his Tohoku aesthetic became the basis of a stereotyped butoh style that continues modishly to the present day in much of the butoh community and in the minds of many critics.[8] Hosoe also continued to devise highly stylized, studio-based abstractions and subjective documentary projects. His seminal work with Hijikata, however, continues to inspire butoh practitioners around the globe and stands, in the words of Rosemary Candelario, a longtime American butoh practitioner and artist-scholar, as "image words that tell me everything I need to know about dance" (2009).

PUNCTUM: ALTAR

I've been staring at a poster over my desk since 1993. It contains a photo of Ohno Kazuo taken by Hosoe Eikoh, and I can't take my eyes off of it.

I'm not sure what I usually notice first. Is it the perfectly upright body broken only by the slightly turned-out left hand and head tilted to the right? Is it the perfectly balanced and subtle tones of gray, white, and black that invite me into this man's universe as well as keep me at a distance with their otherworldly feel? Is it the two cracks in the wall; a thick one emerging vertically from behind Ohno's head and the other traversing horizontally above, evoking a cross?

Or other small details. The old, worn shoes. The cheap linoleum floor. The unbuttoned collar with no tie. The right hand slightly clawing inward. His aged, thinning, crumpling hair. It all leaves me with a feeling of simultaneous desire and emptiness that keeps me coming back for more.

And every time I peer into the viewfinder of a camera to capture a still image, I see Ohno standing . . .

PRODUCT AND PROPHECY: WHAT CAME AND WENT AND NEVER WAS

In his book, *Like a Rolling Stone: Bob Dylan at the Crossroads* (2005), Greil Marcus examines the significance of Dylan's song "Like a Rolling Stone" for twentieth-century American art, culture, and society. Though the song was recorded in 1965, Marcus asserts that its subversive and catalytic cultural inheritance was in play for decades since rock and roll's genesis in the 1940s. He claims that the song encapsulated that legacy into an artifact absolutely of its historical moment as well as its own imagined future. Marcus cites Pisaro in speaking of the song as aspiring to history via prediction and causation: "But like a Geiger counter developing a will of its own, it wavers between trying to record the coming quake and trying to *make it happen*" (8), implying that seminal art works are also self-fulfilling prophecies.

I believe *Kamaitachi* stakes a similar claim. By invoking an archaic cosmology (like Dylan's mutating folk-poetic rock) to fathom an incipient storm, Hosoe and Hijikata became actor-provocateurs, conflating past, present, and future into a social imaginary in which others could project themselves. In times of social upheaval like the 1960s, this message can come as a warning to those invested in normative culture. For others on the margins, it may be a sudden or renewed reason to live. More acutely for butoh artists, Hijkata's Tohoku marks the photos less as designed images with aesthetic immanence, and more as a source of knowledge full of psychic immanence. While Hijikata wrote hundreds of pages of working notes and essays as well as an artistic autobiography, he never published his *butoh-fu* or publicly codified a choreographic or training method. Butoh is an ever-fluid space of idiosyncratic engagement between mind and body, more focused on identity than form. Thus, a few dozen photos, a handful of film clips, and a few oblique writings are all the average practitioner has witnessed of Hijikata in the decades since his death. This has made *Kamaitachi*, as the most widely circulated vestiges from his archive, a key reference for self-definition by countless butoh students and dancers based on who and what they believe Hijikata was. One might surmise that many later-generation practitioners look to these photos, as well as other images of the movement's founding performers, for gnosis from the roots of butoh itself.

This desire drives many practitioners to bestow legitimacy on such images as a kind of sacred text, replete with alluring, obfuscating surfaces and an achingly unresolved physicality.

In analyzing meaning in photography, John Berger states: "Certainty may be instantaneous; doubt requires duration; meaning is born of the two. An instant photographed can only acquire meaning insofar as the viewer can read into it a duration extending beyond itself. When we find a photograph meaningful, we are lending it a past and a future" (Berger and Mohr 1982, 89). Berger points to a symbiosis between photo and viewer. Not only does the viewer interpret meaning, but the distance in time between the death of the photo's instant and the birth of action in the viewer's perception grants life as well.

The stillness of photos—their out-of-time-ness—also allows viewers to control this psychological distance between themselves and the images. On the one hand, this may permit escapism, a lack of criticality, or resistance to certain worlds evident in photos, such as street-level social injustice or the inhumanity of torture, war, and genocide. This ability, however, can access also a deeper sense of witnessing, marking a viewed image, in critic Susie Linfield's words, as "a fantasy that we need—in order to contemplate, to think, to engage" (2010, 164), making photo viewing an act of fantasizing the Other through the photo-object. Bachelard explains this psycho-temporal phenomenon in terms of daydreams, or what we might call "conscious dreaming":

> By the swiftness of its actions, imagination separates us from the past as well as from reality; it faces the future. To the *function of reality*, wise in experience of the past, as it is defined by traditional psychology, should be added a *function of unreality*, which is equally positive. . . . Any weakness in the function of unreality, will hamper the productive psyche. If we cannot imagine, we cannot foresee. (1994, xxxiv)

The relationship between "experience of the past" and "the productive psyche" in photographic perception and identification is what W. J. T. Mitchell calls the "image-text," a visual entity not only capable of being *read* in terms of its past—situating the image in its historical context—but also *made* relevant by the user in a manner desired or necessary for knowledge. In other words:

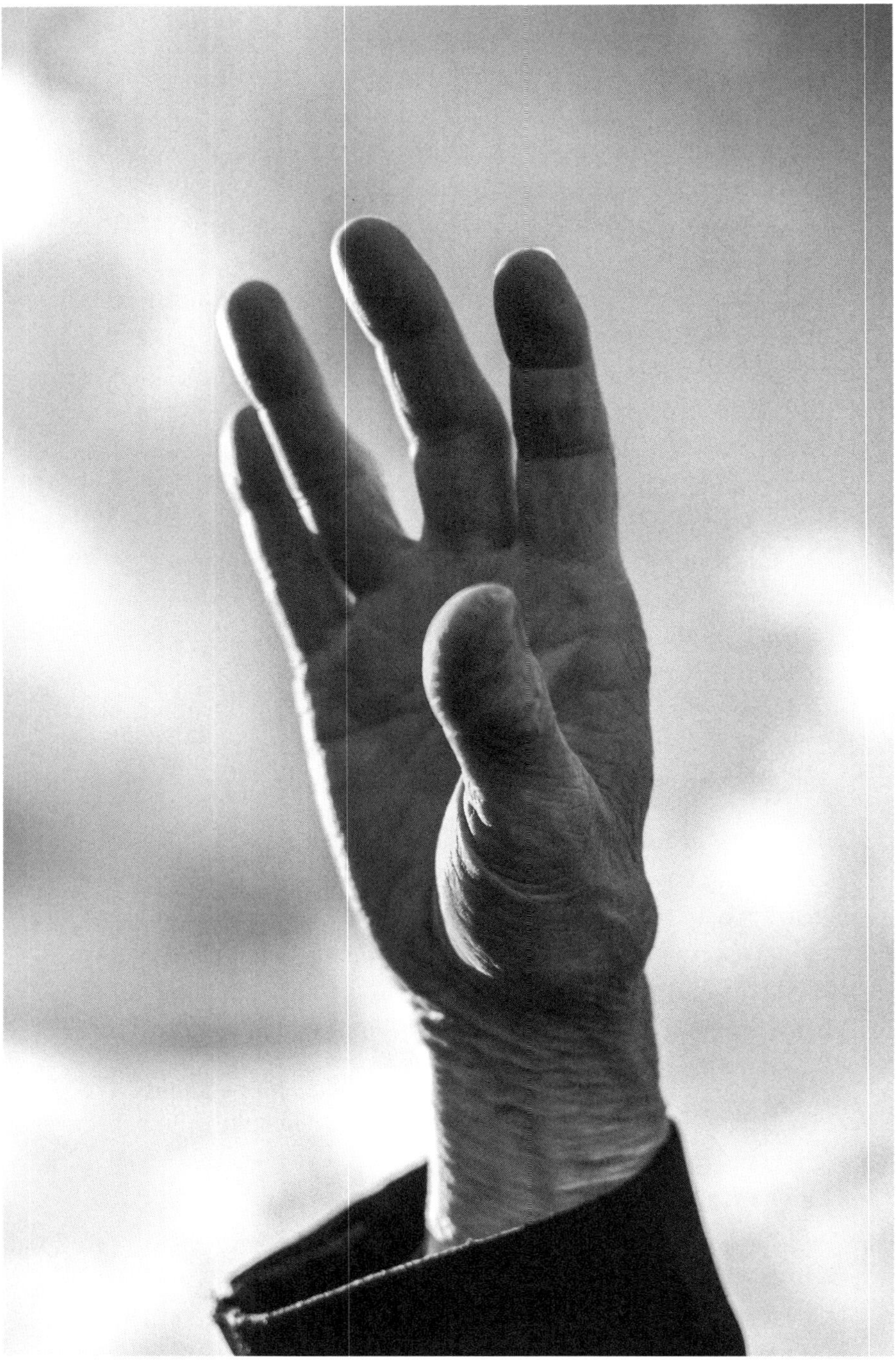

Ohno Yoshito, Yokohama, Japan, 2016.

> To *anachronize*, to bring the image into the present, and perhaps to see what future it opens up. The image, and imagination, "goes before us" as the Israelites say when they ask the artist, Aaron, to create an idol to express their tribal, national identity. It is also what a scientist does when he creates a model, a schematism to explain a phenomenon. The imagination, in other words, is the first step on the road to understanding. (2010, 12)

Such imaging may be our tendency to assign a place in our cosmology to everything we see. Thus, in engaging with butoh photos, practitioners look to the past to create their futures, making their relationship with photos a dialectic between objective and subjective perception, which represent death and birth. By perceiving facts (Barthes's studium), i.e., stasis, we destroy what is there, by nature mutable and impermanent. By perceiving idiosyncratic impressions (Barthes's punctum), i.e., ambiguous, unstable reality, we generate meaning and immanence, which arise in the fertile liminal space between the image and our desires.

All of which makes me wonder, when I consider the photo in the poster that I love, am I killing something, or giving birth?

The face, of course. Pasty white makeup. Eighty years of wrinkles. Eyes sunken and still, yet searching. Lips edging downward, unparted, unsmiling. A clown without a stage. Neither beauty nor beast. More the image of seeming absence while absolutely present. He's there, but in a form of life that most would count as dead and gone.

One thing I know: Ohno's shadow instills in me a soft, gentle viscerality. If his body, his apparition, impresses at all, it is because of the contrast between it and the clarity of his shadow, impossible without the presence of his referent, so ghostlike.

And his hands. Huge, powerful instruments, crawling through the air like wisps of dense white smoke, after the fire is out, but while the embers still burn deep inside . . .

BUTOH IN THE AGE OF MECHANICAL REPRODUCTION

Throughout *Camera Lucida*, Barthes refers to a photo of his mother when she was five years old, standing in a winter garden. His sense of the enduring emanation of love from this image is based on his belief in photo-immanence, a perceptual phenomenon contingent on the punctum rooted in his desires. Barthes seems to assert that photos are ultimately no more or less than what we make of them, highlighting a crisis state engendered by this truth: "I am the reference of every photograph, and this is what generates my astonishment in addressing myself to the fundamental question: why is it that I am alive *here and now?*" (1981, 84)

Like Barthes staring at his mother, I see death and liminality in the poster image of Ohno, not only because of his ghostly visage, but also his too perfectly composed stance in relation to the light, the wall, and Hosoe's camera. Also liminal, however, due to the ambiguity of its subject, Ohno's barely dancing body, an irresolute studium not easily circumscribed. Because my relationship to the image necessarily involves my embodiment—my version—of Ohno's artistic and cultural identity, it also contains elements of identification and desire: a purely imagined longing. This poster has sat by my desk for over a quarter century through five relationships, nine homes, and countless jobs, yet all I know is that its punctum within me alleges a rising from near-death, a perennial state of dying and becoming. This mechanically reproduced object is situated in my life like an altar or devotional image, and as such, it can be said to possess an *aura*.

The cycle of dying and becoming enacted through the perceived sacred energy of aura within visual objects may similarly drive the ebb and flow of negotiating one's place in relation to a social power dynamic, wherein positions become characterized and iconic (e.g., visionary artist, business leader, great politician, etc.), and thereby sacralized and auratic. Thus, such processes may be fundamental to identification. In speaking of immanence within Christian iconography, David Morgan points to this phenomenon as *visual piety*, the power of which "consists in enhancing the immanence of the spiritual referent through the image, reifying it, and merging it with a concept" of the historical person or object (1999, 43). Scholar and butoh dancer Alessandra Santos recalls perceiving such a potency in the *Kamaitachi* images when she first witnessed them: "I saw the photos before seeing films of Hijikata dancing, so the static images of the dancer captured perfectly his movements before I saw him actually moving. The photos demonstrate so well Hijikata's energy and demonic force" (2009). Santos draws personal inspiration from this encounter:

> Hijikata running with a baby in his arms in the fields was etched in my mind forever. . . . I feel that Hijikata is offering the baby to the gods in sacrifice, or maybe he is escaping, knowing that there is no escape from fate. It's very mytho-poetic and perhaps even a little desperate and aware of the human condition, it's existential and sublime at the same time. It's like Hijikata is a messenger, a reminder; through his dance he reminds us there are infinite possibilities and dimensions beyond our understanding, and yet everyone knows it. Hosoe was able to capture the multitudes Hijikata produced in his dance. (2009)

According to Allen and Mary Nooter Roberts, devotees of a sacred practice may even cultivate agency through processes like visual piety, such as in the West African Mourides' active seeking-out of *baraka* (from the Arabic), "a form of divine intervention available through visual imagery," from devotional images of their saint, Amadou Bamba (2003, 24). The Robertses write, "Above all else, Mourides feel that *baraka/aura* does things: it works, changes, and helps" (2003, 26).

Walter Benjamin's conception of aura, as the perceived psychoenergetic quality in an artwork to which society has granted legitimacy, relies on a work's "presence in time and space, its unique existence at the place where it happens to be," or, in other words, "The presence of the original is the prerequisite to the concept of authenticity" (2019, 169–70). Benjamin asserted that an artwork's mechanical reproduction and perceptual repetition necessarily reduced the impact of its aura while also democratizing its remaining immanence and aesthetic effects. This idea, however, homogenizes the mass of public viewers and largely refuses the agency of the individual to idiosyncratically experience the reproduced work. Can we not conceive also of an originary experiential state defined by a viewer's subjective perception and relationship to a reproduction? As the Robertses have asserted about Mourides's assumed agency through active interpretation and use of saint imagery, "What may appear to be the circumstantial details of photographs can be concretized, rendered 'eternal,' and thrust before us as objects of ongoing interpretation" (2003, 47). What if a given photo's aura were experienced, not in relation to its status within a unique print object, or even given its agency accumulated through circulation as a virtual object within digital and social media, but rather through the essential fact of it being framed and displayed, desired and expressed? Perhaps the objectified status of a studium, when taken in by any number of individual viewers, also contains the seed of punctum's effect and can serve as the root and path of punctum's subjective perception.

In her essay "The Survival of the Aura" (2001), Petra Kuppers examines this extension of Benjamin's thesis: "The decay of the aura might just be the advent of another auratic event: the encounter of spectator and work of art. This encounter always has at its heart the 'unapproachable': the inability to fill the void in the subject in search of recognition" (40). Kuppers observes ironically that this inability of the "curiously nondescript mass person" that is Benjamin's anonymous audience for mass-produced art still motivates their desire for "authorship of the art encounter," thereby repositioning the aura away from unique objects into "the specific encounter between the mass person and the reproduced object," an encounter between masses of individuals desiring "completion rather than accumulation," i.e., subjectivity suffused with "desire rather than consummation" (40–41). The death of the aura is also the persistence of desire.

Many theorists have spoken of photography as deadly, causing the death of the moment and, therefore, its aura as well. As Susan Sontag stated, "all photographs are *memento mori*. To take a photograph is to participate in another person's (or thing's) mortality, vulnerability, mutability. Precisely by slicing out this moment and freezing it, all photographs testify to time's relentless melt" (1978, 15). A few months before writing *Camera Lucida*, Barthes expressed his interest in photography as "tinged with necrophilia, to be honest, a fascination with what has died but is represented as wanting to be alive" (Batchen 2009, 9).

The fact, not only of a photo's reproducibility, but of the eventual decay and death of every photographic subject, begs the question of whether it is possible for the image's auratic singularity to draw from the subject. Writing on Derrida's eulogistic essay, "The Deaths of Roland Barthes" (1981), in which Derrida speaks of his own experience of the punctum effect after Barthes's death, Kas Saghafi notes, "For Derrida, it would be more accurate to say that the photograph does not serve as evidence for the Referent itself—as if such a thing ever existed—but for a structure of reference to the absolute singularity of the other" (2010, 88). Derrida comprehends his melancholic longing for his deceased friend,

Barthes, through the fact of Derrida's longing for him; *how* he misses his image. A photo's subject (its referent) and its meaning in the mind of the viewer is inseparable from the process—the very act—of reference committed by the viewer.

This process is evident in postwar Japanese art employing subjective identification and social imaginaries, such as Terayama Shuji's perennially refashioned Aomori, Abe Kobo's oppressively depersonalized Japan, or Hosoe and Hijikata's netherworldly Tohoku. Such artists recast their subjects anew through the transforming modality of the referencing act. In such cases, what readily determines a photo's generativeness is its engagement with the viewer's desire, which may produce not a renewed or revivified aura, but an altogether new aura or imagined immanence. As Saghafi describes, "the structure of *reference* carries or bears the other and carries back to the other. Photography thus refers to *and* suspends that which it refers to, the absolute singularity of the other" (2010, 89). The backward-looking singularity of the viewer/other is what paradoxically engenders the forward-leaning singularity of the subject/referent.

The concept of photography as both deadly and generative in this manner implies a liminal state produced by photographic perception. Within the image viewed, death and life coexist since, just like the viewer's identity, they are processes in constant flux. Such an engagement for butoh artists, however, is not simply one of devotion or worship, but of resonance, of seeing that what one feels in response to an image may somehow already appear in an implicitly sacral context within one's everyday life. Circulated publicly as consumable objects, butoh photos are made to be seen, and this is true even of those images, as Katsura Kan has indicated, of humanity's dark side. Susie Linfield speaks of the necessary individuality of such a process and the need for such images to be seen, to be purposely witnessed, as when viewing photos of incredible suffering:

> The Holocaust was designed to be an event without witnesses: to exterminate a people and erase the memory of the crime. . . . This is why, no matter how searing, repellent, or soul-crushing these photographs, I feel a small sense of grim satisfaction when I look at them. To see, to acknowledge, to study, to know: we cannot bring back the murdered millions, but we can defeat Hitler's plan for a kind of cosmic forgetting. (2010, 97)

These examples of how reproduced and broadly circulated photo-imagery possess utility for various communities further illustrate the punctum effect, whereby the viewer feels their way to the root of the image's aura within themselves. The inseparability of subject and image in the act of reference causes transformation into an altogether new subject with a reimagined aura and immanence. These energies, suspended in the image between death and life, allow the viewer to see the world of the subject anew and charge their viewing with the desire for probing such interstices, of the darkness therein and its generative unknowing.

Butoh photos, possessed by liminality, may dialectically engage body and image, i.e., the performance of butoh's multitude of identities and the visual culture that it represents. Such images may thereby allow viewers to map a strategy to appropriate, transform, and transcend proscribed and commodified identities offered by late capitalist hegemony. By projecting corporealities riddled with damaged visual codes, butoh photos may refuse the meta-normative, categorizing tendencies and mythologizing self-consumption of postmodern visuality. In some sense, despite their ability to be printed, distributed, and marketed, butoh photos do not want to be sold, and their ownership may reside less in what appears on the surface and more in the viewer's desire. Butoh photos, dare I say, are made to elicit punctum.

Moreover, while *Kamaitachi* may have established a template for such a strategy, butoh photos have since become a near-standard element of how butoh students and artists encounter and reflect the practice. Butoh photo-visuality acts as a mirror, a framing device for orienting the body into a psycho-physiological state that reflects and extends the image(s) upon which one is focused.[9] Rather than an escape into anonymity or self-exile into moral oblivion, as in Walter Benjamin's glass universe of the Parisian arcades (Benjamin 1999, 538),[10] butoh photos can create a universe of imagery as a hall of mirrors, serving as a multi-perspectival reflection of being.

MOVING MEMORY

Turning to practitioners' experience with butoh photos, this reflective process manifests in varying contexts. Jay Hirabayashi, co-artistic director of Kokoro Dance in Vancover, Canada, recalls his early practice in the 1980s:

I had a book of pictures of butoh stuff, and I read Jean Viala, who put out a book, and I read what he said butoh was. The first book was in Japanese, so I couldn't read the text, but the pictures were amazing. So we would look at the pictures, and I had done one workshop. We just decided we would try to do what we imagined butoh was. So I shaved my head, we painted ourselves white. I made some dances where I was moving very slowly. And after, when I finally did get to take Kazuo Ohno's class, he said don't imitate me, and don't use any technique. So I thought that actually when we started we were doing the right thing. (2010)

Alessandra Santos recalls *Kamaitachi* as fundamental to her perception of butoh as self-actualization:

> I first saw Hosoe's images in the late 1990s when I was learning about Hijikata and butoh. They were intriguing and alluring aesthetically, but also haunting and revealing Hijikata's iconic identity and dance. Hijikata running through the fields as a demon with a halo of light captures perfectly the "possessed" state of the dancer. I think I only saw a few images from the book then, but what stuck with me was Hijikata dancing hunched forward, stepping like a peasant, or leaping, or playing, emblematic of becoming someone else to dance in someone's steps, again evoking possession or total empathy, or perhaps that is the secret to become oneself fully? (2009)

Heyward Bracey, a Los Angeles-based dancer, reveals a connection to *Kamaitachi* after hearing a story from his teacher about Hijikata's supposed epiphany upon returning to Tashiro:

> In sharing Hijikata's story he managed to include me somehow in a lineage of cultural transmission that had begun . . . when Hijikata encountered something more substantial than he had previously known . . . in the body of his father on the roads of his village. My teacher said that Hijikata had "found his own country." . . . Having a direct connection to a pivotal experience of Hijikata's puts the photographs in a whole other category of experience. When viewing them I'm looking at images that tap into my connection with Hijikata's epiphany, which has had an impact on my own personal and artistic life. (2010)

Contemporary dancer Alissa Cardone has worked with a wide range of artists, including Ohno Yoshito, Kasai Akira, and Tanaka Min. She recalls a very direct photo inspiration during her training on Tanaka's Body Weather Farm in Hakushu, Japan:

> When I was on the farm, Min had a bunch of books at the farmhouse, and I remember looking at those photographs, and one specifically, the photograph that spoke to me the most and that I always think about and that's so amazing is the one with Hijikata on the really really high fence, and he's sort of framed in the corner, crouching like a bird. I spent a lot of time as a child outside on the grounds where my parents lived in the woods. There's something about that photograph that really spoke to me and connected to my inner child. I understood later that he was trying to find his childhood and his body and the sort of residue of the earth, the residue of the experience of growing up in Tohoku, and his finding his sister in his body, and all of that very personal history that he was trying to harvest in order to create dance. (2011)

American butoh artist Joan Laage (also known as Kogut) trained with Ashikawa Yoko, has performed since the 1980s, and founded the Daipan Collective of butoh artists and the Seattle Butoh Festival. She was inspired by Hijikata's nexus of personal history, body, and memory, and how these factors integrate in his photo-images:

> Coming into his public persona was his combination of fact and fiction. Here's an interesting thing about my childhood and his. My body was so close to the land where I grew up. Mine was also a land like his, although not as harsh. Cold in the winter and snowy. When you see him up there on the fence, it's also that thing about nature and animal, which I really connected with. The animal-ness of the human. That's very non-Western. (2011)

As Lippard states, "Photographs are about memory—or perhaps about the absence of memory, providing pictures to fill voids, illustrating our collective memory" (1998, 20). Sontag describes this phenomenon operating even more deeply: "Photographs that everyone recognizes are now a constituent part of what a society chooses to think about, or declares that it has chosen to think about. It calls these ideas 'memories,' and that is, over the long run, a fiction. Strictly speaking, there is no such thing as collective memory" (2003, 85). Add to this notion historian Pierre Nora's cautionary on the authoritarianism of history as a discipline, and we begin to see that the expression of an assertively true, personal memory represents a challenge to such authority:

> From the chroniclers of the Middle Ages to today's practitioners of "total" history, the entire tradition has developed as the controlled exercise and automatic deepening of memory, the reconstitution of a past without lacunae or faults. . . . History's procurement, in the last century, of scientific methodology has only intensified the effort to establish critically a "true" memory. (1989, 9)

In a subjective documentary vein, Hosoe's *Kamaitachi* is a reconstitution of his and Hijikata's pasts with lacunae and faults intact, something ambivalent, insecure, and haunted to satisfy their nostalgic desire:

> I wanted to return back to the country to photograph, but not as a realistic documentary, but from my sight, from my eyes. Because it is a memory. Can photography create memories? That was also my question. Also my curiosity. Maybe yes, maybe not. No one had tried to record memories. Just always trying to record other realities. . . . It's a little bit complicated. It is a matter of photography. It is a matter of just a boy. (2010)

Kamaitachi and hundreds of other butoh photos have settled into the public realm, provoking practitioners and audiences to reflect on their memories. Experiencing the fictional reconstructions of performers and photographers is a communal reinvention of selves that inverts history as a discipline, rejecting what Nora calls a "form of memory" coming "to us from the outside; because it is no longer a social practice, we interiorize it as an individual constraint" (1989, 14). Instead, butoh is a form of memory that comes from inside, a social practice born of individually reduced constriction, and exteriorized as a liberatory gesture. Butoh has become, in its largest meaning, a social movement opposed to history as dominance, expressed through one's body across past, present, and future. It is a practice of framing "collective memory," not as a singular portrait of history, but as an aggregate of individual subjective memories, with each practitioner creating an artistic persona out of such elements. Each artist, in a sense, creates their own *Kamaitachi*, just as Hosoe did in conjunction with Hijikata:

> That was my personal document of my memories as well as Hijikata's, and hopefully it would let ordinary people think that those were part of their memories. This is also a record of, not the reality, but the psychology of the photographer. And your interpretation is free. The purpose of my photography is not to persuade people. It's not to make them think the same way as I do. I'll give you one good example . . . Marc Chagall. When I had the chance to see his retrospective exhibition . . . I came to the conclusion, "Oh, that is *his* Kamaitachi." So I understood his works very clearly. (2010)

Similarly, in *Camera Lucida,* Barthes repeatedly cites the unstable ground on which objective memory lies and makes a clarion call for subjective truth via the viewer's presence as the ultimate mode of comprehension and knowledge production. As he exhorts, "let us abolish the images, let us save immediate desire (desire without mediation)" (1981, 119). Barthes also warns against photos that present the static representation of desire: "Pleasure passes through the image; here is the great mutation" (118). He gives primacy to photos that are the actualization of desire, as the winter garden photo is for his nostalgic desire for his dead mother's presence. For Barthes, if photos are what we make of them, then what we make—what we produce with the labor of our "loving and terrified consciousness"—is "*ecstasy*" (119).

We may ask, therefore, from where would practitioners draw inspiration for the continuing redefinition and renewal of their practice if not from material like *Kamaitachi* as a practical source and motivational force? Just as diasporic Tibetan Buddhist nationals find immanence in any reproduction of the Dalai Lama's photo (Harris 2004, 142), so many butoh-based practitioners find inherent inspiration in *Kamaitachi* and other butoh photos in books, magazines, exhibits, and films. In this way, we come to know iconic personae such as Hijikata, Ohno, and others in the context of our own imaginary of their lives and memories and butoh's postwar roots. For, if Hijikata, as butoh's prime exemplar, did not come from his invented, post-indigenous, Tohoku imaginary, how else might we know from where we come?

August 2010.

I'm sitting in Ohno Yoshito's kitchen, having tea with him and his family. Ishimoto Kae, one of Waguri Yukio's principal dancers, who also performs her own works internationally, is interpreting for us. Yoshito-sensei tells me that when his father was in the middle of creating a new show, he would sometimes ask Hosoe Eikoh to photograph him. In this way, by dancing for the camera and seeing the resulting images, Kazuo-sensei would find enough distance from himself to be able to finish the piece.[11]

Yoshito-sensei also says that his father didn't like to put up the show poster before opening night. He wanted the image to have an impact, so much that it would inspire people to want to steal it if it were displayed before the show. (Punctum.)

I tell Yoshito-sensei that this is exactly what I did in 1993, on the day after seeing Ohno Kazuo perform Admiring La Argentina *at the Japanese American Cultural and Community Center in Los Angeles. I walked into the lobby and stole the tour poster that was taped to a guard desk; the same poster that still hangs over my desk and permeates my psyche. Yoshito-sensei says this story makes him happy.*

"This is the main purpose to print the poster."

Ohno Yoshito, Yokohama, Japan, 2016.

Hijikata's body in crisis was a decolonizing gesture, a body/image dialectic functioning as a generative frame within which to perform a fraught, simultaneously hegemonic and subjective vernacular. Despite butoh's reputation as an underground dance form in Japan, it has achieved acceptance in the West, where artists appear in festivals, contemporary venues, and main stages. Given this circulation, what might be an appropriate lens through which to view the resulting tensions and harmonies in the transnational butoh community?

One possibility is the interplay of identities addressed by Japanese/Asian and American/Western practitioners. Where Hijikata and other artists pushed against American and Western identity, so American and Western practitioners often cite butoh's ostensible identity as a Japanese art form. Transnational identity is rooted in and formed by intercultural tensions between seemingly stable yet indeterminate national and local identities. In discussing the dimensions of modern ethnicity, Arjun Appadurai notes that national and local ethnic identities are often defined as a "primordial" reaction to the hegemony of outside forces, thus positing an inner-outer dialectic that he identifies as *implosion,* a drawing inward in reaction to external forces, and *explosion,* a concomitant outward expression of self-reified national or local identity (1996, 156–57).

Seen in these terms, many Japanese postwar avant-gardists retreated, implosion-like, from late capitalist social structures into an aesthetic and subcultural realm that was at first primitivist and later distilled to premodern and archaic. Butoh's early years in the West, on the other hand, mark the tail end of an explosion of expressivity begun in the 1960s. It is an articulation of ethnicity that many viewers have essentialized as a primordial, "authentic" Japanese body, thus reifying the dark mythos of butoh that began as a reinforcement of nativist identity and a negation of Western culture. The history of butoh, and much of postwar Japanese avant-garde art, was a see-saw of reductive perception and inscription of the other on both sides of the Pacific. With all its complications, it is from this dialectic that butoh gained its power, and from which many practitioners continue to draw.

Such ethnic and subcultural tensions arising from transnational flows may also inspire practitioners to cultivate an ambivalent self-image. Lila Abu-Lughod cites a heightened reflexivity and self-questioning from those whose identities are inscribed by a power structure and situated both inside and outside dominance, embodying both self at the center and other on the margins. This dualism points to the need to resolve crucial questions of positionality, audience, and power inherent in all self/other distinctions: "Standing on shifting ground makes it clear that every view is a view from somewhere and every act of speaking a speaking from somewhere" (1991, 140–41). The commodified/decommodified contradiction inherent in Hijikata's dance points to a hegemonically inscribed exterior and an intuitive, immanent interior.

Whether framed as psycho-physiological schizophrenia or a radically composed mind/body dichotomy, a split self is what butoh is all about and must eventually address. In doing this, practitioners both perform and resist reified binaries, such as racial orientations and cultural exotifications employed by persons inside and outside of cultural and political boundaries. Such deliberate mixing is intended to expose the falsehood of monocultural and hierarchical identity. As performance artist Guillermo Gomez-Peña speaks similarly of borderization and globalization: "Since the arrival of the Europeans to the not-so-New World, Latin American culture and the Spanish language have always been 'impure,' syncretic, and hybrid. Latino culture has always fed on the flesh and form of the other, and this cannibalism might be the very source of our strength" (2001, 119).[12] Gomez-Peña's approach to performance art strongly echoes that of butoh artists: "We are the illegitimate mestizo children of art, theatre and literature, of 'high' and 'low' culture, and our job is to remain open to new influences, not to set fixed theoretical parameters. In fact, the strength of performance lies in its indefinable nature, in its hybrid and ever-changing nature. The day you can define it, it stops being performance" (119).

MY BUTOH

A mysterious journey to my interior, that is butō.
— Hijikata Tatsumi, introducing his last workshop,
November 24, 1985 (Mikami 2016, 183)

Once Hijikata established a regular choreographic practice and dance company by the early 1970s, his art was both rooted in his Tohoku imaginary as well as marked by an archetypal Japanese body. Moreover, many audiences are familiar with the stereotypical image of the butoh dancer that developed: nearly naked bodies covered in white makeup moving methodically, writhing in psychic pain, crazed facial expressions denoting dark primal urges and a loss of reason, and so forth. This increasingly superficial impression has been perpetuated over the decades by much of the viewing public as well as dance journalists to the point where even older-generation dancers, whose own innovations contributed to this style, now reject it. Kasai Akira, for example, bemoans the loss of originality among younger butoh artists: "Typical butoh dance style is shaved hair, white makeup. But if butoh dancers only follow this style, they will forget butoh dance keeps going with history and society. People who only follow traditional style of butoh forget about this second way" (2009). Tanaka Min, who briefly called himself a butoh artist when working with Hijikata in the mid-1980s, steadfastly refuses the label: "Now in the world, butoh is just one of the dances. It's categorized already. That's why people want to call themselves butoh dancers. But it's over. It's become a fashion, and I want to escape from that" (2009).

My own performance work also has been created, presented, and consumed in this context. As an American practitioner, I am my own primary case study, a defined, packaged, and presented self navigating between embodiment and expression. Starting in Los Angeles in 1995 and nationally and internationally since 1999, I have created solo and ensemble works in butoh-based dance theater. At first, I drew on the few stock references I could find in books, newspapers, and magazines and a single live viewing each of Ohno Kazuo and Tanaka Min, and my work reflected this simplistic impression. Since then, I have drawn upon the widest sources, yet also on my idiosyncratic likes, dislikes, obsessions, fantasies, and, especially, body.[13] Just as Hijikata could not make his off-kilter physicality conform to ballet or modern dance conventions, so I could not ultimately make my mostly suburban Los Angeles and fourth-generation Asian American sensibilities genuinely conform to those of the endemically Japanese and Asian Hijikata or Ohno.

I wasn't raised in semi-rural northern Japan as butoh's founders were, nor connected to the landscape from which Tanaka draws inspiration, nor invested in the Western European high culture with which the most globally successful butoh dance company, Sankai Juku, has aligned themselves. My native culture was not so much invaded by Western hegemony as it *is* Western hegemony. From mass-mediated constructs to domestic and foreign Others, most of the tensions I've experienced, and subcultures from which I've drawn inspiration, lie expressly within this realm. I grew up with a steady diet of bland 1970s pop music and MGM musicals, but also funk, hip-hop, and global art house cinema. I learned mime in fourth grade, and popping, a street dance form, as a teenager. The one big dance audition in my life, for a Madonna world tour, ended in a dismal, Jerry Lewis-like attempt at a straightforward jazz routine. I have no formal training in dance or theatre and came to performance late, at age twenty-six, through workshops with contemporary performance artist Rachel Rosenthal, my eventual mentor and director, and Body Weather Laboratory technique class with butoh-aligned dancers Oguri and Roxanne Steinberg, former disciples of Tanaka Min.

Otherwise, I'm largely self-trained and draw from all the aesthetic influences of my life. I have developed my own training based on concepts from butoh practice, hip-hop culture, and Zen Buddhism. I attempt to embody intersectional tensions based on narrative, character, persona, or sociocultural references, while allowing these tensions to play out in the space of the perpetual and signifying push and pull between performer and audience. Contemplation, vulnerability, and dialogue are my priorities on the way to modeling crisis resolution, even if never achieved.

I'm drawn less by the hackneyed image of a fetishized dance of darkness than a dialectic process of cycling dualities, such as aggression/vulnerability, illness/healing, or isolation/dialogue. Exploring one's identification through butoh-based training may address these dualities by unpacking internalized elements of socialized and domesticated behavior. In this sense, my dance practice is a reflection of this project's auto-ethnography, a self-writing of people and culture in my life sphere. Who or what exactly my *self* is holds the key to answering my questions surrounding butoh. If all that concerns either life or death lies within each person, I seek to frame the space/place and time/history of such an entity. If butoh embraces and resists definition, if it both embodies and negates duality, then I seek a theory to encompass this paradox.

I seek an empty room.

PUNCTUM: CHAMBER DANCE

September 2014. Bangkok.

For weeks, I've been developing blind spot, *an autobiographical solo performance. A meditation on the nature of seeing in everyday life through personal narrative, I include my lifelong passion for photography and cinema, my identity as a simultaneously Asian American and global citizen, and the legacy of U.S. imperialism and corporate militarism in East and Southeast Asia in the context of Thailand, where I've lived part-time since 2008 and, for the last four months, under a military coup in one of the most touristic and social media-saturated populations in the world.*

So far, most scenes in the show are saturated with photo and film imagery, layered in a tangled web of colorful places and people from throughout my life. But with the premiere in less than two weeks, the show is also too full of clever distraction. I need a moment of pause. I need a passage of pure reflection, of no escape from my premises, biases, and excuses. As a butoh dance theater artist, I need to find my character's contradictions.

I ponder a way to escape myself by facing myself, within the nature of photography as the show's central metaphor; a dark chamber within which one momentarily lets in the light; memory created from a trace of reality. I remember a koan by thirteenth-century Zen master Eihei Dogen:

> *A monastic asked Zen Master Judan of Longya, "When do the teachers of old get stuck?"*
>
> *Longya said, "When the thief slips into an empty room." (Loori and Tanahashi 2005, 265)*

I turn off the stereo. I change into black pants and a dark gray hoodie. I remove the color gel from a single overhead light.

At that moment, as I step into the center of the circle, I don't know where I am.

From the series, "MuNK," Tashiro, Japan, 2016.

3 : AN EMPTY ROOM

MEMORY: DANCING THE WEATHER

April 1998. Venice Beach, California.

Cows don't generally wade through rapids, stand on their hind legs, or piss into the wind and rain, yet here I am.

My dance teacher, Oguri, has assigned an image to the class. Our only task, however long it takes, is to fully embody it—to follow its story through to its logical end. So here I am, in a gorgeously renovated dance studio around the corner from high-rent boutiques, furniture stores, and hipster bars in Venice Beach, one of the most expensive neighborhoods in the country, standing precariously upright, imagining myself as a bovine being trying not to drown in a raging river, urinating against the tide and a torrential storm.

After a few minutes, my limbs heaving from the strain, I turn away, exhausted, my mind's eye observing my bodily fluid swept away and disappearing downwind. I feel my life force simultaneously escape, humbled by the elements, and energize from the resentment of feeling victimized. I sense a rhythm churning silently beneath the battered and deadened surface of my body, attempting to lift muscles, bones, and skin whose energy and purpose have elapsed, expired in absurdity. In this moment, I know nothing, I am incapable, and I am about to die.

I feel more alive than ever.

Over the next half hour, inspiration seeps in one drop at a time, and somehow, joints, organs, sinew, and blood begin gradually twisting and turning my body to face the elements again . . .

MAKING AND BREAKING

> The theater like the plague is a crisis, which is resolved by death or cure. And the plague is a superior disease because it is a total crisis after which nothing remains except death or an extreme purification.
> — Antonin Artaud (1958, 31)

What am I left with after three decades of corporeal-visual engagement with butoh? If butoh artists perform their truth through a devised lexicon of subjective experience—everyday life filtered through one's idiosyncratic body—then what is that body? We have witnessed many versions of what the body in crisis was for Hijikata, Ohno, and other senior artists, but a challenge for contemporary practitioners is to explore what their bodies and crises are here and now. I believe a half century of practice in Japan and around the world begs a question for each practitioner: What is my butoh capable of being and for what purpose?

My perspective on butoh rests on three core concepts: *chaos, contradiction*, and *crisis*. Corporeal, epistemological, or sociopolitical *chaos* instigates a sense of *contradiction* in one's perceived, constructed, or imposed identity, resulting in a *crisis* state of disharmony, tension, or conflict, out of which one performs this state for further affect among themselves, collaborators, and audiences. I view this process through a range of ideas that address crisis at the intersection of intuition and socialization, including ritual theory. While butoh began as a rebellious gesture against cultural domination, its structure of crisis manifestation is more than a *ritual of rebellion* allowing for institutionalized protest (Gluckman 1963). It is also more than an archetypal *rite de passage* (Van Gennep 2004), rather reaching further back into what Victor Turner called a *ritual of affliction*, in which:

> There is a strong element of reflexivity, for through confession, invocation, symbolic reenactment and other means, the group bends back upon itself . . . not merely cognitively, but with the ardor of its whole being, in order not simply to remember but also to remember its basic relationships and moral imperatives, which have become dismembered by internal conflicts. (1985, 233)

While butoh practice engages crisis similarly through "becoming the thing itself," charging butoh with the power to effect change in practitioners and audiences is something else. Can butoh serve as a template for focusing beyond the personal and enlarge subjectivity into social engagement? Turner's ritual of affliction has a distinct social concern, aspiring to complex identity within greater openness, being "a passionate attempt to heal the breaches caused by social structural conflict and competition and by egotistical or factional strivings for power, influence, wealth, and so forth by reviving feelings of an underlying bedrock *comunitas*, a generic human relationship undivided by status roles or structural oppositions" (1985, 233). While I disagree with Turner's universalist belief in the generic, which allows for the ethical relativism upon which dominant cultures depend, I uphold his ambition of an open, democratic, and just social structure through performative ritual processes and explore the possibility of butoh aspiring to a similar agenda.

While Hijikata did not develop his craft as a primarily political or philosophical practice, he was inspired by expressions of recursively transformed social identity, such as writer Jean Genet's conjoining of abjection and beauty in his novel, *The Thief's Journal* (1949). Another influence was Antonin Artaud, who cited the potential for theatre to manifest a form of crisis that reveals deception and malevolence and elicits personal transformation antidotal to dominant forces. In Artaud's manifesto *The Theater and Its Double* (1932), he speaks of theatre as a disease, the action of which, "like that of plague, is beneficial, for, impelling men to see themselves as they are, it causes the mask to fall, reveals the lie, the slackness, baseness, and hypocrisy of our world," and that such darkness reveals an internal power that invites people "to take, in the face of destiny, a superior and heroic attitude they would never have assumed without it" (1958, 31–32). By the mid-1970s, Hijikata had implemented such a thesis in ensemble performances. In a 1977 interview, theatre director Suzuki Tadashi stated that Hijikata had cultivated a form of crisis more volatile than long-established Japanese arts ostensibly dedicated to the same sense of instability:

> When I see noh and such, I no longer feel that fictional perfection exists based on a sense of crisis or in that sense of terror that if you take even one wrong step you will fall backwards into a dreadful abyss. . . . My first impression of Mr. Hijikata's work was that sense of crisis . . . that going in such a direction is difficult and also that

what emerges from it is quite chancy. Even when a certain relationship comes about, it's really very good because the relationship has a sense of crisis. (Hijikata, Senda, and Suzuki 2000, 62–63)

Suzuki points to the issue of routinization in the making and consumption of any method of collective communication based on expression or "charisma," such as religion, politics, art, or dance (Weber 1991). Classical dances such as Japanese Noh, Western ballet, Thai Khon, or Indian Bharata Natyam are just a few of many forms worldwide in which body positions and movements are objectively codified and predetermined as requisite foundation for any further expressivity and individuality. While numerous variants of even Western Modern or ballroom dance exist, they are still largely codified in terms of proper body positioning, gestural vocabulary, and movement texture.

Genres, styles, and idioms for instigating and embodying ambiguities have developed as well in every medium, from painting to dance to new media and beyond. These forms run the risk, however, of becoming fetishized by adherents desiring to regulate their effects. The French Impressionists broke from Western classical academic painting in the nineteenth century, but their innovations also led to decades of newly codified techniques in the twentieth century. More recent artistic movements borne from postmodern culture's desire to resist late capitalism's postindustrial hegemony have resulted in their own form of ideology. The Dogme 95 international collective of filmmakers, for example, established a "Vow of Chastity" that, while a somewhat tongue-in-cheek gesture aimed at the high cost of feature film production and mainstream commercial aesthetics, held artists to a set of "rules" for nominally straightforward, honest, and "authentic" storytelling.[1]

Dance artists seeking to maintain the knife-edge of indeterminacy, therefore, need to invent ever wider-reaching and more inclusive modes of spontaneity or difference than codifications that set physically specific and indexically permanent forms. While any technology begs the question of routinization—after all, systems are systems—evoking the potent and unfathomable is also always one purview of art. Adding to Hijikata's and Ohno's methods of starting from the a priori, subjectively experienced body, additional structures and concepts may be useful, perhaps starting by stepping back to orient movement practice within the philosophical.

In *Butoh: Dance of the Dark Soul* (1987), critic Mark Holborn quotes Hijikata as saying, "I come from Tohoku, but there is Tohoku in everybody," and "There is no philosophy before butoh. It is only possible that a philosophy may come out of butoh" (Hoffman and Holborn 1987, 9). Taken together, these statements and others indicate that Hijikata was not wedded to a formalist definition of his work. His Tohoku imaginary may inspire practitioners not only to activate a relationship between their bodies and crisis states, but also to invent their own imaginaries. Hijikata's *butoh-fu* was based on *his* Tohoku, implying that other persons' imaginaries could serve as the basis for their own butoh-based investigations. If it is not absolutely necessary to adopt Hijikata's formal imagery and language in order to engage a body in crisis, then perhaps his essential practice may be philosophical as well. Tanaka Min's experience of Hijikata echoes this prospect:

> He (Hijikata) would often say something is *butoh-teki*, butoh-like. "Look, isn't he *butoh-teki*?" he would say or, looking at a dog, "You see, this dog is butoh!" He would find the essence of butoh even in nonhuman creatures including plants. Movement, technique, and *kata* (form) are merely parts of dance but not all. (2006)

Seeing butoh wherever one finds it means one's values, priorities, and practice exist symbiotically. After decades of practice, dancer Mizu Desierto speaks of coming to butoh as the discovery, not of a concretized form, but of a psycho-physiological approach to art and healing. She is increasingly concerned with the larger relevances of butoh as a mode of connectivity between self and other beyond the stage:

> Butoh came to me at a really interesting time. My father had just passed away unexpectedly . . . and around the same time I met a dancer who was . . . integrating butoh forms, so she first gave me the philosophy. I'm more drawn as I age to butoh as a life practice and how it infuses everything I'm doing, and how I continue to offer that to other people who aren't necessarily dancers even. So I think it's coming from an interest or a need I have to continue to dance and also explore the somatic intelligence that I think the world needs more of, but maybe not through just witnessing me. (2011)

Within butoh's legacy as a resistant practice against hegemony, if butoh can also serve as a philosophy, this fact may point to broader activations of a butoh-based paradigm. Just as Hijikata could conceive of paintings as revealing a butoh quality, we might speak of acting or playing music as butoh or through a butoh lens since they are also art forms in which performers may challenge themselves to embody chaos, contradiction, or crisis via language, character, or sound. In the book *A Director Prepares: Seven Essays on Art and Theatre* (2001), stage director Anne Bogart orients her theatre practice around the principles of *memory, violence, eroticism, terror, stereotype, embarrassment,* and *resistance.* She weaves these concepts together to fuel her creativity in collaboration and rehearsal: "The sensation of this walk to the stage, to the actor, feels like walking into a treacherous abyss. The walk creates a crisis in which innovation must happen, invention must transpire. I create the crisis in rehearsal to get out of my own way. . . . In unbalance and failing lie the potential to create" (86). Bogart extends her framework and compares her stage experiences to examples outside of theatre in order to demonstrate how similarly crisis operates in both performance and other situations:

> Most people become highly creative in the midst of an emergency. In the instant of imbalance and pressure, quick and decent solutions to big immediate problems must be found. It is in these moments of crisis that native intelligence and intuitive imagination kick in: the woman who lifts a car because her child is trapped beneath, an inspired strategic choice in the crisis of battle, the quick decisions in the heat of a final rehearsal before a first night audience. (129–30)

Likewise, the body in crisis is more than an approach to performance. The very terms "body" and "crisis" exist on a wider plane of meaning, resonance, and relevance, about which I am speculating. Thus, how may a butoh performance paradigm be approximated in other fields and contexts? One example outside of art making is the performance of crisis in architecture. In *Against Architecture* (1989), Denis Hollier opposes the positivist and utilitarian subtext that drove Georges Bataille to write about the melancholic loss of social value and collective emotion accreted around the cathedral at Rheims, France, severely damaged in World War Two. Hollier speaks of "the veiled ideological necessity controlling" Bataille's eulogistic text, "a far vaster and more secret cathedral in which it is thoroughly trapped and . . . which makes writing only possible *afterward* and against this text, against the oppressive architecture of constructive values" (1992, 15).[2] Implicit within Hollier's thesis is an inherent tension between dominant and subaltern value structures that compete for the use and meaning of architecture.

John McMorrough expands this concept when he speaks of the "genre of the apocalyptic" in cultural thought, or "the shadow of the progressive ideal of the avant-garde," "a description of a new prevalent condition," and "a means of working through the problematics of its era" (2009, unpaginated). The author asserts that the apocalyptic for contemporary society is "both global warming and sub-prime loans, both nuclear terrorism and social ills. All are real, and all are, to some extent, constructs" (unpaginated). Put another way, even in the Covid-19 era, the scale and complexity of both potential destruction and actual suffering are largely determined by what human society has wrought upon itself. The built and designed impression of social structures, which direct public discourse similarly to Hollier's competing value sets within socioeconomic and political hierarchies, makes their destruction within the apocalyptic not simply an end, but also a beginning: "In this sense the specter of the apocalypse is another version of the modernist tabula rasa, a leveling of the past to make way for the future" (unpaginated). For McMorrough, in this era of widespread fears about humanity's collapse, competing ideals are put to the greatest test, and we find that the utopian and apocalyptic both present radical change and an opportunity to recalibrate our collective imagination.

Echoing Bogart and McMorrough, Mark Wigley asserts that emergencies not only inspire, but require creativity, in speaking of crisis as key to architectural and environmental design:

> What happens when emergency turns into crisis as the familiar linear narrative—immediate danger and rapid response followed by careful repair and eventual recovery—does not unfold? What happens when the recovery narrative itself breaks down? What would be the architecture of crisis? Is crisis architecture a contradiction in terms or a crucial unacknowledged force? (2009)

Architecture tangibly exists, making any architecture of crisis something that happens and an example of crisis leading to schism or, borrowing Gregory Bateson's term for an ongoing lack of resolution, *schismogenesis* (Bateson 1972, 68; Turner 1985, 293; Schechner 2006, 211). Crisis is part of what Wigley refers to as society's "familiar linear narrative" in that we expect conflict to ultimately resolve. For Wigley, an all-encompassing, paradigmatic approach to stabilization characterizes most emergency response mechanisms: "The role of emergency procedures is to maintain the limits of a particular space. In a sense, they define the real geometry of that space. The actual condition of a space is not revealed in its visible shape but in the emergency protocols that are used to maintain the shape" (2009). In what other field, for example, are plumbers, electricians, locksmiths, and even paramedics and insurance agents but the conservation, preservation, and restoration of domestic space, of a normative definition of home?

Limited space and stability become codefined in the context of emergency response, or what Wigley calls "crisis management," wherein stability is equated with stasis. Hijikata railed against such a notion in postwar Japan. He posited his Tohoku imaginary's *nikutai* (fleshy/carnal body), refashioned from the *kokutai* (national body) as an alternative to the bland homogeneity arising from the strange brew of the Occupation's democracy by decree, an unleashed Western commercial culture, and an undercurrent of Japanese social conformity. Hijikata nurtured and produced his idiosyncratically refined vocabulary of crisis body imagery by appropriating and juxtaposing archetypes of a hellish urbanism and a mysterious ruralism. His performative body, poised out of balance between these structures, sharply influenced by both yet defined by neither, stands in stark contrast to mainstream American domestic culture in the same postwar period. It was Hijikata's place, his idiosyncratic *home*, undefinable in normative terms, versus society's space, the abstracted *house* to which both the late modernist and late industrial culture and the growing postmodern consumer culture were assigned. Corporeally and spatially, butoh practice sits opposite to the rise of American suburbanism in the 1950s and 1960s. As Lippard states:

> Although for a century the U.S. has not been a rural nation, a single-family house with trees and flowers and a big lawn remains the American dream. . . . City living exists in vibrant defiance of that dream; suburban living compromises it. If the city has stood for

vice, and nature for virtue, then the suburb is morally somewhere in between. (1998, 226)

Liminal in a vacant, noncommittal manner, suburbs are a compromise between movement and stasis. They are redolent with the patina of an imagined socioeconomic mobility, yet static in their occupants' desire for security in the dominant socioeconomic hierarchy. Conversely, engaging crisis provides motivation and rationale for processes leading to either movement or stasis. Both are self-perpetuating: the nature of movement is stimulus and change, while stasis is distinguished by limitation and uniformity.

Environmental activist and former physicist Vandana Shiva argues for the biological and social nature of movement: "Sustainable societies move in a stable state—with, not against, the cycles of life. To be in a stable state is not to be motionless; it involves movement and progression within an orbit, like an electron around the atom or the moon around the earth" (2005, 51). Balance and harmony require motion and a perennial state of *coming-into-being*, also characteristic of butoh practice. Stillness in butoh serves largely to highlight the impossibility of stasis. There are few artists, for example, who claim the butoh mantle and also choreograph with heightened precision or symmetry to the point of actual stillness. Moreover, Hijikata's *butoh-fu* was an attempted codification of his aesthetic, yet it instigated idiosyncratic active and reactive movement within each dancer, so exact movements vary. The teachings of Ohno Kazuo, who functioned during much of his career as a solo dancer, also bred spontaneity in his students. His training exercises stressed creativity and a broad, indeterminate movement vocabulary based on simple, singular images.[3] As Goda Nario highlights, the approach developed by Hijikata, Ohno, and others established butoh as a paradoxically subjective and communal art: "A Butoh method developed, but the experience is individual. A basic attitude or approach is common in Butoh, both past and present, but expression varies. One attitude remains central to Butoh, however; the reaction of the body—it answers the world outside" (Horton Fraleigh 1999, 175).

Butoh's emphasis on self-reflection and coming-into-being makes it an impulsive practice that, in a certain sense, embodies exactly and only momentary form. Unlike the above examples of crisis management or suburban planning, which attempt to circumscribe, contain, and erase crisis within proscribed parameters, spontaneity and improvisation in identity-based performance is crisis embodiment, epitomizing the momentariness of being itself. As Wigley asserts, "Nobody can plan for crisis since crisis is exactly . . . that which defeats both planning beforehand and response afterwards" (2009). Effective crisis response thus also includes that which holds the potential for further crisis. In this sense, just as any attempt to resolve a state of crisis, sooner or later, creates one anew, so any attempt to resolve a performer or character's contradictory state in butoh engenders further unresolved expression.

(RE)MAKING

To where does the production and perpetuation of crisis lead? Was Turner correct that rituals of affliction can instigate communal compassion and sharing? Was Artaud right that theatre most effectively operates in a plague-like manner, afflicting practitioners and audiences to trigger, in his words, our "hidden force" or "heroic attitude"? Is Wigley accurate in asserting that crisis is the ultimate paradox by which society moves forward and repeatedly generates itself? Do these theories possess similar social agendas, and how thin is the line in crisis-based methodologies between benevolent transformation and fetishized manipulation?

To speculate in detail around such questions and how butoh may relate to larger frames of reference, I compare and contrast butoh as a principled strategic approach to addressing crisis with a geopolitical theory, *the shock doctrine*, coined by social critic Naomi Klein in her book *The Shock Doctrine: The Rise of Disaster Capitalism* (2007). Klein details the relentless dismantling of social support systems worldwide where neo-laissez-faire concepts have been enforced via institutionalized chaos and violence, especially those inspired by the theories of economist Milton Friedman, who stated that "only a crisis—actual or perceived—produces real change. When that crisis occurs, the actions that are taken depend on the ideas that are lying around. That, I believe, is our basic function: to develop alternatives to existing policies, to keep them alive and available until the politically impossible becomes politically inevitable." (7)

At face value, this theorem echoes butoh's performance of crisis. The crucial difference is that Friedman's followers have predetermined, hegemonic solutions ready to go when disaster strikes, while butoh responds via chaotic, contradictory, or irrational states for self-empowerment of individuals within a collective. As Maro Akaji, butoh artist and founding director of the butoh company Dairakudakan, describes:

> In Japan, there is a great materialism and a great contradiction in people's attitude toward nature. If the unique economic situation in contemporary Japan is described as a miracle, then Butoh is another Japanese miracle; it is the antithesis of the economic miracle and it is a total rejection of the values of that materialism. We need to stop the accelerated activity of development. We need to block the velocity. Butoh is therefore a dangerous force. (Hoffman and Holborn 1987, 76)

As Wigley asserts, the designed emergency response of predetermined solutions are intrinsically crises waiting to happen. The more structured, enclosed, or authoritarian the solution is, the larger any resulting crisis may be when imbalance or tension occurs, and the more possible a chaotic or destructive result. If mass protest, for example, is a logical response to autocracy, an even more massive and possibly violent quelling is a next logical response, leading to a further, even greater cycle of liberation and oppression. While "Friedman predicted that the speed, suddenness, and scope of the economic shifts would provoke psychological reactions in the public that 'facilitate the adjustment'" (Klein 2007, 8), his economic shock treatment methods undergird legal, commercial, and social control structures via masking and institutionalization. Conversely, butoh highlights and subverts their deleterious effects on individual bodies. Both systems generate newly configured landscapes of cultural, ethnic, political, and economic difference, though butoh stresses horizontal multiplicity and mutual resonances, while the shock doctrine looks to hierarchy:

> Believers in the shock doctrine are convinced that only a great rupture—a flood, a war, a terrorist attack—can generate the kind of vast, clean canvases they crave. It is in these malleable moments, when we are psychologically unmoored and physically uprooted, that these artists of the real plunge in their hands and begin their work of remaking the world. (25)

Butoh also might be said to employ "artists of the real," but they produce by imagining new realities oriented toward the as yet unknown for their own and the audience's sake. As Katsura Kan states:

> It looks like earlier human, before human, or maybe it's a question about humanity. And then he seems to transform into an animal, stone, wind, nature, or whatever. And then for me the most important point is if something can't be identified. It's not a performer forcing his own image onto the audience. I think butoh is freer for performer and audience, who can transform together. (2009)

Shock doctrinaires reduce, decreasing action, diversity, and dialogue alternative to their destabilization by design. They diminish obstacles in their wake to corner the market for financial, psychological, or social profit. Klein's definitive example of the shock doctrine's true colors is the Chilean military's bloody overthrow of the Salvador Allende government in 1972 and the equally violent restructuring of the nation's economy:

> Pinochet also facilitated the adjustment with his own shock treatments; these were performed in the region's many torture cells, inflicted on the writhing bodies of those deemed most likely to stand in the way of the capitalist transformation. Many in Latin America saw a direct connection between the economic shocks that impoverished millions and the epidemic of torture that punished hundreds of thousands of people who believed in a different kind of society. (2007, 8)

The shock doctrine jolts society into determined chaos and submission, with a disabled, defeated, or even exterminated body in crisis as its end goal. Butoh instead primes recursive properties in the body in crisis and extrapolates them into the social realm. This strategy was molded in the crucible of post-World War Two Japan, with Western occupiers and subjectivity-obsessed avant-gardists—two groups of "artists of the real" with contrary tactics and goals—competing to rebuild the country from either the top down or inside out. Klein points to post-coup Chile, post-Cold War Russia, post-invasion Iraq, and a host of other political-historical settings as similarly conflict-ridden contact zones. In the U.S., corrupt government officials and greedy real estate developers looking to cash in on the destruction of poor and working-class neighborhoods in New Orleans after Hurricane Katrina took more than a page from

Friedman's book and gave the shock doctrine a toehold on American soil:

> By the time Hurricane Katrina hit New Orleans, and the nexus of Republican politicians, think tanks and land developers started talking about "clean sheets" and exciting opportunities, it was clear that this was now the preferred method of advancing corporate goals: using moments of collective trauma to engage in radical social and economic engineering. (9)

Post-Katrina New Orleans was a heightened manifestation of the shock doctrine, where globalization met global warming in crisis mode, radically altering social collectives in an authoritarian sweep, denuding the economic, political, and cultural landscape in its wake. Instead of seeking out local diversities within diverse localities, the shock doctrine enforces an abstracting homogenization. C. Tabor Fisher discusses how these tendencies invisibilized such diversity within an insidious tautology in New Orleans in the decades leading up to Katrina:

> The Lower Ninth Ward has been repeatedly called poor, black, and crime-ridden, drawing on racist images of "ghetto" or "slum." Poor blacks become symbolic pseudo-subjects, spatially attached to the ward through a process Charles Mills has described as "circular indictment": if you live in the Lower Ninth, then you are poor and deprived, and if you are poor and deprived, you must live in the Lower Ninth. (2008, 161)

As Wigley illustrates, space delineates and often defines crisis, but it is people that respond to, manage, and resolve it. Similarly, as butoh practice demonstrates, while social and environmental circumstances may instigate crisis, individuals subjectively engaged with it are the ones who transform it. Fisher links these concepts in positing multiplicity to address institutionalized racism and hegemony:

> Spaces do not resist; only active people do. Therefore, in order to represent space in resistance to racism and classism, spatial theory must enable, rather than obliterate, the active subjectivity of the people who live in the Lower Ninth Ward, and it must include the relations among the people in the space and between those people and people in other spaces. Such a representation will be concrete,

multiple, dynamic, and textured, and, therefore, less clean and comprehensive than abstract representations. (161–62)

Enclosing communal space ghettoizes it, eviscerating its power and influence. Opening such space—physically, mentally, and perceptually—makes its identity fluid, variable, and liminal, moving to a broader spectrum of social relations, interdependencies, and cooperation, and increasing its value for constituents. Butoh training frames the body as such a space, thereby modeling relational diversity and structured resistance.

Further, what is required for either enclosure or opening to fulfill its mandate is a certain balance or imbalance between control and freedom. In the case of the shock doctrine, this means unbridled disturbance: "For economic shock therapy to be applied without restraint . . . some sort of additional major collective trauma has always been required, one that either temporarily suspended democratic practices or blocked them entirely" (Klein 2007, 13). The shock and resultant crisis are externally rooted and imposed from outside, with predictably hierarchy-inducing results: "Like the terrorized prisoner who gives up the names of comrades and renounces his faith, shocked societies often give up things they would otherwise fiercely protect" (20). While butoh aims for reclamation and reinvention of identity and self, the shock doctrine results in their destruction and disappearance, where "followers deplore diversity and demand an absolute free hand to implement their perfect system. . . . It is a logic that leads ineluctably toward violence" (23). The Jewish Holocaust following Germany's World War One defeat and recession. Japanese American mass incarceration in World War Two following Pearl Harbor. Ramped-up anti-immigrant sentiment and white supremacist violence in the U.S. following the 2008 Great Recession and Obama presidency.

Such a mindset—the crisis of stasis, the fear of movement and change—and its resultant strategies can be observed in multiple arenas. Thousands of police officers, with the coordinated assistance of the federal government, clearing out Occupy protests nationwide, corralling news cameras into "safe" areas, with batons blazing around every other street corner, hidden from view. Popular music producers never leaving a synthesized instrument or auto-tuned vocal note to chance. Klein points to CIA torture manuals, much of which symbiotically influenced and adopted Friedman's principles:

> They explain that the way to break "resistant sources" is to create violent ruptures between prisoners and their ability to make sense of the world around them. First, the senses are starved of any input (with hoods, earplugs, shackles, total isolation), then the body is bombarded with overwhelming stimulation (strobe lights, blaring music, beatings, electroshock). . . . It is in this state of shock that most prisoners give their interrogators whatever they want—information, confessions, a renunciation of former beliefs. (19)

Butoh performance also often bombards the body with "overwhelming stimulation" (chaos) creating "violent ruptures" (contradiction) between "resistant sources" (practitioners and audiences) and "the sense of the world around them" that has been imposed from outside (socialized sensibilities and habits), thereby causing individuals to reveal personal "information, confessions" (their conflicted inner lives) through a liminal state (crisis). Butoh and the shock doctrine are mirror images of each other, but with opposite goals and concomitant means and ends.

Klein also argues that imposing radical change too quickly or traumatically can have the opposite of the intended effect of breaking the victim's will. In Indonesia, Bolivia, and Iraq, authoritarian plans eventually backfired after the application of "too much direct pain and, instead of regression and compliance, the interrogators face confidence and defiance" (351). This may be one reason why and how methodologies like butoh work, where the pain is inflicted from both outside *and* within, from not only dominant others but oneself, making it not only shocking but intolerable and triggering a psycho-physiological, systemic cleansing reaction, what Goda refers to as "subconscious rebellion" within the "confused self" (Horton Fraleigh 1999, 175). Or as butoh artist Murobushi Ko describes the inherent enigma of his artistic motivation:

> In my identification, there's a contradiction. Sometimes I need this. I don't know if I'm still a butoh artist or not. But I always think about why I like butoh so much. And I said this is the impossibility of movement. This is the most strong possibility and positivity of butoh, I think, for creation. Because I always want to stand in this position, this position, this position, because I can't stop as a butoh dancer, and I'm still butoh. (2012)

Sooner or later, however, the powers that be in any arena get wise, and the dance world is no exception. For butoh, an increased profile has brought overtures to mass commodification, perhaps starting with Hijikata and his dancers as a Dr. Moreau-like villain and his grotesque creatures in the 1968 horror movie, *Edogawa Rampo Zenshū: Kyoufu Kikei Ningen* (English title: *Horrors of Malformed Men*). Popular music acts have employed painted, grotesque-faced, butoh-ish bodies as signifiers of everything from misery to spiritual purity.[4] Even in high art criticism, butoh is often reduced to inscrutable Asian bodies and an essentialized, post-Hiroshima, Japanese psyche. Perhaps this is no different than the commercialization of 1960s counterculture rock bands and 1980s hip-hop DJ and MC crews, or refinement of the shock doctrine in the twenty-first century to commodify crisis itself:

> The next phase of the disaster capitalism complex is all too clear: with emergencies on the rise, government no longer able to foot the bill, and citizens stranded by their can't-do state, the parallel corporate state will rent back its disaster infrastructure to whoever can afford it, at whatever price the market will bear. For sale will be everything from helicopter rides off rooftops to drinking water to beds in shelters. (529)

While butoh is intended to reveal crisis, the shock doctrine predetermines its production. It's the difference between putting your body on the line and having it taken away from you beforehand. If butoh is capable of manifesting a *post-socialized* state of being, then the shock doctrine epitomizes a preemptive strike against such possibility. Unlike temporary or overtly violent crises like the imperialism of postwar and postcolonial eras of the twentieth century, this is augmented, artificial crisis normalizing thievery within an ideological framework of everyday life values. In postwar Japan's enforced liberation and re-engineering of quotidian corporealities, early butoh performance was a fetishized rebellion and apt reaction against a monolithic and impersonal hegemony. While democracy by decree is still attempted (as in the U.S.'s Iraq and Afghanistan conflicts), it is proving less efficient than consumption by decree. Why force people to live within a determined politico-economic system when you can persuade them that a limited set of predetermined choices are all they need or want? In other words, in the face of a new kind of matrix, activists must imagine resistance of a different order. If my contention is correct that butoh's revelation of self-knowledge leading to crisis may facilitate empowerment, then this may be a place to start. The architects of simulacra are intent on preventing awareness that there is ever any other world or body with which to begin.[5] As Klein asserts, however, in detailing the work of psychiatrist Ewen Cameron, the shock doctrine's methodological inspiration, thievery and memory make incompatible bedfellows:

> All shock therapists are intent on the erasure of memory. Ewen Cameron was convinced that he needed to wipe out the minds of his patients before he could rebuild them. . . . But like Cameron's former patient Gail Kastner, with her intricate architecture of papers, books and lists, recollections can be rebuilt, new narratives can be created. Memory, both individual and collective, turns out to be the greatest shock absorber of all. (585–86)

If knowing who you are entails who you have been and can be, then butoh points toward maximizing memory beyond fear and shock, cultivating agency through one's moving body as is, where memory becomes the handmaiden of imagination. This phenomenon may be why butoh dance tends toward the assymetrical, decentered, and broken. Performers assemble themselves before our eyes, not back together, but into new combinations of elements derived from the dismembered-remembered detritus of oppression, passion, marginalization, and desire. They are at once the answer and the question. As butoh dancer Denise Fujiwara states, "Memory plays into my practice because it is the storage facility for our experience and can bring detail and specificity to the work. Butoh allows us to re-imagine and re-invent our memories in fantastic ways. So if you have a good cache of memories, you become a richer dancer" (2018). Similarly, Katsura Kan describes the resonance between what is held in the body and lost in society:

> When your grandmother or grandfather dies, we lose many things. And we can't catch up. But somehow we believe the body has memory. And then the dance only wants to involve some kind of memory. If we're doing something we can't identify onstage, it's interesting because it might be my grandmother's mother's mother's mother doing something like this [*demonstrates a move-*

ment]. So that's why new vocabulary in butoh helps to research something missing or vanishing. (2009)

As Klein states, memory operates as a shock absorber, making it capable of fostering shared reference points between performer and audience. Every creative act initiates a web of details within the dense realms of history and memory, wherein audiences experience the artist's desire for meaning. The more mutually resonant these particles are, the more performer and audience are joined by the weight of history. As Pierre Nora states, "history is a representation of the past," "binds itself strictly to temporal continuities, to progressions and to relations between things," and "belongs to everyone and to no-one, whence its claim to universal authority" (1989, 8–9). The more disparate a performance's elements are, however, the more memory is tasked with making sense of the pieces: "Memory takes root in the concrete, in spaces, gestures, images, and objects" and "is blind to all but the group it binds—which is to say, as Maurice Halbwachs has said, that there are as many memories as there are groups, that memory is by nature multiple and yet specific; collective, plural, and yet individual" (9).

Through its broken-ness, then, butoh charges memory's affect with the task of re-assembling bodies pulled apart by history's authority, the shards of the past . . . *including my own* . . .

FIRST MEMORY, FIRST BODY

(Journal entry, November 2010.)

This is the way it always begins.

I'm no different. A dream from among the first upright moments in life. Grasping the shaky railing of an unstable crib, simultaneously transfixed, fearing, and fascinated by the flood of ghettobird moonlight tracing across my room from a sky too low for heaven above, but still over my head. I didn't understand, but someone was clearly in control. I distinctly remember wondering then and there if, when the light found me, I would become a suspect, a criminal.

Now, four decades on, guilt a foregone conclusion, I know very well how to find my light, but even better how to recede into the darkness, still on my own, still waiting, contemplating, among the shadows in every possible moment.

Flat-footed, I still maintain that first stance from forty-two years ago as an achievement worth repeating, leaning precariously, one at a time, on the outside edge of my feet, an unsure stance entirely assured of its identity. The gravitational clarity of flat feet denied, deferring to a desperate, hopeless plea against Earth's pullout of respect, infatuation.

Forty-two years of stepping, one sole at a time scraping the concrete of a city too familiar and meandering. You see their virgin eyes upon arrival (No center! No there there!), *but you know better, but you can't explain. You can only stand (nobody walks), smile, hope for the best, that they can learn to find theirs in the sea of super lowest common flat surfaces and countless identifications lurking beneath, sand traps of empty form without a mirror.*

In such a forest, no one follows your steps. They can't see a path you've no intention of marking, despite your occasional protestations. Infrequently, finding your dimmest possible light, you stomp out a clearing, a window to let back out your store of ghettobird moonlight, a frame betwixt and between through which you invite infinite peering, a canted, cracked mirror held uncertainly askance; a mute plea for sympathy; a distant, firm, loving embrace.

The author as a child, 1969. Photo by Tillie Sakamoto.

The author performing "Flash Mixtape," Kuala Lumpur, 2011. Photo by Weeling Chen.

THE (NEVER-)ENDING

Rennie: How do you define butoh?
Me: Chaos, contradiction, and crisis.
Rennie: Just like hip-hop.
— The author in conversation with street dance choreographer Rennie Harris (2009)

In his book, *Rhythm Science* (2004), musician Paul D. Miller takes us on a ride through the variegated corners of a postmodern hip-hop philosophy. Taking "the mix" as his central metaphor, Miller weaves a tale of hip-hop cultural practice as the essence of early twenty-first century being, where, through our cyclical consumption and expression of ever-increasing levels of reference-laden cultural lexica, we are fast becoming virtualized remixes in mind and body: "It's an uncanny situation; the creative act becomes a dispersion of self. Back in the day, it was called alchemy, but in the hyperfluid environment of information culture, we simply call it the mix" (29). Many critics skeptical of sampling culture's manifestation of postmodernism's juxtapositional, collagist structures view this global phenomenon with trepidation or disgust. Just as memory and imagination, however, interweave in the mind-body space of the butoh practitioner or rescued victim of the shock doctrinaires, Miller views the digital era as a golden opportunity for anyone to remake their experience of the world around them:

> Sampling allows people to replay their own memories of the sounds and situations of their lives. . . . At the end of the day, it's all about reprocessing the world around you, and this will happen no matter how hard entertainment conglomerates and an older generation of artists tries to control these processes. We're in a delirium of saturation. We're never going to remember anything exactly the way it happened. (28–29)

We can likewise frame the butoh body as a set of contradictory samples drawn from the juxtaposition between our personal experience and socialization, causing a crisis that resolves through liminality and transformation. As Miller puts it, "That's what mixing is about: creating seamless interpolations between objects of thought to fabricate a zone of representation in which the interplay of the one and the many, the original and its double all come into question" (33). Moreover, like butoh, Miller sees contemporary hip-hop as possessing a distinctly therapeutic potential:

> Could this be the way of healing? Taking elements of our own alienated consciousness and recombining them to create new languages from old (and in doing so to reflect the chaotic turbulent reality we all call home), just might be a way of seeking to reconcile the damage rapid technological advances have wrought on our collective consciousness. (72)

If, as Miller further contends, "Sampling is like sending a fax to yourself from the sonic debris of a possible future; the cultural permutations of tomorrow, heard today" (77), then butoh's revelation of chaos may allow us likewise to view the past. By revealing seams and disparate elements in one's bodily landscape, designed by socialization for the perception of seamlessness, one may comprehend the root fabric from which they come and reintegrate them through schismogenetic embodiment, or what Hijikata called sewing our "two skins" back together again (Hoffman and Holborn 1987, 121). This is butoh as remix therapy, where the ever-evolving process of life, death, and rebirth of self via the body in crisis is directly akin to hip-hop's remix; where schismogenesis and resolution cohabit and become, not contradictory, but one and the same in a benevolently self-consuming cycle of reinvention.

Moreoever, training and performance designed to nurture integration and hold space for crisis states may also illuminate and inform discourses in other fields, such as culture, politics, health, or the environment. From the human body to the planetary body to the body politic, the desire to address crisis is perennially urgent, for, as Wigley states:

> A crisis is the moment that the threat is not just inside the space but is actually an extreme challenge to the space itself, from the scale of an individual psyche or body in crisis to that of a family, an institution, a city, a region, a nation, or a planet. If an emergency is a threat within a system, a crisis is a threat to the whole system. (2009)

Crisis is an existential threat capable of manifesting at all scales, and the butoh body in crisis may express such peril in numerous manifestations. Ohno Kazuo's bare body in dance shorts and dance shoes, leaning against a grand piano while a Bach prelude and fugue play, practically unable to move, leaving the audience to process what is and is not being expressed: dancing without dancing.[6] Hijikata Tatsumi presented to the audience on a royal palanquin, dressed in a woman's white silk wedding kimono, stripping down to reveal his body naked except for a long golden phallus sculpture.[7] A Sankai Juku dancer dressed military style as a Japanese schoolboy, desperately unable to eat raw rice kernels or enter temple-like doors twice his height, his silent, deafening scream at the audience.[8] Butoh may serve as a microcosm of both personal and social realms, and how this occurs will differ by each performer-practitioner and viewer-witness.

AN EMPTY ROOM

In *Earth Democracy: Justice, Sustainability, and Peace* (2005), Vandana Shiva lays out a manifesto for shifting society toward an equitable and ecological balance, and her modality for achieving this goal is the democratization of the source material of life itself: "Ecological security is our most basic security; ecological identities are our most fundamental identity. We *are* the food we eat, the water we drink, the air we breathe. And reclaiming democratic control over our food and water and our ecological survival is the necessary project for our freedom" (5).

With this book, I hope to open a similarly futurizing discussion of butoh's potential relevance to a global discourse on crisis by theorizing lived democratization of the performing body. Shiva's concept of Earth Democracy connects people "in circles of care, cooperation, and compassion instead of dividing them through competition and conflict, fear and hatred" (11). My goal is to elucidate a cyclical process of transformative affect made possible by butoh-based practice, positing active witnessing, liminality, vulnerability, and dialogue in opposition to voyeurism, theft, separation, and authoritarianism. I imagine the butoh body as resistant against certain effects of hubris, overconsumption, and hegemony. I posit a method of claiming agency over one's performing body, a commitment to decolonizing and decommodifying one's performative ontology away from bourgeois complacency. In some sense, I aim to provide a path for anyone to become, at least in principle, a butoh artist, marking their bodily space as an idiosyncratic place, cycling endlessly through identity and potential, or what Zen literature refers to as *form and emptiness*, or, in metaphorical terms, *an empty room*.

The theoretical elements of butoh, echoing from the individual to society and back again, are *desire, trickster,* and *the cultural commons,* key permutations of which are the performance of *democracy* as an interactive and generative multiplicity, and *sustainability* as individual or communal capacity for subjectivity or subject-formation. The nature of stasis, conversely, is characterized by *desire, thievery, enclosure,* and the latter's operative mode of *hegemony.* Interwoven and equally possible, these elements are addressed as a series of inseparable binaries in the remaining chapters.

The idea that a radical cultural identity can aspire to social agency and help manifest progressive ideals is, of course, nothing new. Indeed, political and spiritual leaders throughout history are only the most obvious of countless examples. Butoh principles, however, may form a philosophical lens of aesthetic dynamism that offers a particularly tension-oriented frame for knowledge production, meaning making, and critical response within contemporary urgencies and social settings.

In *From Kung Fu to Hip-Hop: Globalization, Revolution, and Popular Culture* (2007), M. T. Kato traces a similar process in the sphere of transnational production and consumption of Bruce Lee films from the 1960s to the present, where differing socioeconomic values and priorities separated by race, class, and hegemony play out on a global stage. Kato characterizes the politically progressive element within this cluster of populations, communities, and industries according to David Solnit's "new radicalism," a worldwide, deterritorialized, multilateral, and multivocal web of thought and action. This movement is arrayed against "the planetary recolonization by transnational capital and radical undermining of national sovereignty by supranational multilateral polity" (2). Kato cites the affective power of personal desire played out viscerally and subversively in social settings as possessing the ability to radicalize democracy in the face of neoliberal hegemony: "The undercurrent of subjectivity that runs from [Emma] Goldman to the global popular movement is a new paradigm where revolution pivots not so much on taking the power of the dominant institution as on reconstruction of society based on radical affirmation of desire and life force both on collective and individual levels" (2). Moreover, Kato echoes the potential for transposing butoh's recursive modality when speaking of the subsequent extrapolation of subjectivity in popular culture:

> Thanks to the progressive aesthetic expressions generated in already semiautonomous subcultures, the popular culture gains its potential for producing affects, aesthetic values, and communal identities autonomously, right in the reproduction process of capitalist social relationship. Accordingly, the mass's appropriation of the progressive aesthetics of popular cultural revolution can render the commodity to "speak" for itself against the grain of its commodity identity. (3)

Butoh's ability to decommodify and recommodify its expression is such a gesture, where "the constitution of progressive artistic expressions assumes a representative expression of the social movement of decolonization" (Kato 2007, 4). Hijikata mugging facetiously through a panoply of Western social dances in *Nikutai no Hanran*. Kasai Akira deconstructing his modern dancer identity onstage through text and movement.[9] Tanaka Min attempting to diminish his individual dancer persona.[10] Subverting the logic of codified form and refusing the audience's expectations of aesthetic familiarity or uncritical pleasure is an avant-gardist's métier and a benevolent sociocultural gesture. Through excision of socialized barriers to cultural inclusion and recursive morphing of perceived and projected identity, butoh practitioners reconstitute the embodiment of culture through dialectically instigated redefinition and perform the results for viewers to witness and reflect in the context of their lives. It's the difference between taking a photo that someone has posed for with an exchange value in mind—images of suffering and selfies, for example, circulated as social capital—and opening the shutter to let in the light that already exists in that moment; awareness instead of acquisition. It's qualitative versus quantitative thinking and behavior, bearing witness individually and communally instead of giving and taking. It is to bear active witness for the other by allowing the instigation, resonance, and consequent activity—life itself—of the other in their self. This is the butoh body's interrelational potential.

Moreover, poetry actualizes desire's ability to lay the groundwork for this progressive state. Kato cites Audre Lorde's claim that poetry is essential for overcoming late Modernism's logos rooted in a Cartesian paradigm through a method, like butoh artists, of "mobile subjectivity":

> When Lorde talks about "I feel, therefore, I can be free," the "I" that can free itself from any constraints through affect clearly departs

> from Descartes's "I" as a rationalized sense of being. It opens an alternative mode of flexible and mobile subjectivity which is singular yet collective, transcending the rigid boundaries of subject formation under the gaze of modernity. (2007, 5–6)

Or as Lorde herself defines poetry, "I speak here of poetry as a revelatory distillation of experience, not the sterile word play that, too often, the white father distorted the word *poetry* to mean—in order to cover a desperate wish for imagination without insight" (2007, 37). She is speaking of and for those who live everyday life without gender or racial privilege, who need poetry, which, because it is rooted in their existential fullness of experience-emotion and language-intellect, speaks truth to power and holds the seed of tangible engagement: "It is a vital necessity of our existence. It forms the quality of the light within which we predicate our hopes and dreams toward survival and change. First made into language, then into idea, then into more tangible action" (37).

Likewise, as cultural critic Lewis Hyde asserts about truth and lies:

> Lies require a liar, and as such they say something about the liar; they are thus better fitted than truths to the task of gratifying the self-regard or narcissism of the individual who makes them. Any work that simply replicates a truth known to others lacks narcissistic appeal. . . . When it comes to truth, however, as the poet Rimbaud wrote, "it is wrong to say: I think. One should say: I am thought." (2010, 137–38)

In *Common as Air: Revolution, Art, and Ownership* (2010), Hyde analyzes the historical development in the West, especially in the United States, of intellectual property as a social and legal construct in opposition to the cultural commons and liberal democracy. He shows that while democracy does not guarantee truth-telling, it makes it possible via multiplicity and dialogue. He also points to the inverse truth that liars and thieves are more vulnerable than truth-tellers because the former have something to hide. Coupling this concept with Hijikata's and Lorde's assertions of subjectivity as an avenue to progressive thought and being, I find an ongoing tension between the production of knowledge and truth via decentered, subjective embodiment on the one hand and untruth, obfuscation, and thievery via self-centered, objectivizing thought on the other. Objectivity requires logic, reason, and clear boundaries at the expense of all else. Subjectivity needs only poetry's infinite resonance. It's the difference between what is and what is possible.

This assertion resonates with the postcolonial urge for identity reformation, where colonization has meant external control of the subjugated entity's body, image, and resources and the reification of static modes of encounter. For an empire's subjects to remain underfoot en masse and long term, they must believe in the reason why. Decolonization thus requires the externalization of internal processes of renewed self-manifestation, or what Gayatri Chakravorty Spivak refers to as a process of both the "colonial subject detaching itself from the Native Informant" and a "postcolonial subject . . . recoding the colonial subject and appropriating the Native Informant's position" (1999, ix).

In the age of globalized, postindustrial borders, and corporatized, transnational power reliant on mass cultural mythologies, Kato asserts that decolonization "necessitates reconstruction of vernacular imagery, narrative, and modes of reception, which can transcend the colonial imagery imposed upon the colonized" (2007, 8). I see this in Hijikata's 1960s postmodern revolt against Western dance and capitalism, woven into the cultural wasteland of his imagined Tokyo, to the premodern Tohoku of his *Kamaitachi*, performed onstage in the 1970s and 1980s. In Kato's terms, Hijikata's sickle-weasels, wind *daruma*, baby baskets in rice fields, and other bristling signs were his vernacular imagery, his mythologized childhood was his narrative, and the staging of both was his mode of reception, all working to transcend an internalized, subjugating, postwar colonization.

In this sense, butoh is the acculturated body dancing in the mirror, accepting what is, while instigating what can be, and circling back to feed itself further: a postmodern process, not of unbridled atavism, but fertility. And the element underlying each moment in this dance of action and life is the same aspect that can lead to passivity and death.

It is desire.

MEMORY: FINDING A GHOST

Christmas Day, 2016. Tashiro, Akita Prefecture, Japan.

At the end of a long day of shooting in various Kamaitachi *sites, there's one more location I want to find: the place where Hosoe photographed the image of Hijikata splayed absurdly on a straw mat, with seven children squatting right in front of him, staring nonchalantly, while a woman from the village stands a few yards distant, calmly taking in the scene. It's always been one of my favorite photos from the series, and somehow one of the most telling; rural Tohoku children examining someone from their former ranks, ostensibly channeling their naïve spirit.*

Yuta says the spot is on the front path of the house of Shibata-san, a village elder, and within two minutes, we pull into her driveway. Shibata-san is outside in her tool shed and greets us with an incredibly gentle smile. Of course, she remembers the photo, she says. I suddenly have an epiphany and ask if she'd be willing to be in my photo as well. A bit shy, she nevertheless quickly agrees. She shows us where Hijikata and the children sat, and where she stood.

I set up the camera. Shibata-san stares at me staring at Hijikata's ghost. Yuta opens the shutter . . .

From the photo essay, "MuNK," Tashiro, Japan, 2016.

4 : DESIRE

PUNCTUM: IN MY HANDS, AN EMPTY ROOM

This is the chamber of desire. This is where it takes place, the manifestation of your dreams.

This is darkness, the space and time of your potential. Without light, you lack energy, impetus, movement forward. Without illumination, your potential diminishes, you accumulate attachment.

Opening the shutter forms an iris, a circle. No beginning. No end. No hierarchy. No separation. Ubiquitous and perennial.

Letting in the light is a decisive act. But will it mean nonintervention or engagement?[1] *Are you creating an image, embodiment, or both?*

Who are you?

In his analysis of psychoanalyst Sigmund Freud's *desire* (*Begehren*) drive, theorist Jacques Lacan situates desire in the indeterminate space between demand for satisfaction and love and the unconditional fulfillment of the subject's perceived need for the object of that love, i.e., the Other:

> For the unconditionality of demand, desire substitutes the "absolute" condition: this condition in fact dissolves the element in the proof of love that rebels against the satisfaction of need. This is why desire is neither the appetite for satisfaction nor the demand for love, but the difference that results from the subtraction of the first from the second, the very phenomenon of their splitting (*Spaltung*). (2004, 276)

This is the state of wanting what we can't have, where the absoluteness of desire exists only in ourselves, outside actuality, where need precludes attainment. Desire is thus liminal, producer and product of its own perpetual cycle of demand and dissatisfaction; of becoming/not becoming. This fulfillment and negation—what Georges Bataille called desire's "excessive violence" (1962, 142)—catalyzes us to imagine and experience the tenuous mental landscapes of perception, knowledge, and behavior driven by desire.

Reflecting on Lacan's spatiality, Slavoj Zizek speaks of the human impetus to somehow connect "the incompatible domains of desire and *jouissance*," even if only indirectly through a third party (1997). This other element he identifies as Lacan's *object a*, which he expansively discusses as "not what we desire, what we are after, but rather that which sets our desire in motion, the formal frame that confers consistency on our desire," and that possesses "a set of fantasmatic features which, when encountered in a positive object, insures that we will come to desire this object" (1997).

In butoh practice, this "formal frame" is the self that one is not, the Other always already within each person, whom we control, are controlled by, and constantly chase. The gap, void, or lack between who we each think we are and who we think we want to be is our dance. Hijikata's premodern Japanese body freed from internalized Westernization. Ohno Kazuo dancing with La Argentina's spirit. This crevice, ravine, or valley, bottomless in its indefinable *ankoku,* and variously shaped as an internalized Other within each practitioner through infinite difference between each of us, is butoh.

Kristeva asks about the other-ed self in its abjection: "Is desire ever anything else but desire for an idealized norm, the norm of the Other?" (1982, 47) This normalized Other is the dark spirit of butoh: the constant and inescapable reflection of mask and inner self conjoined. The butoh dancer is the dualistic entity integrating subject and object, signifier and signified of the irreducible doubleness of cohabitation. Moreover, this entity operates on three levels. One is the relation between performer and audience, negotiating the commodified yet damaged code of the butoh practitioner with the commodifying gaze of the witness that desires encoding.[2] Another is socialized behavior, ranging from innocuous peer pressure intimacies to imperialist decrees, a force-fed frenzy of repetitive utilitarianism and homogenization. Finally, the butoh performer is themselves, peering consciously and abjectly into the mirror in recursive spite and acceptance of all three aspects. In other words, butoh's masked self—its face—contains the *communal, domesticated,* and *intuitive.*

Barthes's memory of the distinct character in each of three gardens around his childhood home also evokes these aspects. He demonstrates how need and want recur in the reflexive mind: "The worldly, the domestic, the wild: is this not the very tripartition of social desire?" (1977, 6) Practically identical to butoh's three faces, these qualities orient the practitioner's desire as a social tripartite as well. Yet another three-fold public practice asserted by Barthes is photography: "I observed that a photograph can be the object of three practices (or of three emotions, or of three intentions): to do, to undergo, to look" (1981, 9). Butoh and photography are not only aesthetically fraternal, but akin in behavior. Each medium in its own way epitomizes desire and action.

Most language for photographic engagement is violent and authoritarian—*hunt, aim, point, shoot, take, capture, freeze, have*—charging them as acts of ownership, hierarchy, and authority (Sontag 1978). There is, however, another tradition, built not on accretion of power, but on subjective presence and a balance between desire, perception, and reality. *Opening the shutter. Letting in the light. Witnessing. Exposing a sensor or film (sheath, membrane) within a camera (dark chamber) to the outside world.* An electronic sensor or strip of celluloid filled with thousands of light-sensitive particles is a fragile medium. Despite Sontag's just protestations against photography's legacy as a tool of patriarchy, the act of photographing is also inherently vulnerable.

Allowing crisis to envelop one's mind-body presence, as in butoh-based training, also makes one vulnerable. In the context of butoh's "desire drive" and its embrace of contradiction, this approach implies a deeper tension between body and image. When image-based desire (attachment to one's constructed vision) is counteracted or balanced by action (what is via what happens), then, like a camera, the body becomes as in the koan that lends this study its name, *an empty room*, an ambivalent space with no clearly attainable state of being on which to hold or depend, but one that is also potentialized. Butoh's broken body is thereby a possibility body.

Examining the interaction of desire, body, and image reveals questions of identity and perception as well. Butoh photos, which frame practitioners attempting liminality or crisis itself, are not simply innocuous snapshots. Their impact—the multiplicity of their *punctum*—derives from the perception of edginess in the performers, from their cultivated impression of darkness, broken-ness, or abjection. Yet perception is just that: not the thing itself. Living between subject and object, between self and other, and intertwined with the performer's projection of their Lacanian *object a*, perception involves the ambivalent push and pull of desire. We feel removed from the subject due to chronology and a sense of otherness, yet photos may stimulate deep-rooted feelings, thereby also making us feel more ourselves. As Lippard describes: "Photographs are seen both as 'facts' and as ghosts or shadows. They are the imperfect means by which we fill the voids of memory in modern culture, to preserve the remnants of a world that has disappeared" (1998, 56).

Photos of violence and death portray a tenuous grasp on life, challenging our desire for knowledge and meaning and tracing the limits of our fascination with viewing the Other. In *Regarding the Pain of Others* (2003), Sontag addresses such challenges by examining how photos of trauma, atrocity, and war are represented and perceived. She cites the example of a 1936 photo by David ("Chim") Seymour that shows Spanish villagers involved in land reform. A Euro-American public sympathetic to the Republicans in the Spanish Civil War, however, readily perceived the photo as an alleged depiction of innocent civilians fearful of air raids. As Sontag puts it: "Memory has altered the image, according to memory's needs, conferring emblematic status on Chim's picture not for what it is described as showing (an outdoor political meeting, which took place four months before the war started) but for what was soon to happen in Spain that would have such enormous resonance" (30). Memory and imagination often conflate in this manner due to familiar markers that evoke common feelings. Desire, especially what is labeled "collective desire," may cause this mental leap, acting as a magnetic force that binds together disparate images and qualities in what is labeled the "collective unconsciousness." Sontag reveals that this force is not a singular entity, but an accumulation:

> All memory is individual, unreproducible—it dies with each person. What is called collective memory is not a remembering but a stipulating: that *this* is important, and this is the story about how it happened, with the pictures that lock the story in our minds. Ideologies create substantiating archives of images, representative images, which encapsulate common ideas of significance and trigger predictable thoughts, feelings. (2003, 86)

Such images instigate the power of viewers' desires in determining expressive behavior, how we construct memory and create knowledge to fulfill such desire. If Berger was right that meaning arises from perception when we assign a past and future to a photo, then are not history itself and narrative, its concomitant language, similarly constructed by our desires? Our stories and truths are driven by what we want from life. Pierre Nora references this condition in speaking of memory, which he states is both collective and individual and behaves according to all that it desires: "Memory, insofar as it is affective and magical, only accommodates those facts that suit it; it nourishes recollections that may be out of focus or telescopic, global or detached, particular or symbolic—responsive to each avenue of conveyance or phenomenal screen, to every censorship or projection" (1989, 8).

Anne Bogart describes the same phenomenon in theatre, where "reality is a construct of thought that desires community" (2001). Speaking of remembering as the corporeal act fundamental to theatre practice, Bogart contends that theatre artists remake the world by refashioning the self: "We create truths by describing, or re-describing, our beliefs and observations. Our task, and the task of every artist and scientist, is to re-describe our inherited assumptions and invented fictions in order to create new paradigms for the future" (2001).

Bogart's thesis and the workings of desire reveal how many butoh practitioners relate their performative identity, rooted in the sum of their self-identity, to their perception of Hijikata, Ohno, or other older-generation butoh artists they admire or with whom they have studied. Each artist may construct a certain persona with which they choose to identify according to their remembered selves. When many practitioners dance, focused as they are on a self-imposed ordeal of chaos and contradiction, they invent a crisis narrative: love and hate, joy and sadness, life and death: stories that live between desire and possession and portray, ultimately and simply, what is in a moment.

PUNCTUM: GIRL

I'm looking at a photo taken by Onozuka Makoto of Hijikata performing in 1972. The dance is called "Girl," and Hijikata is suspending himself barely off the ground by both hands and one foot while his other foot is awkwardly twisted in the air. His decrepit shoes are ready to fall off at any moment. Costume fragments wrap around his waist and genital area, like a makeshift diaper made of old scraps. His long scraggly hair is tied crookedly with a shiny, radiating hairpiece hanging down behind his back. His body is covered in sloppy patches of white makeup and plaster, and his bloodshot eyes stare upward, into the distance.

I say I'm looking at this photo, but it feels like I'm witnessing a totally personal moment.

When I see this photo, I want to stand up. When I see this photo, I want to move. When I see this photo, I want to cry, but the tears never come, just as I am unable to move or stand while staring at the image.

My breath immediately slows past faltering, becoming small, infinitesimal, as if the air in my lungs is all I have left, and I must breathe as gradually as the blooming of a flower.

I see a body forsaken, in shambles, and I want to gather the pieces within myself, unbreak them, dance my way into a complete body in spite of its destitution and destruction.

When I see this photo, I want to become the thing itself.

The author performing "Glorious Day for an Unknown Woman," Los Angeles, California, 1999.

SEEING IS BELIEVING IS SEEING

When I see the Hosoe photo of Ohno Kazuo in the poster on my wall, I sense liminality. I sense that more is always possible. This image of deathliness moving despite itself provokes my subjective desire to live beyond my assumed means. I want to escape delineation and become utter potentiality.

In me, Ohno's photo acts as a metonymic and mnemonic device. Metonymic because it stands for more than just Ohno himself. My love for the photo and the feeling of wholeness it grants me make it a visceral sign of "butoh-ness." Mnemonic because the photo aids in my memory of butoh-ness. While I have accumulated this memory over three decades of butoh in the U.S., Europe, and Asia, it is a remembrance devised in part by the experience of such photos: what and how I wanted to experience based on the images in my mind.

Rooted in its own past and mine, Ohno's photo is "the living image of a dead thing" (Barthes 1981, 79). Instigating and recalling memory and emotion, the image is cause and effect of its own punctum. Interacting with my desire, it is its own raison d'être as an ongoing arousal, provocation, and muse-like image for my practice. My butoh body, redolent with self-regenerative schismogenesis, perennially becomes its own corporeality as punctum, enabled, as art historian Carol Mavor describes, by punctum's inherent irresolution: "Punctum forecloses closure, because desire itself can never be fully attained. Punctum, unlike studium, cannot be shellacked or immobilized" (2012, 43).

The "voice" of a photo—which speaks to oneself from within as punctum—is the voice of one's own God, knowable because purely palpable. As Derrida describes: "The pleasure [*jouissance*] of a continuous and inarticulate presence is a *nearly* impossible experience. . . . The heart is not an organ because it is not inscribed with a system of differences and articulations. It is not an organ because it is the organ of pure presence" (1997, 249–50). Spoken by Derrida as a spiritual metaphor and the psycho-physiological center of humanness, the heart is not in the strictest sense a means because it is always already an end in itself. Derrida's term for the voice of God scaled down to human measure, what speaks through the heart, is *neume*, "pure vocalization, form of an inarticulate song without speech, whose name means breath" (249). Chief among its significations is "the pleasure [*jouissance*] of self-presence, pure auto-affection, uncorrupted by any outside" (250). In other words, subjectivity.

Despite the subjectivity of my relationship to butoh images, I believe my affective experience of them is common among Western butoh dancers of my generation, who came of age in the 1980s and 1990s, after Japanese butoh artists had established themselves abroad, mostly across North America and Europe. We were hungry, with only a handful of books and occasional visiting performers to whet our appetite. Two English-language photobooks, Ethan Hoffman and Mark Holborn's *Butoh: Dance of the Dark Soul* (1987) and Jean Viala and Nourit Masson-Sekine's *Butoh: Shades of Darkness* (1988), were especially instrumental in circulating butoh photo-imagery in America, while Susan Blakeley Klein's *Ankoku Butoh: Premodern and Postmodern Influences on the Dance of Utter Darkness* (1988) was the first scholarly book on butoh published in English and included a few photos.

American butoh artist Joan Laage was affected by these books, and also films and photos, after discovering butoh in the early 1980s, before moving to Tokyo to research butoh, and was invited to perform with Ashikawa Yoko's company, Gnome:

> That rich period. That's when the first documentaries came out. Susan's book came out. Mark Holborn, the two major ones that had all the photos, and I was using those. So early on, especially since I didn't read Japanese, there wasn't much you could read in English. So photography was a huge thing. (2011)

Alissa Cardone recalls that her concept of butoh was "from the very beginning absolutely defined by photographs" in *Butoh: Shades of Darkness*, the first butoh book she encountered (2011). Despite eventually training with Tanaka Min and performing with Kasai Akira and Ohno Yoshito, she was initially mystified and intimidated:

> I saw the images in the *Shades of Darkness* book, you know, they were incredible, riveting. A colleague lent the book to me, and I took it home that night, and I never gave it back! I sat with that book and flipped through the photographs. I couldn't understand how to do that. I think I didn't have an expectation that I would be taught how to do what I saw in the photographs. I don't think I necessarily wanted to do what I saw in the photographs. (2011)

Mizu Desierto, an American dancer trained by Tamano Hiroko, her husband Koichi, a former Hijikata protégé, and Diego Piñon, echoes Cardone's memory: "Of course, *Shades of Darkness*, the others. Everybody knows those books. Those were some of the first photos I saw. I think the most compelling butoh photography that I've seen is by Eikoh Hosoe" (2011). Her relationship with butoh photo-imagery continues to affect her concept of the dancing body and the values she places around it: "I've got a beautiful book of images of Min Tanaka. It's exquisite. I love the images because they really speak to another part of me that's interested in just simplifying and getting more away from costumes and abstractions and into just the human and the land. And I just love that he's so stripped down and bare" (2011).

The intersection of Desierto's photographically inspired perception of butoh practice informing an understanding of the earthly terrain and her declared values as a progressive citizen cultivates a sensitivity to the relationship between humanity and nature. These fuel her desire for developing a method of manifesting sustainable values in everyday life. Desierto has expanded her practice, for example, beyond the stage into a corporeal engagement with organic farming and permaculture, a subject in which she has co-taught university coursework.

American butoh dancer Alenka Loesch studied in the 1990s with the Tamanos in San Francisco and Yoshioka Yumiko and Seki Minako in Berlin, and has produced her own work. She remembers her initial practice as being partly an engagement with butoh photo-imagery as well as *butoh-fu* designed for use in workshop by her teachers. In terms of image-based motivation for meaning in her practice, Loesch mentions photography specifically, and speaks of the *Kamaitachi* images as a template for exploring the roots of one's dance:

> I think those images most definitely take us back to that place where he's from. They've definitely influenced me to go back and investigate our roots and where we come from personally. I grew up in a very rural environment in West Texas. I was born in Lubbock, and we moved every three years all over these industrial wastelands. My grandparents lived on a farm, and I stayed with them quite often, so my memories of childhood are these rural wastelands where it's nothing but big skies and one tree with my swing hanging down from it. So that's the kind of landscape that

I came from. I grew up very lonely in a way because it was only me and my tree. (2011)

Japanese American dancer-choreographer Shinichi Iova-Koga also began his career as a student of the Tamanos, but no longer refers to himself as a butoh artist. He has collaborated with both Western performers and butoh dancers, including Axis Dance Company, ODC Dance Company, Anna Halprin, Murobushi Ko, and Kaseki Yuko, in addition to the work of his interdisciplinary ensemble, inkBoat. While referring to himself as a contemporary dance and physical theater artist, Iova-Koga admits that many of his early inspirations were similar to other butoh artists: "I would say that images of Yoko Ashikawa were very inspiring for me. I think there was something about her visage that, subconsciously or consciously, I would lock onto. It's hard for me to trace, but I would say those were strong in my imagination" (2011).

Desire's relationship with imagery, however, is a double-edged sword, perhaps in art making a necessary risk between perception and projection. In the case of neglecting the assumptions, values, and other influences underlying one's comprehension of what one sees, Barthes's senses of punctum and studium may too easily conflate into an objectified and, eventually, ossified image. Iova-Koga feels that he's witnessed this dilemma in the butoh community:

What we start to get is there's maybe 3,000 images of butoh dance, for example. Well, you can't track all 3,000, right? So you start whittling it down, and you've got maybe five images that have become the consciousness of what butoh dance is. And so many people will say, "Butoh dance, yeah. Shaved, bald-headed men, painted white, hanging upside down," and they're going right to Sankai Juku. And it's like, boom, that's *it*. So they have this idea of butoh that becomes this easy thing to not discuss or to just be able to go, "Check!", that's what it is. (2011)

After an established career as a modern and postmodern dancer, Denise Fujiwara was choreographed by Nakajima Natsu in 1994. She continues to look for ways to employ a butoh philosophy within contemporary Western choreography. This approach makes her wary of being fascinated with early butoh photos, which she feels may impede her progress:

> These photos have become iconic. They are so powerful, they describe what butoh is to so many people. I avoid replicating that imagery in my own work, because that was the butoh of then and there, and I'm dancing butoh here and now. I love them too, but I'm conscious of them as icons, and I know that I should not be seduced by their power. (2018)

Conversely, Onozuka Makoto, who has photographed many butoh artists since the late 1960s, readily admits that his own practice, "looking in" to the dancers "from outside," overtly embraces this fraught relationship between performer, photographer, and viewer. When asked what his objective is in creating photos of butoh artists, he replies, "Life and death. That's it. Imagination or fantasy, eros, or other things. Projecting my imagination into the performance" (2011).

Joan Laage feels that ultimately, practical considerations move beyond any question of authenticity or imagination, stating, "It doesn't matter whether Hijikata's persona is created history or not," and that the value of what is actually created is of prime importance:

> He's up there on the fence. What about gravity? That facility just like a cat to go "Woomph!" That sense of weightlessness. I think when he's running through the fields, that sense of abandon. Out of that, the *kata* (technique and form), that came out of his creative history, the folding of the body, the limbs that are almost independent of each other. He *talked* about that. That's what really sticks with me. (2011)

Katsura Kan believes practitioners must decide for themselves what will aid in their development:

> Everybody can say what butoh is. It's a rocky mountain. Whether a very small mountain or higher mountain, it depends on you. If someone says butoh is finished, it's that *their* butoh is finished. Your mountain is finished, because you cannot go up, or you don't need to. You can go another way. But if someone wants to seek something higher, it needs more steps. So for me, it depends. (2009)

The tensions in butoh imagery point to desire in butoh being a fragile line between active and passive, between perception and projection. It is the difference between embodied crisis and its representation via standardized forms. Desire is the danger of mythologizing to the point of stasis versus imagination leading to transformation. If a mythology is a codified or patterned cosmology, then personal myths, the stories that an individual invents about their world, but draws from communal belief systems, are rife with the potential for either revealing or reifying dominant discourses and ideologies; for opening or closing one's eyes.

Butoh's ability to engage this perceptual binary is what makes it simultaneously attractive, unattractive, or mystifying to many viewers. For Tamano Hiroko, this impression reflects the nature of theater-going:

> The theater is the place to see yourself. That's why people go to the theater. For traditional dancing, people go to the temple or wherever the dance is happening to see their spirit or god or something coming out, or the story of the gods and goddesses. And that's really in their bodies. It's the same thing. It's a mirror. So when you go to the theater, you're sitting inside of the darkness, your darkness, and then the eyes open, and the performer comes through, and you see yourself. And some people stand up, kick the chair, and go home. Sometimes people stay. (2010)

Butoh artist Yoshioka Yumiko, who has regularly performed and taught internationally for over four decades, starting with the first butoh stage performances in Europe in 1977, describes how dancers and viewers need to experience this process in an initiatory manner, so that they can shift perceptions and premises:

> Butoh is a dance of metamorphosis. A dance of transformation, so that our way of thinking can be changed. . . . It's not a dance of darkness. For me, darkness doesn't mean something negative or heavy or serious. We are going in a cave. We have a torchlight. We are giving light into darkness. So what we have: unknown bodies. The unconscious. No words. (2019)

Katsura Kan claims butoh's mystery in performance as an ultimately benevolent gesture to the audience:

> Dance is a kind of dream, and it's very difficult to catch the moment, and if we don't name it, it's gone over time. However, I want to encourage something surreal, like Dali's clock. It's concrete. We can see this clock, but it's melting. So twisting reality. It never happens again in reality, but this surrealism is touching something deeper inside, for the audience, not just the dancer. So the important point is the audience is starting to talk about their own kind of dream, to describe it. If the viewer has a really good interpretation, he finds his forgotten secret that he didn't realize he used to have. (2009)

Resonating with the importance of recall in butoh practice, Sontag qualifies surrealism's affect within the context of memory's function in perception and the artist's necessary fidelity to an unfamiliar yet palpable reality: "The Surrealists misunderstood what was most brutally moving, irrational, unassimilable, mysterious—time itself. What renders a photograph surreal is its irrefutable pathos as a message from time past" (1978, 54). Surreal encounter requires a tenuous balance between the known and the unexpected, such as in live performance that questions the viewer's premises. While the theater may be, as Tamano asserts, where one goes to see oneself, what self an audience member expects or desires varies according to each person's values. While some viewers may resist reflexivity, Tamano sees the butoh artist's responsibility to provide a reflection that is unpredictable and, therefore, uncomprehendingly meaningful:

> Maybe what you do can be a mirror or not. If the mirror is fuzzy or cracked or not clear enough, that's not worth seeing maybe. So you really have to polish it yourself. It's a solid glass. If you put so many ornaments, too much, and you are hiding, then somehow you really should polish it more. That's necessary. Otherwise, who's gonna see a dull dancer? We really have to polish this up. Then there's no limit. Every morning run. There should be no hesitation to practice more. (2010)

Photo viewers, however, retain greater control over their experience. Stillness grants viewers distance, allowing the privilege of restraint. Susie Linfield compares this ability, which creates "a space the viewer can use: to separate herself from, and if necessary resist, the image and its maker," with time-based imagery, especially that of suffering and violence. She cites the execution video of kidnapped journalist Daniel Pearl: "The fact that such propaganda consists of moving images rather than stills is one key to its pernicious power" (2010, 164).[3]

For a viewer faced with visceral body imagery, whether recorded or live, mediated or present, the decision to engage or not in a symbiotic act of mirroring is the difference between becoming a *witness* or *voyeur*. The choice is a matter of either critical comprehension or reception of coded messages as they are. While a witness may testify to the truth or possess experiential evidence, art that engenders witnessing may yet withhold clues. Whether visual, spatial, or time-based, documentary or fictional, creative expressions of intense conditions do not often provide easy rationale for such extremes. These objects implicitly ask viewers to reflect on their sense of responsibility to the objects' historical veracity and truthfulness, urging comprehension through a deeper and broader lens. As Linfield asserts, for example, about Li Zhensheng's brutal photos of the Chinese Cultural Revolution, "They propel the viewer searching for the 'why' into history, political theory, memoir, and fiction; they exemplify the ways in which photographs are irreplaceable documents of history, yet cannot be understood on their own" (2010, 102).[4]

Many 1960s Japanese artists also denied passive viewing, asking viewers to imaginatively or irrationally engage their own referential knowledge and lyrical vision. Moriyama Daido shooting blurry, indeterminate photos of socially marginal figures. Terayama Shuji creating surreal, ethnocentric stage images. Hosoe and Hijikata devising fantastic, mythologizing portraits. All allow viewers to become empowered witnesses via a holistic orientation, requiring them to fill in visual, behavioral, or narrative gaps and witness a projected/perceived place and time of mutual creation.

Alternately, viewers may choose to be voyeurs, distanced observers seeking for no larger frame of reference than the proverbial keyhole to confirm their desires. For Kristeva, voyeurism is elicited by the confluence of abjection and object: "Voyeurism is a structural necessity in the constitution of object relation, showing up every time the object shifts toward the abject; it becomes true perversion only if there is a failure to symbolize the subject/object instability. Voyeurism accompanies the writing of abjection. When that writing stops, voyeurism becomes a perversion" (1982, 46). Kristeva argues such perversion may lead to narcissism, both precondition and coexistent of abjection, even to the extent of prefiguring Lacan's mirror stage (13). To speak of abjection outside a controlled space risks self-obsession and reversion to the solipsism between womb and self-awareness.

Thus, experiencing butoh involves a choice. Butoh performance aimed at a state of cohabitation asks the viewer to become a witness, fostering a liminal viewing context and critical investment. Butoh artists who fetishize chaos and crisis risk eliciting voyeurism to the point of distortion or parody; abject desire as a destructive end in itself. Such dance reifies its embodiments and images, distances the viewer's critical faculty, and indulges preexisting desires. The former choice points to knowledge and potential, the latter to passive observation. Witnesses see what is, looking forward to what is possible. Voyeurs accept what is stated and therefore reify myth.

As Barthes outlined, myth is a semiological system and type of speech beyond ordinary language, its messages delineating exact parameters around subjects (1972). In the case of *Kamaitachi,* the photos are the meaning signifier of the signified Tohoku imaginary and butoh body. For viewers seeking a more absolutist concept of Hijikata's life and work, their consumption of the images moves the pictures beyond form into myth, or, as Barthes defined it, "speech *stolen and restored*" (1972, 125). Further, "Myth hides nothing and flaunts nothing: it distorts: myth is neither a lie nor a confession: it is an inflexion. . . . We reach here the very principle of myth: it transforms history into nature. . . . it is not read as a motive, but as a reason" (129).

For those who perceive Hijikata's *Kamaitachi* presence as a possibility body, however, and despite *Kamaitachi* being flamboyant, declamatory, and ostensibly autobiographical, Hijikata also slips the trap of truly personal revelation to offer a template for practitioners' further imagination and generation of transformative desire. Hijikata's self-fashioning evokes the deeply erotic as a call to personal agency. Audre Lorde describes the erotic as "a measure between the beginnings of our sense of self and the chaos of our strongest feelings," and once one experiences it, the power and depth of the erotic becomes a personal standard of feeling to which one aspires (2007, 54). Similarly, *Nikutai no Hanran* is Hijikata's final performative critique of Westernized styles, habits, and norms in Japanese identity, a summation of the chaos of his "strongest feelings." *Kamaitachi,* however, his first mature statement around a nativist Japanese corporeality and the root foundation for his choreographic vocabulary, indicated, in Lorde's words, a more assured "sense of self." This period was the grand maneuver at the midpoint of Hijikata's career, moving from a preoccupation with the utilitarian urbanism of late capitalism, through the rebuilt and commercially transnational Tokyo of the 1950s and 1960s in which he was immersed, to the premodern, Tohoku body imagery that became his modus operandi. This latter schema produced a fragmented multiplicity of place-based body images and identities to which Hijikata and his dancers aspired, a move away from the totalizing historical present to an image of the past carried into the future as a strategy against domination and an opening to new identities. As José Esteban Muñoz describes such operations:

> The here and now has an opposite number, and that would be the then and there. I have argued that the *then* that disrupts the tyranny of the *now* is both past and future. Along those lines, the here that is unnamed yet always implicit in the metropolitan hub requires the challenge of a there that can be regional or global. The transregional or the global as modes of spatial organization potentially displace the hegemony of an unnamed here that is always dominated by the shadow of the nation-state and its mutable and multiple corporate interests. (2009, 29)

Likewise, through *Nikutai no Hanran* and *Kamaitachi*, Hijikata leaves behind Tokyo and the totalizing indexicality of the corporatist, nation-state metroplex of "the here and now," but not for a global or static provinciality. Tohoku is Hijikata's "then and there," a fetishized province that is nonetheless potentializing. It makes itself possible in ways beyond its root past, to be something more; something utopic. Pointing to the liberatory, futurizing transport to which Muñoz would have us commit, the agency gained from Hijikata's eros moves butoh from trepidatious chaos into greater depths of *ankoku*, where self is emotionally experienced in its fullness.

In Hijikata's first decade of butoh work, such expressions of eros came filtered through themes considered inflammatory at the time in Japan: homosexuality, prostitution, violence, and predation. Yet while provocation may have come readily for Hijikata, he needed strategies for unleashing the erotic in others. Such gestures took shape within the mythological realm of his *butoh-fu* system, which operated in training and rehearsal on multiple levels of stimuli. Bruce Baird enumerates them as starting with physical demonstration, then establishing tone and quality of movement, then indirect prompting toward both the concrete and the abstract, all combining to reveal new ways of moving, with disparate image-words held together in unresolved tension in the performer (2012, 165–69).[5]

Butoh-fu, then, was Hijikata's attempt to codify the transformative potential of eros, from self-image to chaotic desires as an imagistic lexicon of archetypal movement idioms. While *butoh-fu* did not dictate exact bodily forms as such, the words and images constituted a specific cosmology that determined the interpretive parameters of Hijikata's choreography. As his lead dancer and protégé Ashikawa Yoko has written: "Hijikata's dancers, regardless of whether they were brought up in the city or suburbia, without any direct observation, unconsciously began to move like children from the north country, from Tohoku" (Hoffman and Holborn 1987, 18).

Nakajima Natsu, the first female dancer involved from the initial development of Hijikata's butoh-based teaching in the mid-1960s, adds that Hijikata came to an impasse; that he worked for years to codify his practice through *butoh-fu*, but ultimately fell short of his goal:

> Codified dance, like kabuki or traditional dance, it takes time. . . . Only genius dancers can get over the code. This is art. This is their dance. So freedom is important, and Hijikata knew it. Also, living in only his own generation, he can't say this is the code. After 100 years, then the code can appear. For example, Hijikata loved Maro Akaji very much as a student, but he hated his dance. He said, this is not dance, this is not butoh, but also, he had to admit it (as valid). Each true story (like this), he had a very big struggle about it because he devoted half his life to create this system, so he wanted to be able to say, "This is butoh." But he had to deny this because dance is free. (2011)

Murobushi Ko, who trained with Hijikata in the late 1960s and was an original member of Maro Akaji's Dairakudakan troupe before creating his own work from the mid-1970s to his passing in 2015, makes a similar assessment:

> It's Hijikata's contradiction, I think. Butoh doesn't need this tradition. It's most exciting when a new dancer comes, and he can start with just his motivation. Maybe it's bad. Maybe many newcomers are bad. But there's 100 creations, and maybe in one, revolution comes. Maybe that's enough. We must accept this. I don't think Hijikata was a liar, but I think he wanted to make his own style into Yoko Ashikawa. But this way of creation, I think in the final moments of Hijikata's life, Hijikata said, I made a mistake. To make it so clear. (2012)

In 1998, twelve years after Hijikata's death, butoh artist, teacher, and former Hijikata disciple Waguri Yukio published *Butoh-Kaden*, an interactive multimedia CD-ROM (later released on DVD) detailing his experience and understanding of *butoh-fu* from his work with Hijikata in the 1970s and 1980s. Though the project's goal was to preserve and extend the knowledge gained from those years, Waguri still expressed the danger of working a system too rigidly: "What I'm most afraid of is that dancers including myself become slaves of words. If the body were eaten up by words and we danced to explain the words, dance would be dull" (Tanigawa and Waguri 1998).

In Hijikata's system, while the exact shape of dancers' movements are not rigidly set, the specific *butoh-fu* images that dancers worked from were still charged with meanings that he intended, thus setting his subversive poetics in conflict with his desire for expressive clarity. In speaking of the political implications of poetics and mythology, Barthes contends that the two systems proffer differing goals: "Poetry occupies a position which is the reverse of that of myth: myth is a semiological system which has the pretension of transcending itself into a factual system; poetry is a semiological system which has the pretension of contracting into an essential system" (1972, 134). Vladimir Marchenkov extends Barthes's idea, as well as Derrida's contentions around the inherent metaphoricity of all philosophical stances, by arguing that myth and poetry—or, in broader terms, philosophy and art—exist in a symbiotic, circular relationship: "The generation of identity and difference in mythical symbols, aesthetic metaphors, and philosophical concepts is the source of an intricate reality arising from its own interaction with play, of a constantly evolving myth that sustains and, in turn, is sustained by the openly 'unreal' story of art" (2008, 179).

Hijikata's rebellion against Western aesthetics may have resulted in an ambivalent tension in his work between myth and poetics, producing both conflict and cooperation between systems of meaning and meaning-making. Barthes's assertions on the nature of such gestures point to the root of this double bind: "It is because it generates speech which is *fully*, that is to say initially and finally, political, and not, like myth, speech which is initially political and finally natural, that Revolution excludes myth" (1972, 146). In other words, there's a difference between revolution and revolutionary mythology, á la wartime rhetoric, standard American history, or, in Hijikata's case, Japanese nativism. While the revolution in *Nikutai no Hanran* may have been a sloughing off of Western hegemony, Hijikata yet perpetuated his own mythology, perhaps complicating the ultimate efficacy of his art as political gesture. By naturalizing his own version of Japanese politics within the semiological system of his Tohoku imaginary, Hijikata established a practice with its own inherent set of limitations. This bind begs the question, how can you challenge a power structure by creating one at the same time?

BODY STORIES

We can never escape who we are and where and when we come from, but the extent to which we delve into particularities or generalizations—and in the case of butoh, corporeal idiosyncrasies versus cultural universals—is a choice that each artist makes. For those who worked with Hijikata or began their practice during his lifetime, there was probably scant evidence of much choice. Dance critic Sakurai Keisuke cites the work of two butoh groups that came up in the 1970s, Sankai Juku and Byakko-Sha, noting that Hijikata's employment of a culturalist frame around his dance continued into the second generation of butoh artists, even when they attempted to replace his Tohoku body with another:

> They thought it was possible to replace the Japanese body with the Asian body. The fact is you cannot avoid the gap between the young generation and old folk customs of North Eastern Japan. Young people cannot identify with them. Therefore, when they interpret mastery, they look in the direction of Asia. In the past, I guess there were such bodies everywhere but, not today, so they tried to gain ground by reconsidering the time issue spatially. (1998)

These artists attempted to make the body iconic beyond Hijikata's own generalities, reaching their ultimate manifestation through spectacle, which is inordinately defined by widespread, socially dominant, and static desires. As Barthes stated, the consuming public "abandons itself to the primary virtue of the spectacle, which is to abolish all motives and all consequences: what matters is not what it thinks but what it sees" (1972, 15). Even more than the supposed willing suspension of disbelief in theatre and film, the myth-laden image fulfills the desires of the spectacle-oriented public, thus sacrificing internal to external, content to form.

Butoh spectatorship is not impervious to this trap, wherein the liminality of butoh may enter the realm of *liminoid*, i.e., liminality once removed and codified through the devices of theatre rather than the devotional purposes of ritual (Turner 1982). Like any artists, when butoh dancers are marketed and packaged, presenters often sell a static impression and expectation. Most audience members who come to a show have an idea that the exact experience of the work, while often unpredictable, still somehow conforms to the accepted norms of the venue. Katsura Kan, who spends most of his time touring internationally as a performer and teacher, sees this as an unavoidable dilemma:

> American postmodern dance, Trisha Brown and other pioneers, now what are they doing? . . . They're using postmodern dance technique and doing more entertainment and commercial art. So it's impossible for more than 10 or 20 years to keep the avant-garde. . . . For example, Sankai Juku, they have to survive. More than 20 years ago, when I was in Avignon, the Avignon director said it's not Japanese butoh; it's French butoh. "We created it," he said. More of a kind of orientalism. . . . And I don't say this is bad, because Japanese contemporary arts became business in the Western world. That's great. Never happened before. So it's okay. (2009)

Butoh performance engaged in both liminal and liminoid states may be what Richard Schechner calls a dialectic process of "efficacious versus entertainment" (2006), or the adaptation of entertainment forms to create ritualized performances. In some cases, crossing into a liminoid state requires an artist to forego their liminal process, including butoh artists and students who employ gestural, facial, and imagistic stereotypes. Even Kan, who has spent years reflecting on such issues, admits that he occasionally falls prey to high art convention: "Even for me, I made the *Tibetan Book of the Dead* at Naropa University, using a huge black box, a lot of visual images, and music and sound, lighting, and it became beautiful. And I thought, 'Ah, this is too beautiful.' So I need more crisis onstage. So maybe this was not butoh, but more of a kind of normal 'performing arts' work" (2009).

Staging butoh may reveal or cause tensions within the viewer's continuum of feeling, disturbing coherence between normative modes of audience perception and a liminal expressivity. Audience members new to butoh are often unsure of how to see or watch performances, which emphasize irrationality, grotesquerie, or improvisation and challenge expectations around narrative logic or choreographic intent. When this liminality takes on a racialized and culturalized identity (Hijikata's premodern "Japanese" body) and is presented internationally (butoh since the late 1970s), it also brings up issues of commodification of racial, ethnic, and political identities across borders. Hijikata's dance body was designed for chaos and crisis, but within ethnic boundaries. Just as reductively, many Western viewers tend to perceive butoh bodies within an exoticized image of Japanese-ness (*nihonjinron*), but also within the notion of a rebellious, avant-garde lineage working against archetypal Japanese cultural norms. As Miryam Sas states, "In its binarizing mirror, these performances as presented for export come to be categorized and fixed in these limiting gestures or frames" (2011, 175).

The most successful butoh artist in terms of audience numbers and reach, and characterized by spectacular visuals, is the company Sankai Juku. They have toured numerous large-scale, main stage works worldwide since the mid-1980s, all commissioned by the prestigious Theatre de la Ville in Paris. Their hyper-refined aesthetic subsumes the viscerality of crisis or absurdity, with dancers as highly stylized, objectified bodies, exquisitely costumed, made-up, and arranged within gorgeously immaculate stage sets. Amagatsu Ushio, Sankai Juku's founder and director-choreographer, has stated, "Producing unerasable impressions is our business" (Trucco 1984), and repeatedly has advocated throughout his career for a vision of an overarching "universal" (Yoshida 2006, Amagatsu and Watanabe 2013). Nothing is left to chance in their scintillatingly crafted domain.

Many artists and critics consider Sankai Juku's work to be a dilution of butoh's original energies, an erasure of ambiguity, anxiety, fear, or other qualities that complicate the relationship of one's mind-body to a dominant social order. Amagatsu has defended his choice to create "my own butoh" (Yoshida 2006), developing an abstract, minimalist aesthetic that is impressively digestible for audiences that value harmony, universality, and the apolitical. One could argue in response that Sankai Juku's hermetically confined style reinforces and champions bourgeois cultural values. As Japanese dance critic Ishii Tatsuro observes, however, Amagatsu is conscious of such rationale, which has resulted in greater notoriety for butoh in general:

> What Amagatsu is looking for is different. He's not looking for danger or the body in crisis. Whether you like it or not, he looks for a perfection onstage, which completes itself with the performance. Sometimes it works beautifully, and sometimes it's just repetitious. But I think Amagatsu is among the few most influential in butoh, even though Hijikata did not approve of Sankai Juku at all. (2011)

Unlike butoh artists focused on maintaining a crisis state, Amagatsu seeks a mode of perennial coming-into-being that attains resolution: "Butoh dancers' bodies are like a cup filled to overflowing, one which cannot take one more drop of liquid—the body enters a state of perfect balance" (Hoffman and Holborn 1987, 121). His abstract statements in lieu of concrete descriptions ostensibly advocate for a vision greater than the individual self, though they reside in a Platonic realm of ideal forms and mystical beauty. Program notes from the 1999 work, "Hiyomeki," for example, include: "The speed of consciousness and the distance / of movement, / The speed of the body. All carefully treated. / When one arrives at imagining infinity / the body moves nearly at the speed of light, / and nears an almost unlimited stillness" (Samuels 1999). The company performance, "Yuragi" (1993), includes section titles such as "Donmiri—Wind Resembling Air," "Brimming Ripples," and "The Outer Reaches of Tranquility" (Garafola 1997). Even if unintentionally, Amagatsu's words ultimately buttress the group's orientalized performances with a conservative narcissism. In the mid-1990s, just over a decade after breaking into the international touring circuit, Western dance critic Lynn Garafola noticed a marked lack of tension, stating:

> Sankai Juku's new work, *Yuragi: In a Space of Perpetual Motion*, is shimmering and luminous, a vision of sensuous delight that makes

it hard to recall the shock of the group's first performances in this country some ten years ago. . . . Now, only the chalk-white bodies and time-arresting evolutions are left of that expressionist world. *Yuragi* . . . invites us to contemplate a paradise of marvels, each more exquisite than the last. (1997)

By the 2000s, the group's formulaic approach was apparent, even to a critic new to their work and to butoh, such as Catherine Hale in reviewing "Kagemi" for ballet.com in 2003:

The very frisson of *Kagemi* is its inscrutability. We Westerners love confronting the inadequacy of our rationalism, and Amagatsu capitalizes on that, giving us also polished performances and exquisite stagecraft to hold our attention when our metaphysical appreciation wanes. In fact, *Kagemi* is, more than anything, a gorgeous visual spectacle. (2003)

Unlike Ohno Kazuo, in whom the contrast and stimulating tension between the idealized dancer image and the reality of age was evident, Sankai Juku dissolves this divide, solely expressing and reflecting its own rarified concepts. As Sakurai inquires about the group:

Are not the simple body after removing the details or the abstract expression after reducing, hakkoichiu ("one home under the heaven," a slogan used as the Greater East Asia Co-Prosperity Sphere of Japanese militarism)? They removed the outer layer since they thought it was only an outer layer, then to the contrary, the body underneath became the outer layer, so then the reality and materiality of the body no longer possessed a strong meaning. In other words, such "Asian bodies" are only symbols that do not exist anywhere, but there are details in each Asian dance when we look at them. They might have forgotten the fact that details support dances. (1998)[6]

In more direct terms, dance critic Goda Nario views Sankai Juku as a dead end: "For myself, I don't like Sankai Juku. They give too much; there is no room for the audience to play" (Horton Fraleigh 1999, 175–76). In discussing spectacle, Barthes addresses the endgame of this type of viewership:

> This grandiloquence is nothing but the popular and age-old image of the perfect intelligibility of reality. . . . It is the euphoria of men raised for a while above the constitutive ambiguity of everyday situations and placed before the panoramic view of a univocal Nature, in which signs at last correspond to causes, without obstacle, without evasion, without contradiction. (1972, 25)

Gaston Bachelard also warns of "the spectacle complex, which could harden certain values of poetic contemplation" (1994, 190), sensitive to the fetishization of seeing, of holding onto a firm poetic imprint that outlines its borders and encloses itself too clearly. Sankai Juku's stage pictures are immense, Amagatsu's obsessions are ineffable, and their aesthetic sparkles with brilliant clarity. Precise bodies free of ambiguity or ambivalence display the trappings of unfathomability, yet emphasize a harmony shot through with intention. Sankai Juku always already know exactly what they are. This is spectacle as a perfectly distilled impression of reality.

Perhaps a question then arises: Is butoh spectacle a contradiction? Can an artist simultaneously aim for crisis and mass public satisfaction? Perhaps mainstream butoh viewers don't care if crisis, or at least indeterminacy, is actually present. This possibility thus begs another question: Do audiences actually desire butoh?

I believe this paradox has haunted butoh since Hijikata's time: the challenge to be inspired by a revolutionary or revelatory mythology, and yet to move beyond it, for ultimately, myths are parasitic, simultaneously alive and dead: "Myth . . . is a language which does not want to die: it wrests from the meanings which give it its sustenance an insidious degraded survival, it provokes in them an artificial reprieve in which it settles comfortably, it turns them into speaking corpses" (Barthes 1972, 133). Not resolving such tension may perpetuate static modes of encounter and reify false stability. Performing social marginalization while inscribing oneself with the tropes of an alternative center of power may be contradictory, a further tension between the generative and reductive: "The oppressed *makes* the world, he has only an active, transitive (political) language; the oppressor conserves it, his language is plenary, intransitive, gestural, theatrical: it is Myth. The language of the former aims at transforming, of the latter at eternalizing" (149).

Did Hijikata perpetuate dominance by substituting internalized behavioral habits of Western hegemony with performative gestures oriented around his Tohoku mythology? If so, is overcoming this bind a central challenge for butoh in order to move forward as a progressive practice? How might butoh avoid stasis and stay vital as a mode of actively poetic reflection?

This quest is not simple. Unpacking static effects embedded in an artistic practice even as ostensibly resistant as butoh may itself be a cause for crisis. Moreover, no one desires to betray their roots, least of all within a lineage of master-student relations born from a fairly rigid, tradition-minded society like Japan. In the U.S., a Western culture of individualism mostly removed from Japanese essentializations or hierarchies, butoh dancers may feel freer to delve into their differences, but questions of authenticity still bring pressure. Mizu Desierto, for example, reflects on the complex nature of this dynamic in her practice:

> What is American butoh? How is it different? When I go to Japan, I'm often told, "Your expression, everything about you is too loud. It's too much." And I think this is really Western because we're so expressive. So my question is do I try and imitate Japanese and reduce and refine to that kind of nothingness, or is butoh for an American more about I am *more* what I am? . . . I *am* expressive, I *am* emotional, I am all these things that are very different from Japanese culture. . . . I should dance my culture. I should dance my own preoccupations with stress or anxiety or the too much or the too loud. It's part of it. That is American butoh. (2011)

Moreover, Desierto draws from the butoh movement's long preoccupation with root identity through a cultural lens:

> Through butoh, I have become interested in my cultural inheritance. I did a piece in 2009 about my ancestors that came from Italy and the Americanization that happened from my grandmother's into my father's generation. And then me, this person walking around without really knowing her identity or a strong sense of family or roots is the condition of so many Americans. Wanting to find how that path happened and how to integrate the part of me that longs for it. What they tried to create here but was eventually usurped by American culture. . . . I think butoh asks the question, where do we come from? (2011)

While Desierto acknowledges the danger of culturalizing Easternness, she sees this dialectic in relatively optimistic terms. Conversely, Shinichi Iova-Koga views it warily, cautious of tying down an art form defined across the Pacific as Japanese and often labeled as foreign or exotic in an American society comprised almost entirely of immigrant families and descendants, and with its own ambivalences around identity:

> People acknowledged to a certain degree their cultural heritage, and they have some ear to it, but it's distanced. We've become distinctly American, but what is American food? What is American culture? These things exist, but they're a bit nebulous. They haven't been with us a long time, and there are so many families with so many different traditions. So there's this sense of a traditionless nation that has come from so many strong traditions, and yet, there we are. And so when something comes in with a strong cultural identity, I think there's a strong interest. It's very attractive. (2011)

Iova-Koga feels that American students of Japanese butoh artists must guard against essentializing the practice or trying to acquire Japaneseness through butoh:

> I think a lot of Americans say, "Wow," this exotic thing, and you feel like you're participating in another culture's strong identity. I think for Americans that has narrowed the idea of butoh dance. All these trappings of what it is for Japanese butoh dancers is like trying on a suit that doesn't quite fit, right? It fits *them* (the Tamanos) very well. And I think a lot of people start to recognize that after some time, and then they start to try and find their own way. And this for me is much more exciting, when some of the attitudes and the impetus for butoh dance start to become stronger than the forms that people have learned. (2011)

THROUGH THE MIRROR

As many postwar Japanese artists asserted, an individual's personal narrative may shed light on the nature of commonplace and shared aspects within a social structure. In the example of photographer Araki Nobuyoshi, while very few may share his life experience, his work retains traces of the urban, self-conflicted social milieu within which he came of age as an artist in the 1960s and 1970s, and expressed in dozens of books and essays over the decades. Likewise, we may view Ohno Kazuo as a prime exemplar of this approach in butoh. Sakurai contrasts Hijikata's method of attempting to mold his dancers into objectified models of his Tohoku cosmology with Ohno's reappearance in 1977 after a long retirement from performing. He was seventy-one years old, more frail than a decade earlier when audiences last saw him, but somehow all the more effective because of this fact:

> The important thing is not "he can still move well" but the fact "he can no longer move so well," or "he is decrepit." That is "already have become.". . . I think that the "decrepit" body is guaranteed the objectivity and the materiality by the negativity of its disability. This becomes an obstruction to the subject's consciousness, to move the body or the audience's consciousness to reduce it to an "image." . . . I believe that this is probably the congenital talent, old person's talent and disposition of "Kazuo Ohno," which Tatsumi Hijikata envied very much and sought a body that could become object just by standing there. (1998)

Ohno himself alludes to this condition in recalling a performance in Venezuela:

> Butoh's best moment is the moment of extreme weariness when we make a supreme effort to overcome exhaustion. That reminds me of my show in Caracas. . . . My body had grown old and I was working like a rickety old car, but I was happy. Is that what we call wearing oneself out for glory? The dead begin to run. (1987, 36)

Ohno sees himself as is and dances from a sense of unadulterated wholeness in order to manifest his inherent mystery. He must, as Tamano Hiroko describes, polish the mirror of his dancing body, formed by the practice of embodying self-inquiry, to reflect his existential state and resonate with his audience. This polishing reveals a cyclical process leading from the Lacanian *mirror* to the self-recognized *I* to irresolute *desire*, which, through its reflexive reaching toward either maintenance or renewal of self-identity, leads back to the mirror.

Jane Gallop examines Barthes's reference to Lacan's mirror in his autobiographical book, *Roland Barthes par Roland Barthes* (1977). She cites Barthe's sly quotation of the key line from Lacan's essay, "The mirror stage: That's you." ("Tu es cela") (Barthes 1977, 21) to caption a photo of himself as a child in his mother's arms: "Since baby and mother in Barthes's photo are both looking in the same direction, the caption implies that they are both looking at the baby's mirror image. The caption further suggests that the mother is saying, 'you are that,' thus teaching the baby to recognize his image as himself" (Gallop and Blau 2003, 47).

I have, however, an additional reading. Barthes's eponymous book title is already a reflexive gesture, making its contents, over forty pages of archival photos and one hundred and forty pages of text musing on his past and present, a current viewing of his former self. Barthes posits the photo as a mirror in which he sees himself through the image of his mother and infant self. As Gallop notes, "Lacan specifies that in the mirror stage the baby looking at himself in the mirror cannot yet stand on his own, but is standing with the help of some support, human or artificial" (2003, 47). Yet here we witness the fifty-five-year-old Barthes, world-famous scholar, publishing a visual and textual analysis of dozens of aspects—reflections—of his multiplicitous selves: historical, psychological, emotional, intellectual, spiritual, familial, sexual, and professional. While Gallop asserts that Barthes's caption "seems to put the phrase 'you are that' in his mother's mouth" (50), the self-reflexive nature of *Roland Barthes par Roland Barthes* suggests to me that, as the author of the caption, he is also speaking to himself.

I view Barthes's book and *Kamaitachi* in the same way: as subjective documentaries, with the authors all staring back at themselves through the mirror of their poetic imagination. Barthes's text begins with the sentence, "It must all be read as if spoken by a character in a novel" (1977, 1), and follows this statement with dozens of photos from throughout his life, thereby framing these ostensibly documentary images as fictional. Throughout the book, Barthes muses on the mysterious and *possible* significances of his personal and professional insights, predilections, and foibles. Like butoh artists, Barthes looks to the past to create his future in the present. Like Barthes's autobiographical fiction, butoh dancers return to their mirror, each staging their own *Kamaitachi.* Joan Laage dancing her cold, hometown landscape. Heyward Bracey dancing his African American and Native American identity. Alenka Loesch dancing her lonely tree.

Even Ohno largely followed Hijikata's template. Ohno's most successful solo pieces, *Admiring La Argentina* (1977) and *My Mother* (1981), consist of dream-like, imaginary encounters between his body and the spirits of the two real-life women who inspired the works. They are the twin personae that fueled his dance career and artist identity: one his dance mother, and the other his birth mother. The psychic landscape of mother-ness in Ohno's oeuvre reveals him to possess, like other butoh artists, his own *Kamaitachi*.

December 2011. Kuala Lumpur, Malaysia.

I perform two solos for the Nyoba Kan International Butoh Festival. The first is Tsuchi, *a meditation on how the "seeds" in one's body and environment are full of potential to either nurture wealth and plenitude or wallow in lack and poverty. My hybrid costume refers to both farmer/rural/vulnerable and hipster/urban/protective personae. The soundtrack is contemplative koto, guitar, and rain.*

The second piece is Flash Mixtape, *a hip-hop-oriented sketch referencing ambiguous feelings of femininity from my childhood, my discovery of an awkward, disjointed masculinity as a teenager, and a disquieting ambivalence in adulthood toward my identity as an Asian American. The soundtrack is 1970s and 1980s pop and funk music, with "oriental" bigot music from 1904 thrown in for good measure. My costume is b-boy gear, a long black skirt, a vintage American sport jacket, and a big red flower.*

After the show, I meet Singaporean critic, scholar, and performance artist Richard Chua Lian Choon. We talk about dance in Southeast Asia, identity politics, and civil rights. He tells me that he enjoyed Tsuchi, *the imagery, the staging, and the cultural elements in which it's rooted. He says it has all the ingredients for a clear and stimulating interpretation and that, because of this, it was easy for him to make sense of the whole. He felt, however, that* Flash Mixtape *was more effective; that, despite its absurdity, he could really feel my personal identity in it. He says he could tell that he was seeing my body as it is; that it felt in some way like I had lived this piece already.*

After my performance in Kuala Lumpur, seeing images of Ohno onstage made me contemplate Richard's comments about my dance, which likewise point to Sakurai's comments on Ohno's disabled body "as is," all of which brings me back to Hiroko's question, "Who are you?" If Ohno's answer was to dance from the place of seeing himself, how might I, or any butoh artist, do the same? Perhaps what is required is the raw, bodily experience of vision itself. Ohno's lesson is that you must see and show your body as is, making the contrast or complement—the distance—between what you are and what you express clearer and more stimulating. For all its accumulated tropes, butoh has remained a practice of revealing and performing myriad aspects of one's psycho-physiological being and, therefore, desires. Thus, what might performance mean when we are conscious of such motivations?

Barthes points to such a challenge in the conclusion to *Camera Lucida*, framing it as a decision for artist and audience between falseness and truth: "Such are the two ways of the Photograph. The choice is mine: to subject its spectacle to the civilized code of perfect illusions, or to confront it in the wakening of intractable reality" (1981, 119). In the context of action that emerges from crisis, the answer becomes a political moment: a decision to speak through the language of the oppressed, of poetry and transformation, or the language of reified power, of myth and stasis.

It is a decision to become either a trickster or a thief.

From the photo essay, "MuNK," Tashiro, Japan, 2016.

5 : TRICKSTER

I have never been visited by genius and my
appearance is far from that of a certified incompetent.
Not a devotee of ghost aesthetics, I am a mere virgin.
My semen should bring a good price.
— Hijikata Tatsumi (2000, 36)

He was able to adopt a kind of theater about himself.
Actually, first time I met him, he was really acting in a way.
And that was good, because you can go anywhere
when you're somebody else.
— Folk singer Mark Spoelstra on Bob Dylan
(Scorsese 2005)

MAKING AND UNMAKING

The middle plane between the abstract and the concrete, between the living and dead, between what we have and what we want—in short, what we are and are not—is where butoh artists operate, absurdly striving to extract viewers' suppressed fascinations while titillating their normative gaze. It is also the place where tricksters are said to live; a fertile realm of schismogenic crises, and a nexus of past, present, and future. This zone is a hall of mirrors, full of the perpetually signifying histories of real and imagined lives, reflecting a composite image of trickster that shape-shifts and calls itself into question in order to cover its tracks.

To speak of tricksters is to confuse, convolute, and multiply diverge from any single definition. As cultural critic Lewis Hyde posits in *Trickster Makes This World* (1998), addressing trickster mythologies and their sociocultural relevance may be most effective by adopting a trickster-like path: "I work by juxtaposition, holding the trickster stories up against specific cases of the imagination in action, hoping that each might illuminate the other" (14). Or as Bob W. White asserts: "By calling up the trickster figure in a discussion of real people and popular music, I want to suggest that tricksterliness evokes a set of human traits and practices that are socially relevant beyond their status as either structural or narrative conventions" (1999, 157).

In his essay "The Structural Study of Myth" (1955), Claude Levi-Strauss asserts that the efficacy of trickster stories lies in their operative between-ness in the same way that ancient philosophers realized that sound in language creates added meaning (429). He cites Ferdinand de Saussure's differentiation between *langue* and *parole,* between the revertible and nonrevertible aspects of time in language, which allow for historical and ahistorical confluences of interpretation and meaning. Such conceptual unions, as when modern politicians manipulate static impressions of early national history for their own agendas, represent a dialectic process that creates a third level of meaning that is liminal and potentialized (430). Levi-Strauss illustrates how resolution of such duality occurs paradoxically in trickster figures, which are "ambiguous and equivocal" and therefore apt for integrating contradictory aspects of social structures, such as intimate groups rife with oppositional and competitive relations (441–42).

My point is to cite trickster's utility as a useful frame to better comprehend butoh practice. There is a tension between the ideas of trickster as hero or fool (Hultkrantz 1997), making trickster's resultant ability to generate transformative chaos akin to that of the butoh practitioner. In cultural theorist LaMonda Horton Stallings's book, *Mutha' Is Half a Word: Intersections of Folklore, Vernacular, Myth, and Queerness in Black Female Culture* (2007), for example, she warns that heroism implies the performance of and need for rescuing, but that "one of trickster's primary agendas is to resist the act of rescuing so that individuals or societies at large may learn from the chaos" (28). While trickster and hero both act as constructed and abstracted blank slates upon which we project fear and desire, trickster inverts the hero's authority, displacing the skill to cohere by dismantling harmonious structures, thereby producing an irresolution that questions the beliefs underlying such values. As literary scholar Kelly M. Cresap asserts in *Pop Trickster Fool* (2004), his study of Andy Warhol's career-spanning persona of a faux-naif public figure and its relevance to postmodern culture's self-devouring irony, understanding how trickster functions in the real world is a significant challenge:

> What becomes of the epistemological eco-system, though, during an era in which . . . the fools finally get their revenge upon the

> savants, providing . . . a kingdom ruled and run by mockery alone? A sensible response to this scenario is to raise a countervailing voice of critique, after careful study designed to ascertain . . . what mortals these fools be. (227)

It's one thing to be a trickster, another to act like one, and something else to revel in the results or suffer the consequences of their action. In the postmodern era of contradictory, self-consuming imagery in popular culture, trickster elusively confirms, denies, and alters comprehension of self and society: a ghost in the machine in plain sight. Susan Blakeley Klein speaks of butoh artists as possessing a similarly dual appeal, at once premodern and postmodern. On the one hand, they represent "a nostalgic return to the primitive roots of dance" with links "to the uncanny and irrational, to a kind of subterranean reservoir of raw sexual energy tied up in the intimate relation that primitive humanity once had with nature" (1988, 14), while on the other, possessing a "pastiche style, which picks and chooses among modern and postmodern dance techniques, elite and popular forms, with little or no regard for their original context or meaning" (21). Such dualism is liberatory, employing postmodern subversion of spectatorship and premodern destabilization of rigid boundaries. Butoh artists attempt both theatrical and carnivalesque (Bakhtin 1984), liminoid and liminal, creating an experience of simultaneously objective and subjective perception of disability and abjection.

Early butoh's play with premodern and primitivist tropes belies and is subsumed by its postmodern approach to any and all identities, personae, and social structures embodied by the practitioner. Thus, while the validity of trickster as an intellectual shorthand used by primarily Euro-American scholars to generalize about mythic figures from global cultures can be debated, my conceit herein is to employ trickster's qualities of indeterminacy and inspiration as an apt lens through which to imagine butoh's transformative potential within the context of postmodernism's recombinant paradigm. As Gallop speaks of *cohabitation* and Miller of *remix*, so Stallings speaks of *trickster-troping*: "Trickster-troping defers the privileging of one difference over another. Trickster-troping is acts of undecidability. The composition or deliberate use of taboo-breakers, minor gods, cultural transformers, and baad muthfuckas as metaphorical signs of difference and desire signifies trickster-troping" (2007, 10). She asserts that the endemically dualistic nature of tricksters denies "dichotomies that might exclude or limit the development of cultural and social impulses and energies" through a process akin to Derrida's *différance,* which for her creates "an undecidable, a tool to disrupt the entire system of logocentrism founded on binary oppositions" (10). This dualism is held within the single entity of the trickster, embodying a self not only in relation to, but of, *différance* itself. When chaos, contradiction, and crisis "become the thing itself" via juxtaposition, *différance,* and undecidability, the butoh practitioner becomes a postmodern trickster.

MEMORY: NOT JAPANESE JAPANESE

April 1998. In a jazz bar in Nagano, Japan, the post-Winter Olympics glow slowly fades. Outside, Olympic-pin vendors, half of them American, bargain with tourists exiting the train station. An elderly Japanese pianist performs endless variations of "Over the Rainbow," regaling me and my partner with tales of playing for American soldiers during the Vietnam War. I lapse into conversation with an office worker.

"You're Japanese," he says, not as a question, but a statement.

*"No, American," I respond. "*Yonsei *(fourth generation)."*

"Yonsei? We've been in America that long?"

"Well, sort of. But I don't think of myself as Japanese."

"I don't understand," he muddles. "You're a dancer?"

"Yes. A butoh dancer."

"You mean buyoh? *Japanese traditional dance?"*

"No. Japanese modern dance. Ankoku butoh."

"Ankoku?" he realizes, incredulous. "But why? You're not Japanese."

"Many non-Japanese dancers perform butoh in the West."

"But it's not their dance."

"Maybe it's not mine, either."

"But you're Japanese."

"I am?"

He changes the subject and pours another beer.

From the photo essay, "MuNK," Tashiro, Japan, 2016.

Viewed side by side, the roles of trickster and thief represent a range of possible behavior and action taken on the basis of desire. As a liminal entity, trickster is the absence of defined modes of action, or, in some sense, akin to *an empty room*. With nothing to steal, a thief entering such a space is trapped within their own enclosing desire—the anxiety of not having or knowing—and thus avoids it at all costs.[1] Tricksters suffer no such hesitation. In ancient history, Hermes is the God of Commerce and the Protector of Thieves, but "pictures of Hermes usually show him with a little bag of change, just enough to get the trading started. He's no miser asleep on heaps of gold. He loves the fluidity of money, not the weight" (Hyde 1998, 324). Hermes may steal, but he prompts others into motion by any means necessary. His status as a demigod, fully identifiable neither with the gods nor humans, makes him an ideal liminal being to navigate ambiguity, constantly churning the waters around moral or immoral, sacred or profane. The act of upsetting balance, of propelling one out of stasis and into new relations that reflect self and other, is benevolent. Even in stealing, tricksters give.

The myriad pantheons of European gods illustrate this principle. Hyde stresses that for the Norse gods of Valhalla or the Greek gods of Olympus to separate themselves on high means that they have "an ego position to uphold; they can always be pinned down, therefore, caught in a streak of vanity. Hermes is untrappable. It's not that he's humble, he's shameless" (324–25). Moreover, "Unlike the other gods, Hermes is never identified with a place. He can stay 'on the road' because he has no territory to defend" (324). Not only does he know no boundaries, they exist only for him to violate or reconfigure.

By subverting defined states and normatives modes of exchange, tricksters produce a shared space of ambiguity and alter the meaning and value of cultural capital. Identities become destabilized, and borders, differences, and dualities become amorphous until balance, at least temporarily, is regained. Observe popular musicians who undergo extreme shifts in style or genre in mid-career, nonplussing their fans and thereby altering the collective's consciousness of what is possible, at least until a new norm is established, and the icon is reinstated into the popular fold or not.[2]

All such archetypal trickster characteristics are at play in butoh:

a culture hero/fool binary, liminality, amorality, shamelessness, and thievery. Intuitive reaction, vulnerability, and personal truth as a benevolent promise of trickster are active in butoh practice, positing the butoh trickster as an unstable yet compassionate change agent. While butoh artists are known for moving slowly, the truth is we can't keep still.

MANY FACES, ONE BODY

I speak of tricksters as what does not so much exist as operate, and the place they do so is within people who need, want, or do not want them to, making everything told about tricksters also part of their nature (Cosentino 2011). Represented as deities, demigods, spirits, magical beings, or, occasionally, real people, tricksters are not entities as such, but rather what lies between or happens to them since their essence is ineffable. Tricksters are less figures than processes that take place within real lives and communities.[3] We may think of them in many ways:

energy	structure	affect
movement	kinesis	negotiation
tendency	transformation	function
perception	projection	pattern

Such terms are characterized by ambiguity, relationality, and change, implying that we are not meant to know exactly what tricksters are. While the Cartesian "I" remains statically determined, trickster's mutable self constantly produces and reproduces itself.[4] Their only mandate for action is circumstances as they exist, performing different personae and narratives as situations call for them. For example . . .

> "Hijikata Tatsumi" was a semi-fictionalized farmboy in the big city who performed under numerous pseudonyms.
>
> "Hijikata Tatsumi" was a self-centered, autocratic misogynist, who created a subaltern cultural movement to manifest the body in crisis against oppression.
>
> "Hijkata Tatsumi" was a retrograde nationalist who dedicated his life to a politically progressive, avant-garde arts scene in Japan.

In other words, "Hijikata Tatsumi" was a trickster, a public figure consisting of real, perceived, projected, imagined, and contradictory selves that maneuvered in and around his intimates, audiences, and detractors.

Operating synchronically, tricksters like Hijikata are past and future combined; the fiery yang of disarray to the yin of social order.

As a court jester persona, speaking truth to power through the voice of absurdity and Mikhail Bakhtin's *grotesque* body redolent with the transformative power of the human "lower bodily stratum" (Bakhtin 1984), Hijikata was a kind of dancing fool. He made butoh trickster-driven from its inception, refuting mainstream society and setting himself up as an indefinable, sexually ambiguous figure. In Bakhtin's terms, Hijikata embodied an early postmodern expression of *grotesque realism* set within a premodern social imaginary filled with ghosts, farm animals, teenage prostitutes, sickle-weasels, and freezing landscapes. He forged a small subculture, gathering around himself a coterie of misfit performers and social dropouts as well as the crème of Japanese postwar, avant-garde, art circles (Kurihara 1996, Baird 2012). After relegating himself as an "outlaw" dancer by refusing sponsorship from Japan's national dance association after the premiere of *Kinjiki* in 1959, he became like the trickster deity, Exu:

> (Exu) is the Lord of the Limen and Chaos, the full ambiguity of the subjunctive mood of culture, representing the indeterminacy that lurks in the cracks and crevices of all sociocultural "constructions of reality," the one who must be kept at bay if the framed formal order of the ritual proceedings is to go forward according to protocol. He is the abyss of possibility. (Turner 1982, 77)

SUBVERTING MYTH

Mythology as a tool of power refutes transformation. As social phenomena, however, myths lose their efficacy without a dominant group subscribing to their underlying belief system. A corollary void, wherein such power is upended, may be elicited in settings of social tension or conflict via trickster affect, acting as symptom of and reaction to oppression. Mythology as a language reifies distinctions and hierarchies. As figures constantly on the move, tricksters are ambiguous, mysterious, and poetic: a language built for speed. As a means for appropriating resources, limiting the productive capacity of those in opposition, and cultivating dominance through inscription of superior and subordinate identities, myths are the currency of thieves. Conversely, in their terrifying addiction to crisis and liminality, tricksters trade in whatever objects, identities, or materials will accomplish change, while denying that transformation is even possible.

In facing dominance, trickster figures avoid becoming an easy target by playing with their public images as incomplete, thereby confusing myth production. Seemingly evident as an artificial construction, yet performed with absolute earnestness, for example, Andy Warhol's public persona upset many observers when he appeared on the American art scene in the early 1960s. Quickly gaining notice for his commercial and mass-media–style silkscreen paintings, he presented himself as shockingly naïve and inarticulate, rambling through interviews in mumbled, monosyllabic semi-answers (Workman 1990), and actively making himself unintelligible: "he asked interviewers beforehand to tell him what answers to give; he supplied misinformation about things like the year of his birth . . . ; he denied having gone to college; he responded elliptically; he answered through a proxy" (Cresap 2004, 12). Cresap also notes, "Warhol's trickster performance in [the documentary] *Painters Painting* maintains a virtuosic seamlessness, like a joke that never announces itself as such by arriving at a punchline" (75). Whatever Warhol's self-awareness or intentions, viewers are never made privy to what might really be happening, as if someone had distilled the essence of trickster and laid it neatly wrapped on the doorstep of the evening news for no one to comprehend.

In Bob Dylan's early folk music period, audiences convinced themselves that they understood him, perhaps by his design. Having witnessed Dylan firsthand as a teenager in 1963, Greil Marcus cites a liminal mystique at play. Joan Baez brought Dylan onstage unannounced at a New Jersey folk fair that Marcus attended. In photos from the performance, Baez appears poised, in a bright dress full of folk patterns, while Dylan stands in wrinkled, beige shirt and pants, hair mussed, eyes sleepy and gazing (Rudoff 2008). Marcus describes this "dusty and indistinct" Dylan, shoulders hunched and slightly embarrassed, as confusing and transfixing: "Something in his demeanor dared you to pin him down, to sum him up and write him off, and you couldn't do it. From the way he sang and the way he moved, you couldn't tell where he was from, where he'd been, or where he was going—though the way he moved and sang made you want to know all of those things" (2005, 18).

Like Dylan by his mid-1960s pop phase, Hijikata also refused easy comprehension and cultivated a sense of contradiction, even urging others to embrace a split self: "I cherish wet animals and the bodies of the old, withered like dead trees, precisely because I believe that through them I may be able to come close to my desire. My body longs to be cut into pieces and to hide itself somewhere cold" (2000, 56).

Authority for tricksters is a strange bedfellow, something to play with, publicly disavow, and yet cultivate expressly to counter it. Neither Warhol, Dylan, nor Hijikata ever claimed wholeness nor retreated to the shadows. Instead, they plied the middle ground between authority and sincerity, objectivity and subjectivity, art and life. In each case, the dominant culture had no idea how to perceive, let alone address, what each man represented, thus allowing them to continue operating.

At the time, this may have been the only practical option. Throughout history, brute force rarely has been effective in defeating ignorance, conservatism, or oppression. The powerful are simply too powerful. What is required instead is a subversive change agent. Within the Western classical pantheon, Hermes provides the archetypal trickster narrative for anti-oppression. He crosses the threshold between earth and heaven to steal Apollo's cattle and the food of the gods in order to trick them into allowing him a place at their table as an equal. Hyde interprets this gesture, and that of many other tricksters, as anti-hierarchical:

> There is little doubt that in the classical period Hermes is associated with artisans, merchants, and thieves, and the poem itself makes clear that some kind of "outsiderness" is at issue, and that Hermes hopes to change it. To effect that change he has . . . a method by which the excluded can enter a group, change its structure, and give themselves a place at the table. (1998, 207)

Whether involving ancient farmers in a mythological narrative or modern political activists with bodies on the line, such narratives position outsiders as core to paradigm-shifting movements, committing guerrilla acts of civil disobedience that gesture toward social justice:

> Hermes' theft proves the boundary between his world and Apollo's is porous; it implies that the rules by which Apollo operates are contingent and arbitrary. Deftly done, a trickster's thieving calls into question the local property rights. Who gave Apollo those cattle in the first place? Who decided he could set guard dogs around that field? (210)

Hyde also examines the real-world model of Frederick Douglass, who produced and then transformed his own language, both properly and improperly characterizing his social status as a forward-leaning enslaved man, literate former slave, and legitimized public figure. Hyde's central example is a seminal moment wherein Douglass speaks of his reality to a white audience and experiences his body in crisis:

> Douglass, in the North almost three years, still feels the internal prohibition, and must work to break it. (Douglass revised his autobiography several times; his 1855 version of the same scene is even more graphic: "It was with the utmost difficulty that I could stand erect, or that I could command and articulate two words without hesitation or stammering. I trembled in every limb.") Douglass could speak freely in "the colored people's meeting," but that speaking did not make him feel free (it had never been prohibited). It is only when he can speak across the color line, when he can break the rule of silence and contest the white world's fictions about slavery, that he truly feels himself free. (231)

Douglass's crisis makes him vulnerable, which, rather than weakening him, empowers his voice and speaks to the core of a democratic process. While preaching to the choir is less risky, attempting communion across deep and historically entrenched borders may engender a crisis state, the overcoming of which is a liberatory gesture. Even when free speech is permitted in the open commons of a democracy, real liberation still requires real struggle.

Hyde also points to a moment in Douglass's life during his plantation's year-end saturnalia, wherein owners let enslaved people run free with whiskey. By satisfying the slaves' craving and inducing a dispiriting alcoholic daze, the owners lay a trap of internalized shame and naturalized oppression. Douglass's answer is to resist his desire and thereby his master as well: "Refusing his own craving, he cuts the link between the social artifice and the body. To put it another way, because world and body are meant to pattern one another, when he reimagines his body he reimagines his world" (237).

This was also Hijikata's method. By refusing to perform the markers of capitalist hegemony while declaring an archetypal ethnic identity, he redrew the lines around the definition of both. Or as Hyde articulates, "In Douglass's case, all who refuse applejack also refuse the contained contradiction of Saturnalia and thereby create the possibility of *un*contained contradiction" (237). Douglass's idealism may also shed light on Hijikata's use of a primordial Japanese identity. Hijikata invented a mode of Japanese-ness appropriate for his historical moment just as Douglass accommodated his public identity to fit within a civic lineage innovatively linking America's Founding Fathers to the postslavery struggle for civil rights:

> The man who collapsed the shaping categories of plantation culture with irony and contradiction has no trouble promulgating his own set of organizing dualities. Sacred and profane, heavenly and demonic, savage and civilized, just and unjust, decent and indecent—with these and more, Old Man Eloquent shaped and published his vision of a *true* and *real* America" (249).

Trickster behavior and its effects extrapolate outward, sending their surroundings spinning likewise, and without a clear landing spot. Just as Hermes is neither an innate deity nor ordinary human, as the elder Douglass was no longer an urgent abolitionary symbol nor an uncompromising ideologue,[5] and as Hijikata ceased performing once he established his company in the 1970s, tricksters are the reality of elicited change but stop short of explicitly representing it as such. While they engender a new paradigm, they might not be part of it. Once their performative, pragmatic utility has been exercised, their tricks employed, they also may fade back into the folds of the liminal space-time that fostered them.

Ultimately, tricksters may serve to redraw social hierarchies by embodying the arbitrariness of boundaries themselves. Just as Douglass and Hermes each shifted the power dynamic in their respective environments, so Hijikata reoriented the operative paradigm underlying the performative embodiment of the ruling class in postwar Japan. Critics who witnessed *Nikutai no Hanran*, for example, noted the effectiveness of the opening scene, with Hijikata carried into the theater on a palanquin in the guise of a Foolish King character, which juxtaposed processional ritual with surreal set designs and props by the artist Nakanishi Natsuyuki (Maeda et. al. 2009). Okada Takahiko describes an ambiguous event, sharply designed and presented, but unclear in intent: "This thorough-going folly was conducted with solemnity and a straight face, which turned it into a near spectacle" (Okada 2009, 57).

Tone Yasunao states about the scene, "There was a struggle/constraint between the stage art of Nakanishi Natsuyuki and the act of Hijikata here, which could not be reduced into each other. In other words, there was a tension between the action that tries to overcome the spectator's gaze and the gaze that tries to overcome the action" (Tone 2009, 56). Hijikata critiqued and assumed the falsity of the social hierarchy within which he placed his body. His crisis both reveled in and reflexively pointed to its own injustice.

MANY FACES, ONE MASK

Tricksters are often regarded as thieves because they upset the ostensible boundaries defining ownership and origination. Hermes steals the meat of the gods. Coyote tricks the eyes out from other animals, upsetting their relationship to their surroundings and therefore, how they know themselves within a social power dynamic. Warhol denudes the spectacle of, and proscribes tragedy from, newspaper images of celebrity and death, thus stealing away the roots of our collective idolatry and pain.

Highlighting the difficulty in reconciling theft with legitimacy, and in an early career full of stealing, Robert Zimmerman replaced his family name by stealing poet Dylan Thomas's given name, adopted the rough grain of singer Woody Guthrie's voice, and, perhaps most impressively to those in folk music circles, effectively assumed Guthrie's dusty, rootless, bard-like idiom. Bob Dylan then seemingly betrayed all these precious gifts by retooling them for sale in the devil's marketplace, i.e., the pop charts. What does it mean, however, to betray something that never belonged to you; that didn't belong to anyone, least of all the folk music community, which regularly appropriated musical forms and cultural personae for its own sociopolitical agenda? As Greil Marcus describes in discussing American folk music, employing aspects, artifacts, and practices of cultural lineage also works the other way around when the very genre within which one operates already belongs to everyone:

> As they live in an organic community—buttressed, almost to this present day, from the corrupt, outside world—any song belongs to all and none belongs to anyone in particular. Thus it is not the singer who sings the song but the song that sings the singer, and

therefore in performance it is the singer, not the song, that is the aesthetic artifact, the work of art. (2001, 28)

Such circumstances force artists to choose a path. For early butoh artists, subjectivity and mystery were all, and audiences were hard-pressed to know how to react. In both folk music and butoh, artists appropriated the very letter and syntax of their languages from popular culture, constructing aesthetic vocabularies from the social landscapes they referenced: the history of socioeconomic injustice in the United States for folk musicians, and a blend of premodern, traditionalist, Japanese culture with the contemporary trappings of postindustrial consumer culture for butoh artists. Yet each group represents a fundamentally different approach to addressing social issues: the folk artists opting for an idealized everyman, butoh artists for an overtly compromised, contradictory self. The former is resolved and defined, the latter unresolved and indefinite.

The folk movement's mythology and early butoh artists' subversion are differing modes for cultivating meaning. Clothed in earnestness and mythically framed, American folk singers and audiences of the 1950s and 1960s entered into a social contract circumscribed and characterized by a leftist heroic identity in which to believe and its supposed organic existence. Such action mythologizes the heroes desired into a static specificity, turning them from subject to object in order to sustain belief in them. American folk music listeners and audience members wanted Woody Guthrie, Pete Seeger, Joan Baez, Odetta, and others to be who they were supposed to be, requiring their public personae to perform exactly that image. As folk promoter Harold Leventhal describes the collective expectation of the folk community in the early 1960s, "It was Woody Guthrie transitioned to Pete Seeger, who carried on Woody's tradition. Now who was to carry through from Pete Seeger? And in that spot, really, came Bob Dylan. So we began to recognize that Bobby would be the continuation in that tradition" (Scorsese 2005).

But such are tricksters that the febrile social structures from which their provocations arise, built from rigid belief in something amorphous enough to shape to their will, practically ask for their own eventual subversion. As folk singer Liam Clancy states about not just the fact of the folk community's belief in Dylan, but exactly how they invested in him: "In old Irish mythology, they talk about the shape changers. They change voices. They change images. It wasn't necessary for him to be a definitive person. He was a receiver. He was possessed. And he articulated what the rest of us wanted to say but couldn't say" (Scorsese 2005).

Going further, early butoh artists refused the social contract between performer and audience. Hijikata's cohort denied exact meaning in their corporeal image beyond the experience of personal narrative, leaving audiences wanting to know more due to the fact of not defining anything. Thus, this endemically subjective approach to manifesting desire may simply be its embodiment, a radical fulfillment of only its remembered and imagined possibilities. In *Kamaitachi,* Hosoe and Hijikata don't portray universal Tohoku landscapes and bodies so much as their own personal and emotionally internalized images of and bodies from an imagined home. *Kamaitachi* is very much their own private Tohoku.

It is not enough to label someone a thief, for stealing may be either a benevolent or harmful act. Dylan copying forms and appropriating voices from the cornfields and back alleys of the Great American Songbook to capture the zeitgeist of 1960s America is a benevolent mirror and gift while also remaining a mirage purposely disappearing into its own constructed opacity.[6] Conversely, Pat Boone's thoroughly white rendering of Little Richard's "Tutti Frutti"[7] for a white audience to which teenagers' parents in the 1950s could feel safe allowing their children to dance was not only artistic and cultural appropriation, but also an enclosure of Black America within White American hegemony.

"YOU OUGHT TO BE . . ."

Shamelessness is another characteristic of trickster that addresses power. Folklorist Oyekan Owomoyela speaks of trickster tales providing marginalized members of society the means to claim agency through not only commentary around power dynamics, but also by employing personal qualities that enable one to deal with life's difficulties (1997, xiv). Among these is the skill to convert deficiencies to assets without shame or embarrassment, refusing foolhardy heroism, and shame as a social control factor (3). In Hijikata's 1960 essay, "Inner Material/Material," he alludes to limitations on social behavior and its consequences in a postwar Japanese society awash in the superficiality of Western consumerism: "This big Tokyo is rotten with bodies. There is a lethargic generation arrogant with fat and I vomit on its lotioned and powdered pale effeminate skin" (2000, 40). More directly, in "To Prison" (1961) Hijikata shamelessly proffers a vision of a thoroughly abject body, ridden by an earthy carnality and images of dirt, sweat, brokenness, and barely veiled pedophilic and homosexual lust as a form of self-exile into a subaltern netherworld of prisons and gallows. This gated realm was his proposed cure against late capitalism, a ritual of affliction from which there was no turning back:

> No theatre matches this one, which is equipped with the perfect mechanism for my destructive acts against production and morality. I see my own dance in a state of joyful group bathing in prison, and I see inmates on death row in the fall of modern civilization and in the family crest of its good sense. I see the original form of my dance in their walk. (2000, 45–46)

Hijikata exemplifies Hyde's assertion that tricksters subvert moral codes by negotiating boundaries of shame, which are designed to uphold the social order:

> Outside the church, people speak profanely by definition and, if they've been properly instructed, they are silent about the mysteries. Inside the temple, on the other hand, they speak of the mysteries but remain silent as to the profane. Such spheres of speech and spheres of silence, and recognizable boundaries between the two, are thus intimately tied up with any world organized to distinguish between the sacred and the profane. (1998, 156–57)

Tricksters uncover and ply the murky waters between these spheres of speech and silence, instigating each side to intersect with the other, breaking boundaries and revealing social actors on all sides as, in fact, intimately connected. Similar to the manner in which composer Igor Stravinsky and choreographer-dancer Vaslav Nijinsky inspired both hatred and praise by breaking Western classical music and dance conventions with the 1913 premiere of *Le Sacre du Printemps* at the Théâtre du Châtelet in Paris, Hijikata's first butoh performance, *Kinjiki*, spoke aesthetic profanities within a nationally sponsored theater, a temple of high art. In a U.S. context, similarly ambivalent maneuvers had become common by the 1970s in New York City, when street dancers employed the "sacred" dance cypher within the "profane" ganglands of the streets of the Bronx, Queens, and Brooklyn (Chang 2005). Such juxtapositions were also later brought to high-art temples by hip-hop concert dance choreographer Rennie Harris. In his 2002 solo dance, "Lorenzo's Oil," he employed a *butoh funk* style to express dark personal and social themes, and he once choreographed a subversive panoply of racist stereotypes about African Americans, essentially a jigaboo dance on the sacred concert dance stage, which elicited comparable audience reactions as *Sacre* and *Kinjiki* (Harris 2008).[8]

These sacrilegious acts point to why tricksters cannot exist in real life, yet often do: because the self is mutable. The "I" in Rimbaud's "I think" is impermanent. If it is more proper to say, "I am thought," then what follows is an infinite number of possible "I"s that one may generate in every moment. One's ability to cross the threshold between defined realms, each marked by sacred and profane in order to maintain the social order by which they are generated, is largely determined by the capacity for shamelessness or the ability to resist shame's moderating impulses. Moreover, this ability may change over time, even within the same individual. Dylan playing electric loud and proud to an auditorium full of protesting fans in Manchester, England, in 1966 crosses the line and reimagines popular music, altering center and margin. The same man, however, recoiling at the Newport Folk Festival the summer before, just enough to feel compelled to return to the stage and pay penance for his sins by performing acoustically after his now-legendary, first plugged-in set, is a wounded and very human trickster (Scorsese 2005).[9]

With its clarion call for egalitarianism and dreamy civility, the folk movement was dead set against shame, not for the sake of addressing it head on, but in preventing or curing it. Following Dylan's debacle at Newport, however, his solution became shamelessness. Touring the United States and Britain, he restructured his set by reversing the order from Newport, beginning his concerts with a solo acoustic set, then returning after the intermission with his backup band the Hawks (later The Band), as if to say, "I'm still who you thought I was, except I'm not."

Amorality and shamelessness also come together in the example of Warhol. While seemingly more tame and less lucid than Dylan or Hijikata, his lack of shame came in all manner of visible and discrete forms. Framing trickster shamelessness as that which is anomalous, out of place, and therefore confusing and obstructive, Cresap enumerates a laundry list of Warhol's shameless behaviors that people found most disturbing: "His seeming incoherence, quick-fix solutions, social and artistic opportunism; his gestural emptiness, glibness, unfeelingness, and amorality; as well as the apparently rudderless way he moves among images . . . and occupations . . . as if he were channel-surfing" (2004, 48).

Warhol's casual slickness in social dealings illustrates an openness to a variety of identities enabled by shamelessness. Rapidly altering courses through numerous public selves, Warhol was like an actor in a first rehearsal, or a socialite staring into the mirror every morning with a wardrobe full of options. This act was repeated ad infinitum throughout his life, making the question asked by such behavior—"Who am I today?"—also beg the question, "Who do *you* think I am today?" Rooted in the public's assumptions and desires projected onto his public persona, the question is fundamentally centered around the audience's identity.

Bringing this concept back to butoh, if to practice butoh is to ask "Who are you?" then it is also to ask the same of the audience. Thus, "Who am I?" on stage is also implicitly "Who are *we*?" as a performer-audience community inquiring around identity and pushed by the perception and projection of desire.

WHO IS SPEAKING?

The difference between expressing something and manifesting it is the difference between objective and subjective; between the "I" that one projects and the "I" newly produced in every moment. This distinction is essential for trickster's subversive capacity. Too much truth-telling undermines the unacknowledged compromises of collective life. Dominant orders are potentially undone by knowledge of more egalitarian possibilities. To avoid unwanted attention from those invested in dominance and privilege and who may otherwise be made to lose face, the limits on speaking truth to power require the speaker to find an indirect mode of communication. In butoh, this comes in the form of the life, death, and rebirth of the mutating self, fashioned by a mythological, domesticating order, steeped in crisis, and resolved by intuitive mechanisms. The butoh practitioner produces a subjective space of internal logic externally performed for others, a field of existential necessities and detritus from which they express a way of being unmoored from static mythologies tied to dominance. As Barthes describes:

> There is therefore one language which is not mythical, it is the language of man as producer: wherever man speaks in order to transform reality and no longer to preserve it as an image, wherever he links his language to the making of things, meta-language is referred to a language object, and myth is impossible. (1972, 146)

Butoh artists attempt to de-objectify themselves through bodily speech as abject refashioning. From auto-ethnographic fictionalization of self to postmodernism's disruption of false binaries, butoh practice is a constant revision of the rules of perception in social action. When butoh artists dance the corporeality of an irresolute, despairing journey, they speak the language of resistant mutability. As Kristeva states: "In abjection, revolt is completely within being. Within the being of language. Contrary to hysteria, which brings about, ignores, or seduces the symbolic but does not produce it, the subject of abjection is eminently productive of culture" (1982, 45).

This is also the call to trickster, whose subversive maneuvers speak the language of producers and thus communicate beyond myth, cutting through the play of power dynamics. As Dylan asserts, for example, in speaking of the invincibility of traditional music: "Traditional music is too unreal to die. It doesn't need to be protected. Nobody's going to hurt it. In that music is the only true, valid death you can feel today off a record player" (Marcus 2001, 113–14). Traditional music, like butoh, has an indecipherable language all its own, sculpted by and steeped in sociocultural exigencies of countless historical moments.

In his book *The Old, Weird America: The World of Bob Dylan's Basement Tapes* (2001), Greil Marcus explores this world of mystery in the context of Dylan's *The Basement Tapes* recordings from 1967. Marcus traces connections between Dylan's opaque opus and the massive, encyclopedic vision of Harry Smith's seminal LP record set, *Anthology of American Folk Music* (1952), the first great collection of its kind and a bible of sorts for American traditional music enthusiasts. Smith's assemblage was not only an attempt to encompass all that American traditional music had been, but it also evoked another symbolic America, one tending toward essentialization and mythology, but just barely incapable of them. Marcus labels this social imaginary "Smithville," an iconicized nation of human tragedy, triumph, and intense desire initiated by the first colonists and continued through genocide, slavery, revolution, capitalism, Manifest Destiny, class warfare, love of land, and all else wrapped up in America's perennially grand, democratic experiment, full of idealism, terror, hubris, violence, and beauty.

Fifteen years after the release of Smith's compendium, behind a closed basement door in Dylan's Woodstock home, he and The Band took up the mantle of Smith's vision, speaking of its contemporary social manifestations and extending it into their own poetic musical language, one that was yet composed of the same chords, rhythms, and melodies—the very bones and sinew of American traditional music. *The Basement Tapes* show that what was weird about the old America was still weird in the 1960s and beyond; that America's blessing and curse was that it would never be satisfied with what it had. Even in the country's eventual, inexorable decline, it would always see itself as the New World.

Back in Japan, Hijikata and Hosoe were chasing through rice paddies and old barns in Tohoku in the exact same period (1965–68) that Dylan electrified Newport, recorded "Like a Rolling Stone," shouted down jeering concert crowds, crashed his motorbike, retreated to the world of the Basement Tapes, and refined his song craft into a neo-American vernacular. The results of these men's experiences debuted in early 1968 with the release of Dylan's album *John Wesley Harding*, which culled stylistically and thematically from *The Basement Tapes* sessions, and the first public exhibition of photos later collected and published as *Kamaitachi*. Not only did the works reinvent Dylan and Hijikata's public personae, but they wedded backward-looking, ruralist mythologies rooted in their respective national cultures with a contemporary artistic sensibility—reflective yet opaque, serious yet absurd. Both works express an overwhelming desire to know the land that the artists love yet cannot ultimately fathom, and perhaps love all the more for that fact.

Just as *The Basement Tapes* encompass a prophetic vision of an old weird America, *Kamaitachi* does the same for an old weird Japan, buried underneath a chaotic urban landscape (Tokyo as the new boring Japan), with only cracks and crevices to crawl through and relegated backwater farmlands full of empty dreams as the only escape. *Kamaitachi* is the death of old-world values at the hands of postindustrial might. Does this make *Kamaitachi* like Smithville, a photo album of an imagined past as a modernist frame for a new generation to carry forward into the future? Moreover, given the diaspora of butoh artists from Japan to the

West, does that make Japanese butoh performer immigrants to America and Europe like the original Pilgrims, like all American immigrants, eager to hold onto the mythology of their old values yet also transform such tales in their own manner, according to their own experience, to both proselytize and start over at the same time? Are butoh's qualities somehow quintessentially Japanese- *and* American-inflected?

Such questions point with curiosity at the voice with which butoh artists speak in their attempt to encompass the breadth of their personal narratives—contradictions and all. "Kazedaruma" (Wind Daruma, 1985), for example, Hijikata's last public speech and a freewheeling statement on the self-referential nature of his art, is, like *Kamaitachi*, not just an image or memory of his childhood experience of a traditional Japan. The text represents a way of life that wants explaining while knowing full well that no elucidation will ever arrive, just as it never will for love, hate, desire, happiness, or trickster. *Daruma* are talismanic dolls that have become increasingly popular in Japan over the centuries. Hijikata speaks of Tohoku farmers wrapped tightly against the biting cold wind of autumn and winter, transforming them into "wind daruma" that invade their households, "and that already is *butoh*" (Hijikata 2000, 72). He speaks of their walk home being "aerial burial and cremation," after which they can only speak in strange, monosyllabic onomotapeia imitating sounds of nature. Hijikata says that even in summer, Tohoku farmers shake off the intense snow of winter from their sandals. His mother tells him to run with the mind of a blind person, causing his head and the soles of his feet to turn upside down. He stares at toddlers tied to posts, unaware of the meaning or purpose of their hands, soaking in their movements, which, Hijikata said, "had a far-reaching effect on my butoh." The feeling that his arms are not really his arms. His desire to stifle time. To lack technical expertise. To have his long-lost sister living in his body. All of these surreal, subjectively generated images, sensations, and emotions (72–77).

Reflecting on this vast, complex imaginary, I wonder if it matters whether any of Hijikata's source memories were real events. In the end, Hijkata lived, and butoh happened. As Hyde states, "Tricksters use deception to generate material for storytelling, which expresses new worlds, life as it could be, making it also a generative force for the creation of language" (1998, 75–76). Tricksters steal, rename, and reuse through disguise, mystification, or whatever means they need to instigate change. Just as myth is the currency of thieves, poetry is the language of possibility, resistance, and empowerment. And just as butoh may be defined by the question, "Who are you?" so may we ask in manifesting ourselves through butoh, "Who is speaking?"

IMAGE-WORD AS SELF-OTHER

In addressing language and poetry in butoh, we arrive at a fundamental aspect of Hijikata's methodology that was extended in numerous permutations by other artists. In early writings, Hijikata employed provocative, surreal language, which he continued using later in essays, lectures, books, interviews, and personal communications. When he needed a working method for training and choreography, he developed *butoh-fu*, a system of language-based movement composed of an encyclopedic vocabulary of image-words. He reworked this lexicon over the years as he created new performances with a variety of bodies. Waguri Yukio cites Hijikata's method as "to physicalize images through words" (1998). Waguri states:

> Butoh-fu seems like poetry, but is the "physical language" that indicates a dancer's movement, a method for a dancer's physical being, and a way of relating with space. Each word implies a certain movement, condition, a series of movement units, and a drawing reference to a dance image. In other words, it is a kind of symbol for the choreographer and dancer to share image and movement. (1998)

Waguri cites the indexical nature of Hijikata's method from image to word to body, but one in which the referent is more instigator and inspiration than objective source:

> It is observed that there was a process in him, not only to use the drawing to give reference to form, but also to catch "the seeds of dance" that he had found through his unique way of comprehending a drawing with wording. . . . More importantly, throughout the whole of butoh-fu, a word is used as an index to awaken a physical image and, in fact, a word creates dance. (1998)

Thus, language and surrealism mark butoh as a poetic practice. Nakajima Natsu notes that this fact is rooted in an essential difference between Western and Japanese dance:

Japanese traditional music came from religious chanting, so it's more language-based. Japanese dance was produced by language, not music, not melody. This is a very important point when we think about butoh. For example, kabuki came from text language, and Nihon buyo choreography is from singing. Also the foundation of bunraku. In Noh theatre, they sing by themselves. Storytelling. All come from language. In the Western world, movement belongs to dance, and action belongs to theatre. After the Second World War, we all, the original (butoh) dancers, danced Western dance, so we all learned and copied melodic movement. But Hijikata said, "No, this is not our dance." So butoh is body and language, and Western dance is music and dance. Our dance is a kind of action and language. (2011)

Still employed by many artists, *butoh-fu* oriented butoh as trickster-like. By telling lies through stories replete with contradiction and hidden intent, tricksters produce new linguistic connections in order to produce new realities. Butoh language does the same by instigating embodiment of surreal imagery. Expressive ideas are choreographed, but their exact manifestation in detail is ultimately up to the practitioner's body. No two mental images of ants crawling up one's leg, for example, will ever be exactly the same between dancers, causing the same body over repeated instances to differ as well, with the only definite repetition being the instigating image-words.

The butoh body's multiplicity results in multiple images and bodies interacting with each other, producing a singular dialogue in the dancer's body between multiple and competing aspects of desire and reality. This expression thus returns us to butoh's political nature. I see our dance as a democratically engaged process reflecting a spectrum of relational influences, concrete and imagined, on self-identity. Moreover, if a core notion of liberal democracy in our time is to surpass majoritarian norms for the sake of a broader civil society defined by space for inclusiveness and difference, then I view butoh in a similarly philosophical and contemporary vein, but with a trickster-like disposition toward unpredictable manifestations. Political scholar Jeffrey C. Isaac reveals this notion as lying at the heart of liberal democracy's potential for nurturing social multiplicity and its generative insights into power and justice in speaking of Hannah Arendt's positing of a "rebellious politics" that highlight the essence of democratization: "Its principal concern is not with the legal organization of the public authority of states but with the possibilities for embodying and sustaining a spirit of independent association and initiative outside of the state, with generating nonjuridical forms of power and resistance to authority" (1998, 9). Ultimately, democracy at its core is how everyone in a given society lives it.

Isaac acknowledges that while liberal democracy in the twentieth century defeated totalitarian, communist, and fascist ideological forces, it failed to live up to its utopian ideals of universal political freedom. He advocates keeping sight of practical and inspiring models of democratic behavior while recognizing "the forces of resentment, acrimony, and authoritarianism equally latent within modern civil society" and "the dehydrating effects of modern consumer society, particularly the ill effects of the mass media and the forms of cynicism that these media promote" (13).[10] Looking back at butoh through this lens, it is neither the province nor obligation of butoh artists to offer practical solutions to sociopolitical tensions. Yet their capacity for holding space for the chaos and contradiction inherent in the psycho-physiological experience of radical democratization recalls Hijikata's fashioning of butoh as a site for recursive, schismogenetic realism around discrepancies within and between self and other. In other words, butoh is always already difference as lived.

Similarly, in the conclusion to Bruce Baird's monograph *Hijikata Tatsumi and Butoh: Dancing in a Pool of Gray Grits* (2012), the author summarizes butoh practice as operative within a paradigm of variance between one's internal and external life, one that we aspire to transcend:

> Properly speaking, in so far as butoh has any essence at all, butoh is an art form that demands that artists put themselves into continually new relationships and allow themselves to be invaded by others as a way to tirelessly search for actuality. Most of all, it demands that the artists express and experience the pain of others and particularly those who have been hurt by the diffuse customs and conventions of society. (218)

In our attempt as butoh artists to embody absurd and surreal images and enter a crisis state, we allow ourselves to experience a falling short of our desires, a visceral performance of not being able to have what we want, which forces us to observe what we do or can have, just as those in dialogue or opposition with one another in community must do. And in our reaction to the distance between the two, this *différance* between self and other, we thereby learn some truth about our selves, enabling us to operate with greater clarity about and sympathy for others.

LIES AND "I"S

As a subjective documentary, *Kamaitachi* stands as something between novel and ethnography, a fiction ostensibly depicting cultural realism. This makes Hijikata, as coauthor and performer, i.e., subject and object, something between novelist and ethnographer, or author and topic. "Hijikata" is in-between and nowhere. He is a trickster.

But, like "self," where does "he" lie? There's a difference between Hijkata the person and the cultural construct. The latter is a collective fiction. With a reputation as an iconic wild man of the Tokyo avant-garde, Hijikata was idolized by some, reviled by others, and perhaps seen as confusing or absurd to the rest. Simply put, in the public eye, he became a product of the witnessing imagination, a situation defined by and leading to projection of desire and fear. In fiction, such emotions reveal images of what we want and don't want to experience. When such feelings are projected onto a liminal entity like Hijikata, both deity and demon, we are at odds with our desires. If Hijikata's duality makes him both signifier and signified, then his reflection of our desires implies the same dualism within each of us.

This then is trickster's moment. The instant when they become real, when our boundaries are upset, and when we no longer know who we are because the fictional construct of culture upon which our identities were built goes awry. Trickster points to this construct as fiction, forcing us to see ourselves in the mirror, in all our fragmented reality. Ultimately, for all their deviousness, aggression, and play, tricksters are agents of the real. As Hyde says, they make this world. Despite what we want or don't want them to be, they are amoral because reality is amoral. Neither takes sides; they simply are. In terms of democracy, this fact is also what cultural scholar Cornel West refers to when he states, "the challenge is mustering the courage to scrutinize *all* forms of dogmatic policing of dialogue and to shatter *all* authoritarian strategies of silencing voices" (2004, 7). Moreover, by trickster's framing of himself as naïve or imperceptible, others' critiques of his supposed naiveté, blankness, or opacity force people to show their hands; to voice real opinions, to be vulnerable, realized, and reintegrated. This is the proactive promise of trickster.

Each in his own way, Hijikata, Dylan, Warhol, and others crossed the thresholds of high and low, center and margin, perhaps rubbing shoulders at the crossroads and taking a bit of each other's conjuring *juju* for mutual protection. At its most benevolent, Warhol's stripping away of all veneers of authenticity left only post-trammeled surfaces for those with eyes to see to be horrified, fascinated, or moved to prophetic insight. Hijikata's revivification of bodies and spirits lost in a cultural black void deadened by suits, televisions, and aircraft carriers was a postmodern Promethean gesture. Each man provided an opportunity, a gift, for society to view itself, warts and all, and see its lowest depths and highest potential.

Trickster is not only the need for the meat to be stolen, but also for someone to cut the fat, to remove what's unnecessary so life can move on. Trickster is the need itself for shamelessness, lest the world fall into a somnambulistic, mirrorless chamber of fearful, unshared secrets. Without trickster breaking rules, there can be no right or wrong, no life or death. Without the crossing of boundaries, those very walls would not exist, for only by violating that which is inviolable may all things within and without be experienced as valuable or worthless. Without a conductor to shuttle our minds, bodies, and spirits from here to there, from Heaven to Hell and back, how might we perceive what lies in our own backyard, right here on Earth?

In the context of contemporary challenges against social cohesion, mutuality, and sustainable values, trickster's notion of contingent identity becomes socially empowering, revealing how what is needed for survival also changes. The mutability of every self and social body begs a communal paradigm that holds space for all contingencies, regardless of culture, geography, language, or history. Such a world is produced from fragmentation, accretion, and unconscious assemblage by everyone involved in the development of culture and who themselves begin as fragmented, accreted, and unconscious. Trickster is the nurturing potential of space created for difference and redress. Behind the veil, trickster calls for *democracy* and *sustainability*.

Before such processes can manifest, however, a space is needed in which sharing may occur, where definitions and borders are anathema, else division and objectification take hold. A social setting potentialized by trickster must maintain conditions that allow for democratic actors in the face of encroaching boundaries fomented by ever-lurking power dynamics of hierarchy and dominance. Trickster's dance must choreograph opening in the face of entrapment.

In the space where shared assumptions become absurd jokes, where the usual way of doing things becomes the cause of immediate downfall, and where the tense pause of crisis management must eventually give way to the ballasting onrush of crisis resolution, tricksters and those affected by their actions are faced with stepping forward into the unknown or backward into a fortress.

For butoh artists, this means asking not only "Who are you?" but also "Who are we?"

The result of such effort is either a commons or an enclosure.

The author in a production still for the performance, "blind spot," Bangkok, Thailand, 2015. Photo by Yvan Cohen.

6 : IN THE SOIL

Do I contradict myself?
Very well then I contradict myself,
(I am large, I contain multitudes.)
— Walt Whitman, *Song of Myself*, 51 (1855)

Late capitalism loves diversity, but it doesn't know
what to do with difference.
— Ananya Chatterjea (2016)

WHO ARE WE?[1]

Butoh dancers' capacity for trickster is central to their ability to navigate the ethical codes of a given social context. Mutating identity through liminality via chaos, contradiction, and crisis, butoh becomes a contrapuntal play of inquiry and discovery of self—or, rather, selves. Through reflections and contradictions, the body in crisis may generate new selves to recontextualize one's environment.

Like Tamano Hiroko defining butoh by asking, "Who are you?" the question, "Who are we?" is her notion's wider extension and moves butoh to a communal space, where ongoing lives complement, impede, inspire, diffuse, or build on each other. Parallel to this notion, and in light of ongoing environmental, economic, and political crises, the *commons* has gained currency as a generative concept for realizing ideals of cultural renewal, social support systems, resistance to hegemony, and sustainability (Benkler 2003, Goldman, et. al. 1998, Parr and Zaretsky, et. al. 2011, Harney and Moten 2013). As modes of crisis resolution, butoh-based practice and philosophy have the potential to engage discourses around these topics. While my project does not explore the practical history of the commons nor its inverse, *enclosure*, with its consequences of exclusion, I take inspiration from their structures and meanings.

Early butoh subverted notions of legitimacy and authority, claiming access to cultural discourse for marginalized social actors. Butoh practice is generative of shared liminal space, which has the capacity to engender communal engagement, such as in Victor Turner's concept of *communitas* (1985). Such a space allows for multiplicity and pluralistic dialogue—for *democracy*—to become a psycho-physiological ecology enabling the ever-evolving individual and community desire for subject formation, or *sustainability*. In socioeconomic terms, I posit a form of sustainability in opposition to the historically based, Western sense of the term; that which undergirds development of sustainable management, frameworks, design, and financing of capitalist production (Spivak 2012). A butoh-based strategy for sustainability aims to renew and revitalize, not to reinforce or preserve.

Enclosure defies the shared space of communitas, instead defining and marginalizing communal space, debilitating its power and influence. First framed by Hijikata as an individualized response to hegemony, butoh practice may speak back to similar social trends such as rampant corporatization and commodification of multiculturalism, as well as a legally enforced, neoliberal globalization that ossifies authoritarian control into privatization. Such phenomena are enclosures with vast social and ecological consequences (Goldman 2006, Klein 2007, Leitner, Peck, and Sheppard 2006, Shiva 2005).

Opening space for physical and mental connectivity makes it fluid and variable, allowing for a spectrum of social relations, interdependencies, and collaborations. By focusing on practitioners' subjective experience to fire their revelatory power, butoh transforms the space of the body into a "place"—liminally sited between the wider landscape and the concentrated artwork (Casey 2004)—of structured resistance and relational diversity.[2] By examining this process in the context of social discourse and communal engagement, this chapter asks how the butoh practitioner may avoid fetishizing crisis and move toward increased social benevolence.

DOMAINS OF SHARING

In Western political and scholarly discourse, the commons has been discussed primarily in practical, economic, and legal terms. I speak of the commons, however, not only as what is actively utilized or shared, but as sociocultural capital permeating a collective. Social and environmental theorist C. A. Bowers describes the commons throughout history as nearly synonymous with culture:

> The commons, even in ancient times . . . included the air that people breathed, the language they spoke, the narratives that intergenerationally renewed their sense of identity and values, the craft knowledge and technologies that had been refined over generations. . . . Their games as well as their forms of aesthetic expression. . . . In effect the commons encompassed every aspect of the human/biotic community that had not been monetized or privatized. (2006, 2)

In debates around the politico-economic ramifications for globalized society of both the transformative utility and dangerous weaponization of intellectual property, the concept of the *cultural commons*, as both metaphor and practical framework, has become a rallying point for resistant and subaltern discourses as well as an object of criticism. Paolo Fiorentino, Martha Friel, Massimo Marelli, and Walter Santagata define the cultural commons as a "social dilemma" oriented by "culture, space, and community" that can be physical or virtual, possess infinite "carrying capacity" due to its intangible nature, and is subject to either being nurtured or remaining stationary depending on how actively new ideas arise within its field (2010). Bill Ivey criticizes the looseness of the concept's overabundance of definitions that each feel static, historical, and "musty in its connotations" and in need of clearer operative parameters (2009, 25–26). Kimberly Christen decries the repeated default to a public/private binary in debates about the nature of control or authorship within the cultural commons (2005). More recently, in the midst of the COVID-19 crisis, the authors in the rapid-response journal, *Cultural Commons* (Kay and Wood, 2020), unpack a multitude of both reactionary tendencies and restorative justice ideals among the global surge in demand for access to communal resources for bodily, economic, and cultural survival.

My rationale, however, for wading into a discussion of the cultural commons has less to do with its broader ontology than what performing it implies about social interaction; how what is allowed or disallowed affects how we perceive and learn from each other. My admittedly utopian goal is this: if some form of butoh practice can maintain an inherent desire for cultural sharing, it may serve as a model for how to cultivate and express certain empowering tensions inherent in a cultural commons. This may be possible if such sharing demonstrates a nonrivalrous approach to cultural resources that are understood as a common pool of knowledge and ideas, from which various groups are able to draw, implying that greater awareness of and engagement with one's social nature is always in order.[3]

Butoh practice orients itself in this manner by performing seemingly irreconcilable conflicts between diverse identities. Each performer embodies competing desires—aesthetic, cultural, ethnic, political, economic, and personal—in the same bodily time-space, thereby manifesting the essence of a cultural commons. At root, butoh represents what Lewis Hyde speaks of as "the comedy of the commons," a custom "whose enactment is social life itself. Community and common ground cannot be separated here; the latter is the stage where the former has its merriment, a reward that could be called 'returns to scale' but is more simply named 'the common good' or better yet 'the comic good'" (2010, 175–76).

The absurdity in Hijikata's dance reveals and activates this open terrain. Hijikata and his gold-painted cabaret dancers posturing in the high kitsch of self-exotification (Baird 2012, 81–85). Maro Akaji and another Dairakudakan dancer fencing to the death with their tongues (Velez 1989). Amagatsu Ushio clad in a traditional Japanese schoolboy outfit begging for entry into a monolithic, temple-like doorway while desperately flinging uncooked rice into his mouth (Amagatsu 1980). In realizing that socialization often pushes an individual to enact competing agendas, thereby making them untenable, one may be obliged to laugh it off and into another level of dialectic being.

More fundamentally, butoh's absurd tendencies claim a certain position within the field of political aesthetics, and are sited within what philosopher Jacques Rancière calls "the distribution of the sensible," which "establishes at one and the same time something common that is shared and exclusive parts" and "determines the very manner in which something in common lends itself to participation and in what way various individuals have a part in this distribution" (2006, 12). In speaking of alternative political paradigms in contemporary art, Adrian Parr extends Rancière's concept of this commons of knowledge and experience:

> The political condition of art struggles to visualize, give a voice to, and render audible those who remain excluded from the dominant organizational system of knowledge, law, and social position. . . .

> Art can be a mode of political subjectivization. That is, when art redistributes the coordinates of how the sensible is distributed it can transform the hierarchical system of social and epistemological organization. (2011, 8–9)

Thus, artistic action within the commons can reimagine social relations. This is the cultural commons as not just collectively and generally pooled, but inherently active within idiosyncratically positioned persons who actuate this field in relation to themselves. As a form of "political subjectivization" in the postwar Japanese avant-garde art milieu, butoh became an example of what Lawrence Lessig calls forms of *disruptive technology*. More than simply implying a paradigm shift through innovation, such modalities purposely interfere with normative modes of communication, commerce, and control for the sake of building new markets and forms of social interaction (2001, 91). While incumbency tends toward stasis, disruption produces movement. Just as disruptive technologies lead to less control and greater choice in the marketplace of ideas and goods, so butoh does not necessarily prescribe specific codes of movement or behavior. Butoh does advocate, however, through embracing contradictions and cohabiting opposites, for multiplicitous being. In some sense, butoh practice is designed to allow anyone, regardless of their place in a hierarchy, to embody *the public domain*, if we frame the latter beyond legal limits and instead as a cumulative store of knowledge. Hyde describes how the public domain, "that great and ancient storehouse of human innovation," embodies multiplicity via shared ownership: "The public domain surrounds us, but almost invisibly so, as if it were the dark matter in the universe of property. To illuminate but one case in point, every time you drive your car to work, you unwittingly take a ride on the public domain. Exactly how many inventions of the human mind are bundled in a working automobile?" (2010, 47).

I view Hijikata's *ankoku* as another form of "dark matter" seeping through the cracks of "the universe of property," which in capitalism is nothing more or less than the marketplace. Just as the public domain is an implicit force driving innovation, so butoh's darkness is the invisible force that drives its constant mutation. As market productivity feeds off the public domain, so the butoh artist is inspired by paralyzed social conventions. In *Nikutai no Hanran,* with Tokyo's cultural elite in attendance, Hijikata broke the choreographic codes of Western dance embedded in his training, reinjected them into his performance with seams torn and the connective tissue destroyed, and celebrated the resulting disorder for the audience's amusement, repulsion, and wonder.[4] As a trickster engaging the cultural commons, Hijikata steals the conventions of mid-twentieth-century Western dance, reproduces them for a marketplace of ideas, and sets a standard for butoh artists transforming their public identities from myriad elements in the public domain.

Through their incessant physical and identity shifts, butoh performers make and unmake themselves, modeling ways in which butoh philosophy can inform our interpretation of contemporary social phenomena. We might employ a butoh-based frame of reference to understand, for example, how to view subject formation and social resistance in the online realm. Greg Goldberg examines how mass participation in the internet and social media produces in users an ambivalent relationship between communal knowledge production and meaning-making and the hegemony of global capital (2010). Because the latter is part and parcel with the nearly unfathomable amounts of data flowing through billions of people's lives, its dominant power structures overwhelmingly define global economic exchange and cultural identity. Yet Goldberg sees in this paradigm an opportunity for greater cultural invention:

> Vital power does not simply affect users and their lives from outside, but is constitutive of the user and its life, not to mention the liveliness of the data it generates and which often exceeds its boundaries. . . . Put another way, online participation does not express and affect a pre-existing self (user, agent, etc.) but rather is a form of self-making and self-unmaking. (2010, 750–51)

Thus, just as butoh practitioners adapt forms of dominance as elements of their anti-hegemonic behavior, so do self-aware and socially conscious netizens use the corporatized social structure of digital media to fashion their everyday lives in recursive, progressive, or resistant ways. Members of each group look to their cultural commons as a space of identity and intention as well as immanence of cultural potential. If we understand the benevolence of such constructedness through the transformative agency of butoh's collage of identity shifts, so might we better understand a range of social actors.

Enclosure is related to the way historical narratives become collectively embraced. Edward Casey speaks of how "public memory" is dangerously reinforced and made static when individual and social memories—fluid by nature—become framed and codified into history under the aegis of a commodified "globalization without localization" (2007, 85). Butoh's genesis as a vehement rejection of the United States's institutionalization of its own historical determinacy in postwar Japan thus makes history, property, and the body key factors in discussing such resistance.

In speaking of history's disciplinary task of determining human understanding, Pierre Nora states: "At the heart of history is a critical discourse that is antithetical to spontaneous memory. History is perpetually suspicious of memory, and its true mission is to suppress and destroy it" (1989, 9). Such a concept makes tradition, history's tool for maintaining order through vague yet authoritative connotations, also the enclosure of the body, which, in its every gesture, is the manifestation of everyday life. As social theorist Michel de Certeau asserts, just as history is written by dominant ideologies, so is the body:

> The law constantly writes itself on bodies. . . . These writings carry out two complementary operations: through them, living beings are "packed into a text" (in the sense that products are canned or packed), transformed into signifiers of rules (a sort of "intertextuation") and, on the other hand, the reason or Logos of a society "becomes flesh" (an incarnation). (1984, 140)

In this sense, even in the absence of slavery, bodies are "owned" as property through dominant forms of languaging. LaMonda Horton Stallings discusses the dangerous tendency of even mainstream academic and literary critics ostensibly supportive of neo-slave narratives to "fetishize the word or privilege literacy" (2003, 189), thus reifying the dominant mode of controlling corporeal identity.[5] Speaking at a further remove from the body, Rosemary J. Coombe and Andrew Herman cite enclosure of private property taking place even in the virtual realm and intentional commons of the World Wide Web:

> (Property) is a social relationship between socially recognized persons with respect to real and intangible things . . . that is authorized and legitimized in particular cultural contexts. It is also a relationship of profound social power. The generalized failure to see the social relationships that produce the value of things we consider property—the constitutive misrecognition that Marx referred to as commodity fetishism—is one manifestation of this power. (2004, 561)

Coombe and Herman point out that mass consumption of private property as a trope of capitalist ideology allows for the marginalization of those whose actions are not commodity based: "The ability to claim something as one's own is ritually performed in social interactions which operate to render the owner suitable and fitting to appropriate that from which he or she claims the right to exclude others. In the intrinsic alterity of claiming property as a function of propriety, the nonowner is a person who is not appropriate" (2004, 561).

This system makes de Certeau's legally enclosed bodies possible and also makes noncommoditized modes of interacting, sharing, or knowing irrelevant. As Anthony McCann asserts about the threat to traditional music's noncommercial modes of cultural transmission in the age of globalized commodification: "The musical practices that support traditional music transmission abide by models of creativity, collaboration, and participation that together add up to the antithesis of the text-based, individualist, and essentially capitalist nature of intellectual property regimes" (2001, 90).

Intellectual property is wielded globally as the lever by which multinational conglomerates acquire patents to every imaginable product. Vandana Shiva cites the case of India, where the federal government pushes nationwide adoption of genetically engineered, corporate seed while mandating registration of all farm seeds—locally and communally cultivated or otherwise—thereby making it illegal to use noncorporate seed and commodifying the codes of nature itself (2005, 151).[6] Likewise, Naomi Klein shows that chaos is an operative component of an increasingly cynical and lucrative cycle of social bust and corporate boom: "Now wars and disaster responses are so fully privatized that they are themselves the new market; there is no need to wait until after the war for the boom—the medium is the message" (2007, 16).

If crisis and its response, crisis management, are privatized, then crisis itself is enclosed away from dialogue and communion, thus allowing for dissolution and destruction. Capitalism inherently divests mind and body as well as the earth itself from noncommercial social interaction. As Shiva describes, this commons/commodity binary possesses threatening implications: "It deprives the politically weaker groups of their right to survival, which they had through access to commons, and it robs from nature its right to self-renewal and sustainability, by eliminating the social constraints on resource use that are the basis of common property management" (2005, 29–30).

What we witness in principle through the historical progression of capitalist enclosure is the inverse of butoh's potentializing methodology. The desire for capital wealth can lead to the thievery of productive knowledge through the enclosure of practical resources. Such a process is predisposed to subvert democracy, undergird hegemony, and minimize sustainability. Patenting seeds for exclusive use by corporate conglomerates, for example, prevents other farmers from further cultivating longstanding relationships with the seeds and their tangible and intangible benefits. Future commons are lost through scorched earth prospecting that mostly benefits prospectors and their bottom line. Such actions constitute thievery as preemption: stealing a natural entity and its productive usage by demarcating its natural properties within legalized boundaries. It is the opposite of butoh artists' approach to manifestation: rather than looking to the past in order to create their futures and realizing proactive identity, transformative behavior, and social justice, it is stealing the past in order to limit the future by reducing cultural memory and forestalling imagination. If, in a social sense, we define people by who they are, what they do, and where, when, how, and why they do it, then enclosure is death itself.

It is no wonder then that Hijikata's butoh was so immersed in *ankoku* from the start. His innumerable references to this shadowy zone evoke not simply death but an entire netherworld existence, speaking, for example, of the idiosyncratic bodily awareness cultivated by growing up in Japan's rural north:

> Inside my body even now is this feeling that I grew up with my head and the soles of my feet turned upside down. If you don't do anything else, however, you'll turn into mud. And you can't

> make do with mud alone. But I can, I know, declare that my butoh started there with what I learned from the mud in the early Spring, not from anything to do with the performing arts of shrines or temples. (2000, 73–74)

Hijikata utilized his sense of exclusion and marginalization to refashion himself into a liminal subaltern. As Murobushi Ko describes, "He doesn't want to dance for the spirits or the gods. And he said if he's feeling happy, he's not dancing. . . . Maybe his starting point is sadness or breakdown. Separated from the mother ground. I say this feeling is broken, like an orphan" (2012).

Circulating outside of the mainstream enclosure, Hijkata's butoh was part and parcel of the cultural commons.[7] His impetus to resist late capitalism's materialist schema by decommodifying the body was a utopian gesture, making the body in crisis the butoh artist's strategy for recursively negotiating the textually delineated landscape of capitalism.

Is this approach, however, meaningful in contemporary transnational localities? In claiming a negative space in relation to a dominant center, one also plays by the rules of those in power. Political theorists Francoise Lionnet and Shu-Mei Shih describe the way in which centers of social power are reified simply by resistance to them: "Critiquing the center . . . seems only to enhance it; the center remains the focus. . . . The deconstructive dyad center/margin thus appears to privilege marginality only to end up containing it. The marginal or the other remains a philosophical concept and futuristic promise" (2005, 3). Shiva cites the danger of overlooking such distinctions as leading to a negative self: "Ecological and economic identities are linked to roots in a place and a community. When secure occupations and livelihoods are destroyed, the vacuum of the loss of sense of self is filled by the negative identity, an identity of 'not the other'" (2005, 81).

Hijikata's early works were posited in reaction to a similar phenomenon in postwar Japan and were similarly negative in character. Is nihilism his method's ultimate result, or are there broader schema possible for manifesting bodies *who* exist not only in opposition to hegemony, but within an antidotal, alternative paradigm? This challenge was implicit from Hijikata and Ohno's first experiments. The American Occupation Authority and postwar Japanese government feared the possibility of leftist, Communist, and anarchist revolutionary efforts

(Dower 1999). Early butoh needed imaginaries, not just *ankoku*, as an alternative: they needed hope. It matters that the time-space exists to embody and participate in a cultural commons and not simply as an infinite darkness of loss, absence, and disappearance.

How can butoh move beyond its root parameters of ruralist, absurdist, and abstract abjection as a negative reaction to capitalist hegemony? Can the practice maintain a generative, crisis-driven mode of resolution-irresolution, yet reach toward a wider field of guiding principles, as a positive, even inspiring response to individual or societal affliction? What are the necessary conditions for such processes to occur? Moreover, how can the collective butoh community navigate these indeterminate waters through the ever-present risk of increased commodification? As McCann states:

> We need to be aware of the human dimension of intellectual property application, the human dimension of individualist possessiveness, the distancing effects of increasing professionalization, the drive to convert folklore into spectacle, the change that all of these effect upon relationships, upon community, and ultimately upon the transmission process. (2001, 98)

Butoh faces the danger of becoming a globalized art form with pressure toward homogenization and ready access by the mainstream, in which core intangible aspects of any cultural practice may be marginalized, devalued, and eviscerated by a stratifying value structure based on consumer entitlement. While answers to this line of inquiry are for a larger study, in this chapter's last sections I look more deeply at how butoh itself manifests the cultural commons in order to suggest two possibilities, *democracy* and *sustainability*, as particularized discourses that butoh practice may generatively engage.

On the one. All in.

Hip-hop artist Rennie Harris and I are onstage, performing Flash, *our butoh/hip-hop dance theater duet, exchanging ribald, ironic memories of a childhood spent fulfilling heteronormative tropes of the desired, racialized other. I watched Soul Train and wanted to be Jeffrey Daniel. Rennie watched* Fists of Fury *and wanted to be Bruce Lee. He instructs me on how to strut like a Black man. I guide him how to follow his breath like an Asian martial artist.*

Suddenly, as the flow of Rennie's popping waves course visibly through his limbs, torso, and face, his lungs suddenly erupt, sending a swell of energy up his arm, out his fingertips, and into my chest.

I body wave back, falling into the sound of my own voiceover amplified throughout the theater, each word soliciting another body image from inside, a multiplicitous self made of infinite others.

"Breath . . . Center . . . Chest . . . Hip . . . Shoulder . . . Knee . . . Elbow . . . Foot . . . Hand . . . Neck . . . Waist . . . Jaw . . . Lips . . . Tongue . . . Eyes . . . Drop . . . Lift . . . Pump . . . Kick . . . Jack . . . Wave . . . Hit."

I hit Rennie, who sends an even more intense body wave back at me.

"Bruce . . . Fred . . . Shrimp . . . Pete . . . Jimi . . . Kid . . . Glenn . . . Eric . . . Eihei . . . Breathe . . . Push . . . Pull . . . Resist . . . Care . . . Oppose . . . Embrace . . . Know . . . Make . . . Love."[8]

As the voiceover ends and the first notes of a classic funk tune begin, Rennie and I dance an old-school popping routine. Once again, we have circled around to our beginnings.

Left to right: *The author and Rennie Harris performing "Flash," Los Angeles, California, 2012.* Photos by Janelle Traylor.

Embedded in the postwar Japanese, avant-garde art movements out of which butoh arose was a resistance to the Western capitalist ideology imposed on the country by American occupation forces and a string of oligarchical Japanese government regimes complicit in the determination of postcolonial development on the country. After unsuccessful mass protests by leftists, unions, and student groups against the 1960 renewal of the Japan–U.S. Treaty of Mutual Cooperation and Security, the government worked assiduously to present a depoliticized, economically comforting image of the country that foregrounded a homogenized, consumerist rebirth narrative. Published a few months later, Hijikata's essay, "To Prison" (1961), in which he declared, "I will no longer be cheated by a bad check called democracy" (2000, 43), further established his alignment with fellow avant-gardists opposing the state's dominant socioeconomic paradigm of "an everyday defined by forms of consumption as the complement to an administered, closed political realm" (Marotti 2013, 139).[9] Butoh's embrace of chaos and contradiction posits an embodiment of absolute difference and rejects uncomplicated diversity.

Similarly, political theorist Chantal Mouffe advocates, not for the mere fact of *pluralism*, which alone is vulnerable to outflanking, reduction, and disintegration by hegemony, but for a complex political dimension that balances difference and alliance and "questions the objective of unanimity and homogeneity, which is always revealed as fictitious and based on acts of exclusion" (2000, 19). Mouffe's progressive dimension asks everyone in a social structure to join in a difficult intersection of nondominant identities and positions, where "no social agent should be able to claim mastery of the *foundation* of society. This signifies that the relation between social agents becomes more democratic only as far as they accept the particularity and the limitation of their claims; that is, only insofar as they recognize their mutual relation as one from which power is ineradicable" (21). Such a possibility calls for a simultaneous connectivity, not despite, but within difference; a unary state defined by multiplicity.

In Gilles Deleuze and Félix Guattari's critique of capitalism *A Thousand Plateaus: Capitalism and Schizophrenia* (1987), the authors argue for the existence and utility of such a status, a metaphysics of the oneness of being and a system opposed to capitalism's inclination to separate and enclose:

> It is only when the multiple is effectively treated as a substantive, "multiplicity," that it ceases to have any relation to the One as subject or object, natural or spiritual reality, image and world. Multiplicities are rhizomatic and expose arborescent pseudomultiplicities for what they are. There is no unity to serve as a pivot in the object, or to divide in the subject. There is not even the unity to abort in the object or "return" in the subject. A multiplicity has neither subject nor object, only determinations, magnitudes, and dimensions that cannot increase in number without the multiplicity changing in nature. (8)

Deleuze and Guattari connect this framework to the artistic process:

> An assemblage is precisely this increase in the dimensions of a multiplicity that necessarily changes in nature as it expands its connections. There are no points or positions in a rhizome, such as those found in a structure, tree, or root. There are only lines. When Glenn Gould speeds up the performance of a piece, he is not just displaying virtuosity, he is transferring the musical points into lines, he is making the whole piece proliferate. (8)

Butoh dancers performing multifaceted contradictions of a crisis state operate likewise. Just as Gould's voice and fingers famously outflanked each other in myriad simultaneities, so Hijikata's multiply gendered, sexualized, primitivized, modernized, culturalized, and nationalized valences all existed in his unary mind-body, where interior/exterior, animal/human, animate/inanimate, and beautiful/grotesque are so many proliferations. This is the perennially schismogenetic dialogue that the dancers have with themselves. This is the butoh artist's *One.*

Deleuze and Guattari's entities are simultaneously multiple and singular, existing beyond integration, yet composed of systemic elements: "Unity always operates in an empty dimension supplementary to that of the system considered (overcoding). The point is that a rhizome or multiplicity never allows itself to be overcoded" (8–9). To the authors, there is only the One, and everything else is concept or power reliant on coding. When an artistic process defined by oneness takes place, the artist transcends dualism, integration, or other dichotomous frames. Deleuze and Guattari describe what then takes place:

> From chaos, *Milieus* and *Rhythms* are born. . . . Every milieu is vibratory, in other words, a block of space-time constituted by the periodic repetition of the component. . . . Every milieu is coded, a code being defined by periodic repetition; but each code is in a perpetual state of transcoding or transduction. . . . The milieus are open to chaos, which threatens them with exhaustion or intrusion. Rhythm is the milieus' answer to chaos. What chaos and rhythm have in common is the in-between—between two milieus, rhythm-chaos, or the chaosmos. (313)

The chaosmos is the constantly liminal state incessantly mutating in a process of perpetual recodification through the code of each milieu that it passes through, relates or refers to, or temporarily embodies. In butoh dancers' liminal crisis states generated from the attempt to embody or resolve contradictory, coded identities, they perform such rhythms within the chaosmos running between and through the social milieus from which they draw inspiration. Hijikata juxtaposing and deconstructing Western social dances through his imagined Tohoku childhood. Ohno miming La Argentina's flamenco femininity through his German Expressionist training. By diving into the heart of being of the One by juxtaposing distinct or even contradictory codes within their singular selves, butoh artists simultaneously and enigmatically embody, preclude, and transcend the overcoding of unity. By performing the socialized boundaries and connections of whatever milieus they are attempting to express, they reveal their One-ness and, by implication, everyone's as well. They express the paradoxical nature of being, what Buddhism refers to as simultaneous form and emptiness, where absolute being and utter impermanence inseparably coexist.[10] The butoh dancer's every rise, fall, breath, desirous failure, or near-resolution realizes yet another milieu, rhythm, and rhizomatic position.

In other words, the butoh dancer's every gesture is everything and nothing.

MEMORY: A PORTRAIT

August 2016. Bangkok.

After a couple years of mostly long-distance correspondence, dancing around ideas for collaborating, photographer Cedric Arnold and I are finally in town at the same time and in studio for a session. His work has graced museum walls and magazine pages throughout the world, and now he's working on a portrait series of artists in the region.

And now here we are, lighting set, costume on, camera ready . . . without a plan.

Cedric asks how butoh dancers normally move. I launch into a long-winded explanation about how the butoh stereotype of moving very slowly is a misnomer, that we are moving actually quite fast, but within an altered time-space continuum, that there is no such thing as moving in slow motion, which is an artificial construct from filmmaking, even though lay observers keep perpetuating this idea, and that, in any case, I do move faster than most butoh dancers because I've internalized the funk rhythms and street dance of my youth—of needing to run, hide, evade capture, and never stay in one place or identity for long—so the chaos, contradiction, and crisis that I'm portraying is similar to but not the same as Hijikata's, and that I remix and sometimes recreate my own butoh-fu every time I dance.

Cedric nods silently, and smiles. "Well, just do all that, and we'll see what happens."

I breathe in and out, drop my head, raise my left hand in staccato fits and starts, and, for the next half hour, lift my eyes . . .

Portraits of the author, Bangkok, Thailand, 2016. Photos by Cedric Arnold.

Deleuze and Guattari advocate for a nondichotomous multiplicity and thus, by implication, an embodiment of the commons. There are various and variable aspects of the One, but no separation. Sociopolitically for the butoh artist, this frame allows for the metaphysical reality of the commons to combine with the dialogic multiplicity of democratic behavior and the call for sustainability, all via the practitioner's simultaneous multiplicity and oneness. The rhythm at play between milieus and chaos in Deleuze and Guattari's paradigm is akin to what Derrida, in "The Deaths of Roland Barthes," describes as the "rhythm" by which Barthes's inexpressible punctum "scans" every detail of a photo's inherent studium and takes inspiration from them as needed for its overall effect (2001, 42). Both rhythms are driven by the tension between known and unknown, the desire of either a milieu or chaos to know or un-know the other in the contact zone of the chaosmos.

Mark Wigley argues that Derrida's essay reveals the nature of photography as representative of the binary structures endemic throughout Western culture via the haunting of the frame, i.e., the "rhythm" produced by the ineffable tension of punctum within the "haunted space" of the studium (1993, 190–91). Wigley asserts that this tension is especially true of the binary of internal/external space within the hegemony of Western social institutions: "It is the haunting of a space that organizes the conceptual structure of the institutional codes of reading (and institutions are never more than codes for reading, culturally enfranchised systems of representation) that are applied to that space but cannot recognize its phantoms" (191). Meta-action that reflects such patterns, however, speaks directly to the nature of such codes and systems of power: "Inasmuch as deconstructive discourse is always a 'reading' of institutional space, it must disturb the institutions of reading sustained by, and in the end, indistinguishable from, that space," which eventually leads to "a question of the point at which the two are conflated, the point at which Derrida's reading of space addresses the space of reading" (191). With its liminal expressivity between states of clarity and knowing, butoh is such an action.

This haunted space between codes, then, of knowing and unknowing, of the chaosmos, is where butoh lives, and the rhythm flowing through the space is the dance itself. Butoh animates the multiplicity inherent in the milieus that it symbiotically activates and is activated by as the commons that each artist embodies. As Hijikata developed his craft, he did not simply question or spit in the eye of certain ideologies, but he embodied also the friction itself between numerous binary milieus: urban/rural, industrial/agrarian, Eastern/Western, Japanese/American, modern/primitive, spiritual/material, translation/mistranslation, and others. Murobushi Ko believed Deleuze's final book, *Critique et Clinique* (1997), was illustrative of butoh's multiplicity and a crisis-oriented philosophy that encompasses deconstruction of the body's normative behavior:

> This kind of position, it's in crisis. Not only one identification, maybe you must break yourself down and listen, listen, listen, listen. Many fragments, or many organs, start to connect with different directions. In this case, very difficult to make one movement. It's not possible to go straight. And because I understand Hijikata's choreography, the face becomes like a Francis Bacon picture, it's not possible to keep one facial expression fixed, but Hijikata's moving a lot—Ah, uh, ah, uh—and one face becomes a thousand faces. In this case, your facial expression becomes drowned. (2012)

Miryam Sas's analysis of butoh and postwar Japanese photography resonates with this concept. She examines how contradiction, crisis, and subjectivity allow for a wider scope of origination and expressivity beyond the individual and in any given social setting. She hints toward a mode by which butoh artists may embody and activate the cultural commons (2011). Sas describes Hijkata's form as a space-time instant of resolving contradiction:

> Hijkata condemns the moment of erasure, of forgetting, where the point of contact between an act and its refusal, between a person and her acts is lost. *Buto* becomes the effort to confront the moment when that terror or awe is still vivid . . . from a place of paradox that consists of an act and its negation at once. . . . The term Hijikata uses, *kigen*, implies a genesis, a beginning, a traceability. Expression . . . comes figuratively to encompass all kinds of creative acts, but also . . . a liminal place . . . between internalization of something from the outside and externalization/exteriorization of something from within. (2011, 163)

Such action is facing the time-space instant of crisis (actualizing desire), liminally suspended between dualities (trickster), as the moment and place of origination, and becoming what you need and can be in an open environment of possibility (cultural commons).

In speaking of the Japanese avant-garde photo magazine *Provoke*, published in 1968–69, Sas views the photographer's process of subjective envisioning as the lever through which origination, and thus individual selfhood, is transcended: "With the idea of the 'anonymity of the real' . . . there is an attempt to get to the bottom of the act of seeing, which vacillates between the subjective and that which belongs to no subject" (2011, 183). She quotes Moriyama Daido as an example: "I suddenly grasp and put out . . . that thing which is most real . . . to me. After that has ended, it no longer matters at all who took the photograph; it's that kind of an act" (183). Sas also cites photographer Narahara Ikko's view of Moriyama's work as further evidence of the paradoxical transcendence of self via reflexivity:

> Your seeing is the foundation. For example, you saw the special edition newspaper about Kennedy's assassination blowing in the wind, and if you had taken a picture of it, that would have been a completion of your act of seeing. . . . However, instead, it sinks deep inside you, with yourself standing there included—and that there might have been someone (else) looking [possibly at you]—and you try to put that out there to the world as well. . . . And you systematize the whole [aggregation] of these relations of seeing and being seen that envelop you, and what one could call the "one who systematizes these gazes" becomes that which would replace the photographer. (Sas 2011, 183)

This is audiencing, framing the terms for dialogue, via subjective engagement. Subjectivity becomes a means to establish mutual sight and acknowledgment and thus the conditions for multiplicity and dialogue. If establishing a commons requires redefining origination and property, then subjectivity as a means to opening one's originating vision to the wider communal context is a means to the end of interpersonal connection as well. Coupling this subjective mode with Hijikata's crisis state as the space-time of origination opens the practitioner to communal knowledge, a psycho-physiological-temporal resource of being in multiplicity, i.e., a cultural commons.

Such a mode of encounter through mediated vision also becomes a means to challenging the authority of indexical truth, which is ultimately the tool of dominance. As Sas points out:

> It is not the "originality" or "indexicality" of the work of photography that is emphasized, because it could just as well be a recropping, a photo of a photo, or a reversed negative—nonetheless the eyes "gain a hold" of things—an interest in "actuality" not in the documentary sense but in some more asymptomatically liminal sense, an "encounter," detonation, or provocation that breaks existing concepts but that also emphasizes a lack of mediation: the eyes themselves "grasp" reality and then "present" it (the camera's cut) as a certain kind of evidence. (2011, 184–85)

In this sense, a commons may be a recursive space contextualized by liminality as encounter. If one's frame of perception is primed for orienting experience as a juxtaposition of elements that incite new knowledge, then liminal form becomes a provocation referencing its inherent multiplicity. Such a commons gives the lie to indexicality's positivism, as with a personally experienced photo (á la *Provoke*) or body (á la butoh) as evidence of a photographer or performer having phenomenologically experienced a moment of their reality. This commons resets the terms of indexicality as it indicates the artist's lived experience, which is significant for an audience concerned with witnessing "truth" apart from the dominant order. Such entities, in other words, are *subjectively indexical.* They suggest the possibilities and multitudes of lived experience and are generative of such, both within and as the cultural commons.

IMAGINING INCLUSION

In *The Poetics of Space* (1958), Gaston Bachelard speaks of subjective origination in a manner similar to that operative in postwar Japanese art: "The essential newness of the poetic image poses the problem of the speaking being's creativeness. Through this creativeness the imagining consciousness proves to be, very simply but very purely, an origin" (1994, xxiv). When such a consciousness acts upon "the spaces we love," those that nurture and provide us with a sense of security, it alters our experience of such spaces as "eulogized" or "protective" (1994, xxxv). Our subjectivity creates "imagined values, which soon become dominant" when the space is "lived in, not in its positivity, but with all the partiality of the imagination," thereby creating "an attraction. For it concentrates being within limits that protect" (1994, xxxvi).

In other words, lived space becomes inherently subjectivized over time. If, moreover, as Lippard describes, we are not only in, but also of a space, then lived space transcends its objective qualities to become a place. Combined with Bachelard's assertion of such space as protective, then the push and pull of opening and closing—of the commons and enclosure—are at work within us through our sense of *home*, a felicitous metaphor for place as activated space, a refuge and realization of self, and the sincerest manifestation of how people protectively structure their lives.

The desire for security, however, may in other instances lead to a sense of home conflated with an objectified self, validated by dominant paradigms that compete in the rationally delineated worldscape of convention. As geographer Yi-Fu Tuan observes, "Place is security, space is freedom: we are attached to the one and long for the other" (2001, 3), and notes an ambivalent human tendency to physically objectify this notion of liberty: "What does it mean to be in command of space, to feel at home in it? It means that the objective reference points in space, such as landmarks and the cardinal positions, conform with the intention and the coordinates of the human body" (2001, 36). As Bachelard describes, domestic inhabitants often look for validation of their intimate lives through external means: "In fact, they know the universe before they know the house, the far horizon before the resting-place; whereas the real beginnings of images, if we study them phenomenologically, will give concrete evidence of the values of inhabited space, of the non-I that protects the I" (1994, 4–5).

Ironically, in such cases where the "I" that lies close at hand becomes overdefined out of an abundance of caution or fear, this external "non-I" becomes like Barthes's punctum to a studium-like, internal "I"; the trickster provoking crisis to the dismay of the emergency manager; the perceived and interpreted voice of poetic truth that gives the lie to the designed self. How we navigate the difference between such alternatives affects how our imagination constructs the psycho-physiological-virtual space within which our social efficacy operates. An open perspective invites intimacy, while fearful desires may situate the self at a voyeuristic distance, fomenting a competitive, oppositional relationship to perceived others, thereby rationalizing an overprotected personal space made static.

Even this latter state, however, lying within us as we are, may resonate with intuitive tension between openness and closure in what Bachelard calls a "Motionless Childhood," full of "fixations of happiness":

> We comfort ourselves by reliving memories of protection. Something closed must retain our memories, while leaving them their original values as images. Memories of the outside world will never have the same tonality as those of home and, by recalling these memories, we add to our store of dreams; we are never real historians, but always near poets, and our emotion is perhaps nothing but an expression of a poetry that was lost. (1994, 6)

For Tuan, cultivating critical awareness of the dialectic play between these alternate tendencies toward either determinism or poetics is central to social progress: "What kinds of intimate places can be planned, and what cannot—at least, no more than we can plan for deeply human encounters? Are space and place the environmental equivalents of the human need for adventure and safety, openness and definition?" (2001, 202)

As in butoh, we see here the competitive tension between the contradictory selves of I and non-I. It is the pull between memory, charged by life's challenges with notions of safety and surety, and poetic imagery, full of potential beyond the self, one that steps inward and outward with the same motion. Is this not the innate step of butoh, resonant with ambivalent, poetic connotations sought by Hijikata and other pioneers? Tamano Hiroko, for example, speaks surreally of butoh's etymology:

> *Toh*. Sunshine. Reflection in the ricefield. So you step on it. *Bu* is spinning, so it becomes trance. In the dance, you enter a trance, so something else is going through, like when you do traditional dancing. You become somebody far away. Dancing lady is coming through your body, and you yourself are just rented out. We pray for you. You are searching for why it's so different. If you get really into it, and get into trance, you can see there's no border. (2010)

The psycho-physiological experience of butoh movement reduces boundaries while yet acknowledging their immensity and strength. The implicit *home* expressed and shared by the butoh performer is their unique commons reflexively defined by this intimate, unresolved space, the tone, texture, visuality, shape, and movement—in short, its *rhythm*—charging it as that dancer's ever-shifting *place* as well.

Imagination thus serves memory better than any reified image within a solid frame. Why else would Hosoe and Hijikata have imagined a subjective documentary of their childhood, a fictional version of their youth? Hosoe initiated *Kamaitachi* out of his desire to reimagine his memories of Tohoku as a photo-visual experiment, "not as a realistic documentary, but from my sight, from my eyes. Because it is a memory. Can photography create memories?" (2010) Hosoe and Hijkata's childhood memories were conjured from the stuff of their adult lives. The imagined sickle-weasel of childhood appearing through Hijikata's dancing body. The coldness of urban devastation and rural, destitute mystery during wartime displayed through Tokyo's oddly malevolent streets and back alleys and Tashiro's barren farmhouses and poor village children. As in the experience of the eleven-year-old city boy Hosoe lost in the countryside, or the farm boy Hijikata stomping through the Tokyo wilderness, imagination drives our reactions and responses to desire and fear. This vision guides us, as Bachelard describes, into, out of, and through our mutating vision of home, starting in youth, surrounded by a house's dynamisms of past, present, and future, and continuing later in life: "Before he is 'cast into the world,' as claimed by certain hasty metaphysics, man is laid in the cradle of the house. And always, in our daydreams, the house is a large cradle" (1994, 7).

Thus, we return home as the cast and cradle of our real and imagined being: cast and shaped from our desires, and cradle and bosom of its felt presence. At home, we cultivate what we know and want, making it the source of our greatest fulfillment and deepest disappointments. Just as in Hosoe and Hijikata's passionate anxieties and ecstasies that permeate *Kamaitachi*, perhaps nothing is more joyous than having our self-identity validated or more sorrowful than our domestic sphere poisoned by disease, failure, or death. Such feelings affirm our most private memories: "the spaces in which we have suffered from solitude, enjoyed, desired, and compromised solitude, remain indelible within us, and precisely because the human being wants them to remain so. He knows instinctively that this space identified with his solitude is creative" (Bachelard 1994, 10). If memory is to achieve generative relevance to our lives as lived, it must elide its precious cargo of remembered sensations, textures, connotations, overflows, abscesses, cadences, and intensities into the realm of imagination in order to attain a wider relevance beyond the self, achievable only through embodied perception and projection, desire broiling in the chaotic mix of contradictory recall and critical mass.

This is the solitude that produced Hosoe's hesitant dread of other farm children, undisciplined, unregulated, and feral in the eyes of his city youth. This solitude is also the base of Hijkata's Tohoku home space: something neither living nor dead on a barn shelf captured by Hosoe's camera; curled up like a pill bug all day in his farmworker mother's baby basket; the trauma of not recognizing his reflection in a water basin slashed by a sickle.[11]

We see that Hosoe and Hijikata's memory-images do not evoke safety, but rather insecurity, imbalance, decay, absurdity, and raw desire; in short, the unknown. In the precarious path between the protection and exposure that solitude evokes, the image of the unknown pushes us to recall and create a space of wonder where we can connect not only to our own memories and fantasies but also those of others. *Kamaitachi* is thus a prime example of the porous nature of a cultural and creative commons that stimulates subjective dialogue and exchange between social actors experiencing, remembering, and expressing within Deleuze and Guattari's flexible "milieu," Bachelard's punctum-like "space," Lippard and Casey's fashioned "place," or, simply, a particular community and its aspects. Hosoe and Hijikata's respective inventions of Tohoku-ness in *Kamaitachi* were mutual and dialogic affects and affectations within the aesthetic-cultural-historical space that they shared with others in the period the work was created. They concocted their *Kamaitachi* selves as much as they were such entities already by drawing upon memories, their historical moment of the 1960s, and their emotions, surrounding an imaginary that both artists would employ in the future. This gesture was their gift to the wider culture, or as Hosoe describes, "That was my personal document of my memories as well as Hijikata's, and hopefully it would let just ordinary people think that those were part of their memories. This is also a record of, not the reality, but the psychology of the photographer who did it. And your interpretation is free" (2010).

Hosoe is thus in agreement with Bachelard about the ability of memory and imagination to stimulate inclusion and a shared wellspring of imagery, knowledge, and being, i.e., a cultural commons. Or as Katsura

Kan states in comparing butoh's rhizomatic nature with Claude Levi-Strauss's idea of embodying a *topos* of thought, belief, emotion, and behavior:

> When he (Levi-Strauss) wrote down something in a book, afterward he forgot what he wrote. Because he believed, "I'm a place, I'm a topos. I'm just a place that looks like a junction." In a junction, we have a lot of things happening, but it's just a moment in time. Many ideas and many other things are going through the head. It seems I have my idea, but my idea consists of or is created by language, or culture, or ancestors, or tradition. (2009)

Through butoh's performance of mutating junctions of harmonious or disparate elements, a communal labyrinth of cultural identities and permutations comes into being. Metaphorically and metonymically, the body in crisis is always already the cultural commons. Moreover, the practitioner's journey through resolving tensions provides a template by which others may perceive or structure their own route with similar goals. As Elizabeth Carothers Herron describes the artist's ability to contribute to a sustainable civil society:

> The artist must descend into the dark, follow glimmers and intuitions, and find the way back, and, in the mysterious alchemy of creation, both discover and *make* an image as the journey's yield. We can trace the path of the artist through the work of art. Through the artist's image, we are offered a way of transcending the opposites to become more conscious and to expand the limits of our empathy. (2009, 112–13)

Given this larger calling, discussion beyond butoh and into other identities and practices is needed. A next step toward an imagined interdisciplinary practice of devising a democratic, culturally sustainable body may be an investigation of, and experiment with, an imagined intercultural way of being; a step outward across an ocean, or inward into the soil.

November 2015. Four artists spread around a dance studio in Iowa City, not knowing which way to turn.

We've been in residence for a week, funded by a National Dance Project grant to develop and tour Soil, *an intercultural dance theater trio, directed by me and featuring one dancer each from Vietnam, Cambodia, and Thailand. We've made progress, devising dance and text scenes, childhood memory dances, and intermedia choreographies, and revising group dances, solos, and dialogue scenes.*

But suddenly we're stuck. I've told the performers, not without irony, that as Asian foreigners in a Western contemporary work, they need to take back some agency from me. We try the full range of standard postmodern performance strategies: direct address, voiceover commands, sculptural objectification, overblown costume changes, understated microgestures, and everything else in the playbook. Finally, Nguyễn becomes exasperated.

"Let's just leave it alone. Leave us alone. Let us figure it out."

Nguyễn and Waewdao improvise some lines while Kethya deconstructs classical Cambodian dance vocabulary off in the corner. I just watch. For an hour.

And suddenly it clicks. "If you're not going to join us onstage, you need to stay with the audience," says Nguyễn.

"Are you like just another audience member, bong?" asks Kethya.

"You have to leave us alone," says Waewdao.

"I'm gonna tell you what to do without telling you what to do," I respond. "Keep talking. In your own languages. Just be yourselves. Be your own bodies."

They walk as if in flip-flops. They squat. They tell dirty jokes. They imitate middle-aged housewives doing calisthenics in the parks of Chiang Mai, Phnom Penh, and Saigon. They don't understand a word each other is saying.

I type everything I want to say, not to, *but* about *them. I read each line methodically, as if they are silent supertitles on a screen upstage . . .*

Taking a break now.

The director thought the performers should have a scene just for them.

Have you ever felt like this walking into a restaurant, sitting in a nail salon, or stepping off a plane?

Don't assume they're talking about you.

It's OK not to understand everything.

They're not speaking to you.

Anyway, Southeast Asians don't always mean what they say.

We couldn't translate this scene because they never say the same thing twice . . .

. . . or remember their lines the same way.

Even if they spoke the lines in English, it would still sound the same.

(That's a joke.)

And they speak faster than most people can read subtitles.

Do you want in on the conversation?

Is this going on too long?

Should we keep doing what we're doing?

Is this a good time to dance?

We enter the crossroads.

Left to right: *Waewdao Sirisook, Chey Chankethya, and Nguyễn Nguyên in opening scene in "Soil," Iowa City, Iowa, 2017.*

Premiered as an evening-length performance in 2017, *Soil* was conceived, directed, cowritten, cochoreographed, and video-designed by me, a Japanese American butoh dance theater artist, and cowritten, choreographed, and performed by classical Cambodian dancer Chey Chankethya (known as Kethya); traditional and contemporary Thai dancer Waewdao Sirisook; and Vietnamese American dancer Nguyễn Nguyên, who is trained in forms of Modern, contemporary, Korean folk, and West African dance. Work-in-progress and final versions of the performance and related scholarship were staged, presented at conferences, and published in 2012–18 throughout the U.S. and in Bangkok, Thailand.

Soil begins with the performers' identities and identifications, affected by historical influences between the United States and normative Western culture on the one hand and their home countries on the other. The performers grew up in traditionalist societies cultivated over many centuries, but now adapting to rapid change in an era of global culture. They play autobiographical characters whose lives continue to navigate transnational hybridity between Southeast Asia and the U.S. Thus, the work's central concerns are: how place and history form intercultural identities in situations of crisis; the imagination, performance, and sustainability of such identities; and how they circulate and transform in transnational settings and for what purposes.

As with all performances, *Soil* is a contact zone between the overlapping and often competing desires of artists and audience members, and our approach to embodying *Soil*'s themes is the activation of these desires. By the dancers performing their mutating and fraught identities through their desire for and against such distinctions, we invite audience members into active spectatorship, a reflective dialogue about the real-life effects and ongoing political legacy of the U.S. in three societies on the Southeast Asian mainland. For its creators, *Soil* is a dialectic engagement with our positions as transnational artists of color born into ethnic and national populations historically dominated by the U.S. through race-based legal restrictions and mass imprisonment (Asian immigrants, families, and descendants in America from the mid-1800s through the mid-1960s), undeclared, clandestine, and civil wars (Vietnam and Cambodia in the 1960s and 1970s), and geopolitics since the Cold War (Thailand from the 1930s to the present).

The work is dialectic for us in the manner of resolution/irresolution among the disparate influences driving each performer's autobiographical and historical narrative. Local, national, and transnational aspects of culture and socialization possess myriad qualities, which reify each other in opposition and reflection. As Walter Benjamin proposes, a "cultural-historical dialectic" contains the potential for positively resignifying its constituent elements "ad infinitum, until the entire past is brought into the present in a historical apocatastatis" (1999, 459). The families and professional lives of the performers in *Soil* are torn asunder by conflict, yet they strive to arise anew as authorial voices via poetic embodiment of historical trauma, reliving and remixing their pasts in the present moment on stage.

Soil is also dialectical in the sense employed by Stuart Hall, a process "which is never merely a 'desired' synthesis or reconciliation of contradictions but the recognition and embodiment of struggle at every level" (Grossberg 1996, 164), with the performance of such struggle as a liberatory gesture. Through their actions, the dancers show themselves as distinctly culturalized by familial, linguistic, and geographic factors, yet with myriad shared cultural resonances as Southeast Asians. *Soil* is thus designed to model a cultural commons, a living wellspring of identity markers that serves as its own perennially mutating source of sustenance.

As with all aspects of living culture over time, however, any cultural commons is also always changing. Lineages and legacies, whether occurring on the local, global or personal level, follow paths of desire and intuition at least as much as those of intention. Our challenge, therefore, was to perform what the dancers have been, are, and want to be. For three interculturally active persons, this means living in and through multiple places and identities.

LEAVING HOME

Soil begins with each performer standing on a straw mat of the kind typically used in daily life throughout Southeast Asia. As they stare into the distance and at the audience, an oncoming monsoon and then a clap of thunder are heard. Their bodies unsettle, and each performer begins tending to their personal belongings and the mats as awkward signifiers of home. Scenes reveal the performers' backgrounds and lives as dancers and global citizens. Dance sequences, dialogues and monologues, and video and photo imagery mix with an original cinematic-style soundscore by Japanese composer-musicians Imanishi Reiko and Isohata Shinichi, with additional hip-hop music by Raphael Xavier.

The dance forms in which each performer is trained or expert are shown not simply as their specific practices, but as character traits that influence their physical, psychological, and emotional makeup. We learn that Kethya has trained and performed as a classical Cambodian dancer since the age of five, when she began lessons with one of the country's oldest teachers. As she says onstage while twisting her body into rigorously disciplined positions, she has committed her life to creating "movement that connects with the gods and communicates their spirit. I have to make my body ready for this at all times." With a similar sense of tradition, Waewdao is tempered by the colloquial and nonchalant attitude of her regional Lanna (northern Thai) culture. Her dance poses, depicted in *Soil* as extra rigid and obvious for the foreign tourist gaze, alternate with an acute earthiness forbidden in classical Thai dance, revealing a perennial intracultural tension within her expression of an often nationalized culture. Nguyễn's sense of rhythm from West African and Korean folk dance training are revealed in his monologue about arriving in America, being physically shocked by a cold climate, and witnessing his brother adopt a "gangster" persona as protective coloring against suburban racism in Southern California.

As the performance unfolds across space and time, and the characters' narratives become more layered and complicated, metanarrative strategies are employed as necessary. Kethya and Waewdao phone home to update their mothers on daily life performing and residing in the West, while Nguyễn dances his contradictory feelings around familial obligations in a letter to his father still imprisoned in Vietnam underneath film footage of his present self recreating his childhood arrival in America at the airport. All three performers suddenly break character and the fourth wall to speak about the typical ignorance of and exotification by Western audiences around their languages and customs before just as suddenly performing a group dance of sexualized and passive Asian female tropes. The dancers later enter into a kitsch track race against each other on camera while arguing whose home nation has suffered more from war, genocide, or internal fascism.

On this broader level, the performers in *Soil* perform national legacies of trauma. In the last half century, Vietnam, Cambodia, and Thailand

Left to right: *Chey Chankethya, Nguyễn Nguyên, and Waewdao Sirisook in disco dance scene in "Soil," Iowa City, Iowa, 2017.*

have experienced humanitarian, political, and economic crises, many rooted in international causes and consequences. After centuries of colonialism and numerous recent and devastating wars, Vietnam remains plagued by environmental trauma, while a large expatriate community comes to terms with the ambivalence of globalization. In Cambodia, the civil war and genocide of the 1960s and 1970s still resonate through socioeconomic uncertainty and competing historical narratives. In Thailand, after thirteen military coups over nearly nine decades of a constitutional republic, the populace remains deeply divided within intransigent political ideologies, class warfare, endemic corruption, and regionally culturalized racism. Moreover, in the age of climate change, natural disasters exacerbated by political stalemates and systemic corruption continue to devastate Southeast Asia, with floods, typhoons, and drought as perennially increasing threats to stability. The identities of the nation-states and local populations referenced in *Soil* have consequently undergone fundamental and often severe upheavals and transformations.

Further, the performers in *Soil* have a lived connection with Western culture and the U.S. At age seven, Nguyễn settled with his mother and siblings in Westminster, California, a predominantly Vietnamese immigrant suburb within the multicultural urban sprawl of Southern California's Los Angeles and Orange Counties. Residing largely in America for eleven years, Waewdao speaks from the ambivalence of a binational life, performing and teaching in two countries and languages. Kethya maintains a career as an internationally active, working dancer and choreographer throughout Asia, the U.S., and Europe, thereby experiencing cultural heritage, diaspora, and artistic development firsthand as a singular practice.

The performers attempt to manifest a dialectical engagement with these lived realities by connecting quintessentially American stories of migration and cultural transformation with the transnational realities of the Southeast Asian archipelago, which represents much of the U.S.'s complex international presence, especially since the 1960s. From the public war in Vietnam, to the secret war in Cambodia, to the military, political, and economic domination of Thailand, the history of all three nations over the last half century is fundamentally affected by American foreign policies and realpolitik. Based on the dancers' lives and crises of recent decades in their home countries, *Soil* addresses broad issues of contested social values and bodies politic, authorial agency around cultural heritage, commodification and embodiment, and, perhaps most acutely, an ambiguous and somewhat self-fashioned "East/West" transnational identity. Additionally, the work reflects the writing, dancing, and circulation of diverse cultural identities in contemporary global society.

As director, I employed and examined our creative process of dialectic embodiment around butoh-based principles. *Soil* continued my ongoing exploration of training, artistic, and philosophical principles beyond the confines of the butoh community. The dancers and I spoke of the *chaos* of their societies' recent histories, the seeming *contradiction* of embodying both past loss and future possibility, and the goal of performing the resultant *crisis* body onstage. In effect, we worked to craft a butoh-inspired, Southeast Asian body in crisis. My butoh-based narrative preferences and directorial methods used to develop *Soil* emphasized image-based movement vocabulary and contradictory tensions within socialized personae. We also integrated body images, interpersonal situations, cultural behaviors, and the strain of overlapping multiple languages within the theatrical space of the show to create a remixed vocabulary of simultaneously distinct and shared movement, largely composed of visual-textual elements from each person's dance form, culture, and history.

Throughout the development of *Soil*, we explored how a multiplicitous identification may be generated through this interplay of body, crisis, and dance. For Kethya, the answer was clear: "I'm dancing democracy. Coming to the West, learning what's possible, bringing the knowledge back to my culture. Just to dance for us is a statement. We lost so much after the Khmer Rouge. Just to dance is to show what's possible and how you can be many things at once" (2012).

Nguyễn performs a series of dualities that he continues to live with on stage and off, including Modern/Postmodern, Vietnamese/American, and gay/male. As a young dance student, he was first drawn to West African and Korean traditional dance because of "their spiritual and rhythmic qualities," which enabled him to connect his body "to something wider and bigger" (Nguyên 2015). Nguyễn gained a connection to somatics from these forms, leading to later training in release technique, the dominant approach in Western contemporary dance. Having fled Vietnam at age five, he arrived in America at age seven not fully acculturated as Vietnamese, yet perceived as such by classmates and neighbors. He was thus forced to negotiate the immigrant pressures of a new language, social structure, and educational system as a simultaneously foreign and domestic entity. Moreover, as a gendered and culturalized Asian American citizen, his character looks to the past to recreate his future in a constant state of incomplete becoming:

> I play "Nguyễn" represented as a certain idea or nostalgia. His grappling or coming to terms with his cultural heritage, while maneuvering through the contemporary art landscape, being a modern dancer in a white form. How do you find ways to express your identity when the form is not necessarily suited for Asian-ness? I also fluctuate between feminine and masculine. Part of that subtext is the question of identity and being a gay man in Western society, but also in Vietnamese American society, which in some ways has adopted a hyper-masculinity as a way of compensating for being immigrant, never truly incorporated into American society. (2012)

For Waewdao, performing her multiple selves as a traditional dancer rooted in the history and culture of both her native region and the dominant Siamese culture in Thailand is an ambivalent act in which competing narratives are in tense, layered dialogue. As a working artist who has performed locally, nationally, and internationally, often under the auspices of government and private tourism agencies, she embodies competing cultural desires for a living:

> We always behave like this. We want to show off. We don't actually care whether people are okay or not. We just want our nation to look good. This is my character in the piece. She just ignores what matters, caring more about how she looks but not how she feels. But she also tries to tell the truth whether or not anyone is listening. It's heavy and painful to try and be who we are not. At the end of the piece, she's not resolved, but she's not trying to pretend anymore. (2012)

Politically speaking, *Soil* is an attempt to resist the force of cultural enclosure by employing the existing contradictory expressivities of all three dancers, who gradually accrete behavioral gestures and personality traits through reflection on their lives and interactions with each other. Toward the end of the piece, Waewdao performs a solo dance in which the competing narratives embodied by the choreographed and codified typologies of her local/national and traditional/global dancer personae come to confrontation and cohabitation. Performed to "Pratana" (Desire), a sentimental pop ballad from her youth, Waewdao's increasingly awkward and pained gestures reveal an identity riddled with ostensibly rivalrous values, from national cultural ambassador to folk performance inheritor to postmodern dance artist. She resists the multiple enclosures being inscribed upon her body and actively assumes this tortured body, a simultaneously made and unmade self. Like Kethya and Nguyễn, Waewdao is dancing her own idiosyncratically democratic process.

Many scholars have criticized or offered alternatives to contemporary expressive forms via changes to copyright and intellectual property regimes for the purpose of "democratization of cultural production" (Goldberg 2010, 740–41). Creative Commons and other open source, consent-based frameworks, for example, exist to increase greater circulation and everyday usage of intellectually copyrighted works. In a complementary manner, the dancers in *Soil* and other global artists and activists have reappropriated and remixed baseline elements in their historical and expressive identities for the sake of heretofore unknown and unpredictable manifestations outside the dominant influence of globalism's litigious structural forces.

Just as the dancers in *Soil* required the fashioning of their own modes of crisis resolution and expression, remixing myriad voices of social participants allows their multiplicity to support a thriving dialogic process of becoming. Hijikata's dancers pandering to Japanese salarymen and American servicemen in postwar strip clubs while appropriating characteristics of these environments for their incipient, antihegemonic, dance of darkness. American-born butoh artists problematizing their immigrant family roots while plundering the richness of such backgrounds for expressive material. And similarly, outside of the butoh realm but inspired by its strategies, Nguyễn Nguyên flowing smoothly through his Horton-based, modern dance training and postmodern quotidian gestural vocabulary in order to deconstruct his postcolonial/postwar Vietnamese, subaltern identity.

For all these artists, operating in a butoh-based modality, multiplicity and dialogue become necessary partners in the context of embodied democracy—not as a system, but rather as behavior. Often misunderstood by audiences (and even many students and practitioners), butoh's core is not some vague, idealized "nature" hidden in the dark cogito of *ankoku*, but what is socially repressed, oppressed, or marginalized. This array of states of being may be more generatively considered as the manner in which practitioners' desires operate in tension with habits and modes of socialization and marginalization in everyday life. Manifesting the democratic body here means escaping systemic order and instead being dialogic engagement itself between multiple embodiments, ideologies, spiritualities, languages, and timeframes. In this sense, the body in crisis, redolent with the rhizomatic rhythms that arise between these myriad factors, is democratic behavior that only needs itself to transcend its mix of both humane and false premises in the way that Stefano Harney and Fred Moten advocate within the realm of marginalized yet always present social actors and action that they characterize as the *undercommons*:

> We're already here, moving. We've been around. We're more than politics. More than settled, more than democratic. We surround democracy's false image in order to unsettle it. Every time it tries to enclose us in a decision, we're undecided. Every time it tries to represent our will, we're unwilling. Every time it tries to take root, we're gone (because we're already here, moving). (2013, 19)

Lewis Hyde asserts that the often contradictory internal dialogue between one's multiple selves is a kind of trickster state of "motley-in-motion" (i.e. lack of firm identity), which can be positively "refigured as the babel of tongues, and its mental reflection as the polyglot mind. Regularly we hear of tricksters being involved in the origins of linguistic multiplicity" (1998, 299). Once a trickster charges the space around them with liminality, what is initiated is not conversation, which takes place between parties speaking the same language and carrying the same values, but dialogue, an attempt at communication between systems of knowing.

Moreover, this liminal state, between crossroads and marketplace, between contemplation and action, or poetry and myth, lays a destabilizing groundwork for the democratic process by manifesting a "polyglot mind" and employing "linguistic multiplicity" in the face of dominant power. How clearly and effectively people arise from this chaos-induced hall of mirrors influences their future strength in dealing with social challenges. Or, as in the way Cornel West explains the blues, the social value of reconfiguring and reversing internalized abjection is not unique to butoh:

> The blues professes to the deep psychic and material pains inflicted on black people within the sphere of a mythological American land of opportunity. The central role of the human voice in this heritage reflects the commitment to the value of the individual and of speaking up about ugly truths; it asserts the necessity of robust dialogue—of people needing to listen up—in the face of entrenched dogma. . . . The stress the blues placed on dialogue, resistance, and hope is the very lifeblood for a vital democratic citizenry. (2004, 93)

Lila Abu-Lughod points out, however, that culture simply defined by multiplicity—while less hierarchical, more accepting of real differences, and clearly learned and mutable—is still not an answer to hegemony, in that it can also lead to or reify rigid binary thinking, as with reverse Orientalism or purist cultural feminism (1991, 144–45). "Culture is the essential tool for making other," she states, thereby giving "cultural difference . . . the air of the self-evident" (143). This makes any use of the term for defining identity, even for ostensibly just purposes, potentially divisive. Or, as Francoise Lionnet and Shu-Mei Shih describe, "authenticity" is "the 'othering machine' (Suleri) . . . that produces in the minor a reactive notion of authenticity in the form of cultural nationalism" (2005, 9).

Ultimately, these thinkers argue for a more diverse representation and embodiment of self as well as transversal communication and interplay between minor identities and groups. Abu-Lughod posits the concept of *connections* between researcher and subject on all levels, thereby increasing mutual understanding of each other as active and inquisitive "real" beings (1991, 148). Lionnet and Shih also propose, in place of yet further major-minor relations and postnational identifications across borders, the proliferation of minor-minor relations, where marginalized, subaltern, or local groups may relate directly with each other, according to their own ontological systems of knowledge and communication (2005, 8).

I would propose that these modes of connection take place already in the form of, not simply cultural typologies or narratives, but through social imaginaries that travel diasporically through immigrant populations and mass media. Many butoh artists have come to know the *Kamaitachi* images as a mythical landscape within which Hijikata already, so to speak, lives. Just as butoh is a bodily actualization of the cultural commons, so images that engage its imaginative perception and expression also manifest a democratic process.

Photojournalist Gilles Peress, in conversation with Susie Linfield, identifies exactly this phenomenon, especially in the globalized virtual realm, where, more than ever before, a multiplicitous viewing and interpretation of photo-images is taking place:

> Peress envisions the Internet as a potentially antiauthoritarian tool in what he calls our "post-postmodern" era. "We are entering into an age in which visual language is defined by a dialogue between photographers and audiences," he says. "This means not just the democratic posting of images but the democratic *interpretation* of images. . . . There is no longer a voice of authority, with univocal images created from above. . . . We need deep humility, humbleness, in relation to our formulation of reality now." (Linfield 2010, 257)

Such humility is also necessary when dealing with internal and external sources of abjection. Hijikata made visceral and common currency of his abject emotions and dealings with marginalization and culturalization. Expressing little patience for the false promise of democracy by decree, he created a modality for rhizomatically conjoining desire, expression, and perception from all sides—that of the center-subject, margin-other, and everything-everyone between. Fred Moten speaks of how the production of such moments conjoins both the residue and erasure of subject-object (2003). In discussing Sadiya Hartman's attempt to transcend the "hypervisible" abjection embedded in the collective consciousness of Frederick Douglass's recounting of his Aunt Hester's torture, he points to the inherent but necessary ambivalence of reciting and embodying oppression *and* healing:

> Douglass and Hartman confront us with the fact that the *conjunction* of reproduction and disappearance is performance's condition of possibility, its ontology and its mode of production. . . . Like Douglass, she transposes all that is unspeakable in the scene

> to later, ritualized, "soulfully" mundane and quotidian performances. . . . This is to say that there is an intense dialogue with Douglass . . . opened by a refusal of recitation that reproduces what it refuses. (2003, 5)

Hijikata's template for democratic behavior—to speak oneself by not being able to do so—accomplishes such a maneuver. The dialogic nature of oppositional desires is transposed to performative technique, revealing what was and can be, and what is made and unmade, all in the body's present space-time. By answering capitalism's false, universalizing, and homogenizing democracy with a broken body regenerative of multiplicitous subjectivity and difference, Hijikata initiated a mode for democratic behavior, rooted in life as lived, in all its oppressed, triumphant, conflicted, and mysterious glory.

BODY, SOIL, SUSTENANCE

In speaking of butoh's relevance outside Japan, Hijikata suggested that there was a Tohoku everywhere, an *ankoku* inherent in any place, and people may discover it for themselves.[12] Such a concept parallels transnational and globalization theories about the relationship between the local and global and their productive inseparability (Appadurai 1996, Arnove and Torres 2003, DeKoven et al. 2001). Likewise, much sustainability discourse is grounded in advocacy for local growth, production, and consumption as a matter of not simply reducing and refining our industrial footprint, but entering into a maximally symbiotic relationship with the environment and reducing intellectual, cultural, and legal boundaries between humans and "nature" (Asch 2007, Bratspies 2006/2007, Faber 2011, Parr 2011, Shiva 2005). Similar to the dialogic behavior that engenders the democratic body, interactive and holistic behavior may support a *sustainable body*, one that frames itself around and responds simultaneously to local and global conditions.

A butoh body attempts the same through employment of its given status, i.e., its body *as is*, the raw material for engaging crisis and resolution. In the binary terms of butoh's dialectical political process, this body is the local to late capitalist hegemony's global. In socio-environmental terms, butoh practice is an internalized embrace of the value of the local, though it is incumbent upon each practitioner to manifest according to their own "local," i.e., personal, conditions.[13] A deeper question remains, however, around the nature of the practitioner's behavior in relation to the environmental systems and social ecologies in which they operate. Butoh began as reactionary mostly in relation to Western hegemony and capitalism, but its specific form of negation also provides entry into a wider discourse as much as it has spawned compulsive behavior of lineage-obsessed acolytes and modish imitators.

Philosopher Jeffrey A. Bell demonstrates how Deleuze and Guattari's analysis of capitalism (1983 and 1987) reveals the system's tendency to foment both the "institutional violence" of quantification within hierarchical power structures as well as the "nomadic violence" of market-driven chaos inspired by capitalist aspirational behavior (2011). Bell interprets the pair's writing as identifying capitalism's propensity for oscillating between these extremes due to its paradoxically authoritarian and open-ended structure. Further, the artist—especially the martial artist—may effectively negotiate this paradox via the "warrior" method of doing and not-doing, which undoes the subject "by affirming (capitalism's) very tendency to undermine and undo codes, subjects, and axioms, but affirming it in a way that does not lead to a collapse into stratification or chaos: it allows for 'ways'" (230). Bell concludes his arguments by asserting, "Instead of an unsustainable subordination of productive processes to the demands of the extensive quantifications of the global subject of capitalism, the task is the undoing of this global subject and the creative invention of 'ways' that swing between unsustainable alternatives" (239).

Following Bell's thinking, I draw parallels between butoh philosophy and how capitalism's limits and potentialities may be elucidated by the functionally uncodified "ways" that artists negotiate their communal presence and interaction with others with whom they are in cooperation or opposition. Butoh's uncodified philosophical frameworks of resolving/not resolving crisis may allow us to inventively comprehend how intra- and interpersonal tensions in society may be addressed. The butoh artist's "way" of embodying crisis by appropriating contradictory modes of being for transformative purposes echoes Bell's call for a sustainable method of balancing—if not resolving—capitalism's violent swings between quantification and chaos identified by Deleuze and Guattari. If sustainability requires what Adrian Parr describes as "a historical frame of reference to combine care for other than human species with social justice concerns as a way of invoking the emancipatory potential of the future" (2011, 9), then butoh does likewise to fulfill its potential.

Roland Faber points to such a mode in his discussion of the potential for cultural symbolizations to aid in our imagination of sustainable futures. Faber identifies the production of a "dangerous" place where perceptions, symbols, and values between humanity and "nature" are decomposed through a process of negotiating their shared contingency—their sameness—within the vastness of Deleuze and Guattari's chaosmos (2011, 249). Faber asserts that human sustainability is dependent upon this process of engaging the dissolute "risk" of such a process:

> Sustainability may only be addressed *from* this dangerous place and, hence, is *necessarily* arbitrary because of this *decompositional connectivity*. Accordingly, the art of valuation is a negotiation of fire: in this fire, values, virtues, and virtuals are created and dismembered. The *art* is to go through the fire of decomposition such that permanence, but not intensity, might be lost. (2011, 249)

A similar assertion can be made about butoh practice, which fosters the image and expression of impermanence through visceral performative means. Hijikata sought to energize and sustain a culturalized corporeal identity in opposition to a homogenizing modernization. Ever since, myriad practitioners have struggled with their individual perceptions and interpretations of butoh's foundational principles and forms. Now, butoh-based artists globally are faced with the challenge of identifying transnational, intercultural, and interdisciplinary modes rooted in the pioneers' establishment of an artistic approach to sustainable culture via, in Faber's terms, the "decompositional connectivity" of butoh's schismogenetic engagement. Butoh's chaos, contradiction, and crisis "decomposes" arbitrary schemes embodied in socialized and domesticated corporealities, thereby allowing for intuitive "connectivities" to form from the ashes of one's artistic "fire."

Soil was my attempt to model such a process. I chose the title as the word's myriad connotations may serve metaphorically for the ubiquitous yet vulnerable potential for knowledge, identity, and action that is the cultural commons. Soil is symbolic of the earth, landscape, or environment within which life events take place. How such a realm is imagined, enlivened, and utilized determines the health and sustainability of a society.

The beneficent inter- and cross-cultural richness embodied by each performer in *Soil* charges their presence as liminal and therefore apt for their depicted life situations. Similar to the manner in which many postwar Japanese avant-gardists entered into an oppositional engagement with dominance, each dancer in *Soil* was born into a culture cultivated over centuries yet forced to adapt to rapid change in a modern era of competing transnational paradigms and politico-historical narratives. In negotiating the interplay of inherited and invented selves, the dancers and I sought an alternative approach beyond mere reaction that speaks to the effects of cultural dominance, even when such qualities are already internalized into the "selves" of their respectively marginalized "others."

The inherent tension, moreover, between embodiment and expression of such dualism begs the question of under what assumptions an artist is operating. In other words, when the dominant discourse encloses one within a definition of the less valuable other, the historical and cultural paradigms from which such categories are derived come into question. On Broadway and in Hollywood, for example, from classic, blockbuster musicals like *The King and I* (1951) and *Miss Saigon* (1989) to films like *Apocalypse Now* (1979), *The Year of Living Dangerously* (1982), *Da 5 Bloods* (2020), or almost any Vietnam War movie, the experiences of Western characters and performers are given narrative primacy, intellectual superiority, and emotional sympathy over those of their Southeast Asian counterparts, despite the fact that the stories take place in Southeast Asian societies and wholly involve and affect the latter in body, mind, and spirit. The legacy of exotified and culturalized tropes about Southeast Asia still runs deep and weighs heavy in the lexicon of American popular culture. Indeed, when Waewdao was offered a guest teaching position in a college dance program in a major American city, the program director mentioned, without irony, that while their department had not previously offered Thai dance to the students, they had exposed them to Thai culture by presenting a production of *The King and I.*

Performance studies scholar Royona Mitra states that what is typically referred to as "intercultural theatre has focused on creating a very particular kind of mise-en-scène where diverse cultural traditions, texts, artefacts and people coexist within a predominantly Western dramaturgical framework," and where elements rarely interact with each other or become extremely diluted (2015, 14). When beginning the *Soil* project, we were wary of wading into an indigenized Asian localization or the dangers of inadvertently developing a vague, simplistic, non-Western identity. Neither did we want to accept yet another standard Western contemporary lens on the characters we were positing. We also knew we had to avoid not only a classically authoritarian subtext typified by a traditional ethnographic approach (e.g., Margaret Mead on Bali) or a Western-style, presumptuously "color-blind" staging, such as Peter Brook's *Mahabharata* (1989), a major stage and film production famous in the West, but rather more infamous among performing artists of color for its reductively multicultural aesthetic (Mitra 2015, Bharucha 1990). We also hoped to avoid an evocative, literary approximation from afar, such as with Indochine/Vietnam in many of Marguerite Duras's novels. We also refused a stance of moral ambivalence, such as in *The Act of Killing* (2012), Joshua Oppenheimer's haunting film about Indonesian mass murderers called to account for their deeds, as revealing and ultimately engaged as that course of action may be.

Our method was based rather in an incongruous mixed bag of influences that each performer-character, rather than being born within, gradually grew into and chose. In the act of coming together as an expressive trio, the dancers embody the dialectical elements already imbricated within their everyday lives, displaying and wielding these traits to perform tense variations of themselves traversing transnational lines, across a simultaneously lived and imagined continuum of Southeast Asian and American influences. Nguyễn, for example, portrays a prototypical Vietnamese child émigré to the U.S. in the post-Vietnam War era. He is filled with cloudy yet intense memories of infant years in the home country, a tortuous and life-threatening refugee period, and ambiguous teenage years and young adulthood in the U.S.A. He eventually self-fashions not so much a purposely syncretic identity, but one accreted by time itself from disparate cultural, linguistic, familial, and nationalistic strands.

Based in her birthplace of Phnom Penh, Cambodia's political and cultural center, and self-identified as wholly Cambodian, Kethya yet remains fascinated by and creatively focused on Western contemporary performance concepts and practices. She is primarily supported by Western arts funding and a dance and theatrical touring circuit dominated by Western contemporary aesthetics and discourse. In *Soil*, her character stretches, moves, and presents herself within the strictly delineated, almost two-dimensional lines of her classical dance form and speaks of being complicit in perpetuating traditional gender roles in Cambodian society. Her repeated efforts to expand the scope of her life, however, through leaving home, being educated abroad, or performing nontraditional theatrical roles, are driven dramatically by the Western trope of the quest for individualized self-realization through heroic journey.

The performers are not so much in a lineage of activist postcolonial creatives that seek to undermine a "corporeal colonization" (Burns 2008) delineated by a Western imperial framework, but rather act to acknowledge the lifelong intercultural hybridity that each has embodied in their own way. Neither is *Soil* simply a depiction of subalterns resisting hegemony, though that subtext is at play. More significant for the actors was inquiring reflexively into their identities and fashioning a performative mode of being by which they might sustain benevolent aspects of their traditionalist yet always mutating cultures. They navigate through aesthetic, cultural, and political conventions on both sides of the Pacific, through multiple environments largely defined by binary categories that reify hierarchical distinctions. The dancers do not represent simply commodities that speak for themselves nor simply *other*-ed selves gazing back at a masculine or heteronormative center. Our desire was to move beyond the schizophrenia of "double consciousness," which is never exactly integrated and always put upon by mainstream American culture as either/or (Du Bois 1903). These bodies speak paradoxically but also consciously and explicitly *as* subjectively identified *and* externally inscribed entities. They purposely cohabit, sample, and remix all aspects of their contradictory selves.

Just as butoh artists employ memory and imagination to reorient themselves, the dancers in *Soil* submit themselves to their respective crises rooted in personal and collective trauma. The soil under their feet is not just physical, but temporal as well. Creating their future is rooted in their experience of the past. Nguyễn was born in Saigon in 1975, the year "The American War" ended and just as his father was sent to reeducation camp by the Communist authorities. He escaped in 1980 by boat with his mother and two siblings, and spent his sixth and seventh birthdays in refugee camps in Malaysia and the Philippines before arriving in America, where, as he says onstage, "I stepped off the plane and saw my breath in the cold air for the very first time."

Trained as a classical dancer from the age of five, Kethya was born to an upper-middle-class family involved in the reform government in 1987, eight years after the end of the Khmer Rouge genocide, in which over ninety percent of artists and cultural workers in Cambodia perished. When Kethya dances, she invokes not only the gods and spirits but also the lost, found, preserved, and reconstructed traditions of her forebears, which are again in danger of being lost in the midst of globalized culture:

> This is a question I ask myself and that other people in Cambodia ask themselves. Should we forget about the past and just move forward, or should we respect the past and tradition only? So it's a big question for my generation in Cambodia right now because we are about to lose the tradition, what we've been handed so far, and we want to catch up with the world and everything. So how can we balance all that? It's my crisis. (Chey 2012)

Waewdao was born in 1977 in northern Thailand, the so-called Lanna region, where a contested historical narrative has brewed for almost a century and a half since the unification of Thai-associated kingdoms and lands and the suppression of Lanna culture. Northern Thai schoolchildren, for example, are often not allowed to speak *gam mueang*, their regional dialect, but video games, mobile devices, and social media are a given. Lanna dance is taught in school but not included by name in discourses of national cultural identity. Lanna dancers, especially pale-skinned females arrayed in languidly choreographed spectacles, are regularly employed as exotic visual elements marketed for the international tourist gaze, an enclosed, static space devoid of imagination. In the case of Thailand—marketed internationally as "The Land of Smiles"—commodities don't so much speak as constantly beam a vitiated, depersonalized welcome. Or, as Waewdao states in *Soil*, implicitly commenting on Northern Thai–style cultural negotiation, "We love to be peaceful, but when the time comes to fight, we smile and spread our legs."

For each dancer, embodied crisis instigated by chaos and contradiction is not merely a performance, but a way of life. But what to do about this? Leave the status quo unchallenged in a downward spiral of

Left to right: *Chey Chankethya, Nguyễn Nguyên, and Waewdao Sirisook in multiple languages scene in "Soil," Iowa City, Iowa, 2017.*

increasingly disenfranchised solipsism, or resolve crisis by any means necessary, even if it means codifying that which is spontaneously generated (Deleuze and Guattari's "overcoding"), thus reifying a new hierarchy? Or is there a middle way that not only embraces the dancers' paradox, but allows them to navigate the disorderly liminal terrain of nationalized and globalized marginalization?

Each scene of crisis in *Soil* leads to a transition where the performers are forced to move from one straw mat—from one way of knowing, being, and expressing—to another. Kethya sings the Buddhist chant she has recited since childhood, her core of stability in a sea of chaos. Nguyễn employs every movement discipline trained into his body, swimming from one place to another, just as he did at five years old with dozens of other Vietnamese refugees when their boat capsized as they approached the Malaysian coast after drifting at sea for three weeks. Waewdao holds her traditional dancer body erect and proud, her actions framing a mythologized national image of strength and grace in the face of a desensitized, exotifying tourist industry. Each character enters into a dialectical mode, reimagining personal narrative as a circuitous route through cultural, linguistic, physical, emotional, and identity crises: tempted by globalized self-commodification of Cambodian classical performing arts, adrift on a Vietnamese refugee boat, or code-switching between sanctioned and marginalized Thai languages.

Movements that cross borders and trouble dominant orders navigate liminal states, marking out nonhierarchical frames of reference. In *Soil*, rigid, binary frames of gender are gradually reoriented. In an early scene, Nguyễn's character adopts the feral machismo of an archetypal Vietnamese American, immigrant male, but then reveals his underlying desire to fully realize his equally imagined queer and Vietnamese femininity. Emerging from a precise choreography of gendered gestural codes, Nguyễn's semi-improvised cabaret dance, performed to the sound of air raid sirens and actual gunfire from Southeast Asian conflicts intruding on the disco tune, "Don't Leave Me This Way," leaves him traversing uncharted emotional and transnational territory that he must newly map in front of the audience during each performance.

Likewise, we witness Kethya reasoning her way through to the logical result of always being a "good Asian girl" when she is also a powerful dancer capable of classical roles that she is forbidden by heteronormative rules in her classical discipline from performing. In Cambodia, as in many cultures in South and Southeast Asia, the Monkey King, Hanuman, is considered a strictly male role. By asserting her right to perform this dance in public, but in a foreign country, in informal costuming, and for only ninety seconds, Kethya also places herself into a liminal state, suspended tenuously between firm cultural traditions and her desire to manifest a diverse, dialogic self. For her, *Soil* represents who she is, has been, can be, and yet may never be.

In another scene, Waewdao performs a similar balancing act of critical reflection. Since the 1970s, the "Neo-Lanna" movement of artists and cultural workers in the north, and especially in Chiang Mai, has explicitly embraced the tension between tradition and desire. Working over two decades as a dancer performing both living and newly reconstructed traditions of Lanna culture, Waewdao emerged as one of the leading artists of the so-called "Lanna Rennaissance" (Cummings 2006, Farrell 2011). In her solo dance in *Soil*, she positions herself squarely at the crossroads, between the weight and expectation of the dominant national Siamese culture, the liberatory empowerment of contemporary Lanna arts, and her character's fundamental desire to express her own humanity beneath the surface images of history, privilege, and marginalization.

By adopting butoh's body in crisis to perform seemingly irreconcilable conflicts between competing identities, each performer attempts to generate an explicitly and idiosyncratically self-problematized, Southeast Asian body in crisis. The dancers embody competing desires—aesthetic, cultural, political, economic, personal, or otherwise—holding them together in the same bodily time-space, producing individual manifestations of a cultural commons. Throughout *Soil*, the characters gradually mobilize behavioral gestures and personality traits through reflection on their lives and interaction with each other. Nguyễn and Kethya claim more multiplicitous body images, Kethya and Waewdao gain both increased distance and intimacy with their gendered selves, and Waewdao and Nguyễn care less how others perceive them. By the last scene, in which the actors perform a dance of communal identity, they have realized a methodology of activating and employing the cultural commons via their own idiosyncratic bodies in crisis. Nguyễn's multicultural rhythms, Kethya's subtle visuality, and Waewdao's visceral aesthetics blend into a hybridized dance built from the witnessed moments, accumulated behaviors, and consequent personae

Left to right: *Nguyễn Nguyên, Chey Chankethya, and Waewdao Sirisook in final trio dance in "Soil," Iowa City, Iowa, 2017.*

of their life stories. Choreographed from the gestural vocabulary of the performers' combined paradoxical, self-contradictory movements, the final trio becomes a manifestation of a cultural commons—personal and collective—that they always already share throughout the performance.

We owe each other the indeterminate. We owe each other everything.
— Stefano Harney and Fred Moten (2013, 20)

Seminal events create legacies that are developed and carried on through communal accretion of individually acute resonances. While historical narratives are contested between variably interested parties, subjective truths are manifested and sustained through real lives. The performers in *Soil* depict this process and speak their truth by offering themselves to the audience through multiple bodies, languages, and emotions. They root their unfixed, ever-mutating presence in historical and social crises to which they are directly connected, speaking to notions of sustaining civil society. Along with butoh practitioners, they ultimately seek to help and nurture the field of socially conscious performance, a continuum of dialogic sustainability from the microcosm of the individual to the macrorealm of the collective. My hope is that an artistic consciousness may arise from such endeavors that is akin to what Charles Price, Donald Nonini, and Erich Price Tree have termed "grounded utopian movements":

> By grounded we mean that the identities, values, and imaginative dimensions of utopia are culturally focused on real places, embodied by living people, informed by past lifeways, and constructed and maintained through quotidian interactions and valued practices that connect the members of a community, even if it is a diasporic one. (2008, 128–29)

These movements' groundedness—their lived, practical relevance—infuses their utopian ideals. As with Hijikata's implosion from capitalism, Tanaka's moved conversation with the elements, or the *Soil* dancers' transcendent potential embedded within their cultural limitations, manifesting subjective utopian desire may not always be pragmatic, but its personal and collective truth is its social function and reward.

My repeated reference in this book to "become the thing itself" is a plea for what Zen Buddhists describe as *no separation*, which underlies the concept of *anatta* (no-self), or no individual existentially separate from all else. As environmental philosopher Val Plumwood asserts:

> As the discipline of ecology . . . has shown us, humans are indeed in the ecological drama, not as an audience looking on but as actors on the stage, and the great task of sustainability is desegregation, to accept our ecological identity and situate human life and settlement in ways that maintain the long-term functioning of the ecosystems we participate in. (2006, 142)

As practitioners of the contemporary body in crisis, butoh-based performers must become more conscious of this project of desegregation within their developing modes of sustainability, making it a requisite corollary, as Adrian Parr characterizes, of the larger project of cultivating the cultural commons: "The proposition is that activating the global commons will not just happen once we become more open to sharing a variety of different viewpoints, approaches, and experiences; it also involves being able to play with various combinations of these differences with a view to carving out innovative directions that will constructively move us forward" (Parr 2011, 11).

Diversity may be a necessary starting point for a society built on mutuality, but difference is the space where the hardest realities are learned. Butoh practice charges this dark, irresolute region, this *ankoku*, with both concrete and ineffable possibilities rooted in the interiority of personal narrative, yet with the potential for shared multiplicities throughout countless permutations of space and time manifested as myriad places and historical moments.

It was in this spirit that my director's statement for *Soil* emerged. These are words on which I reflect daily, and with which I hope to warn, provoke, and inspire:

> We can only live within the means of our nature, but this holds endless potential. The body fearless in crisis must learn to sustain itself. This is the world's lesson to itself in this historical moment.

Thank you for reading.

Ohno Yoshito, Yokohama, Japan, 2016

NOTES

INTRODUCTION: (MY) BUTOH

1. For an examination of butoh's diasporas, see Rosemary Candelario, "'Now we have a passport': global and local butoh" (2019).

2. Darkness as a metaphorical space of ineffable knowledge is a recurring metaphor in numerous philosophical and spiritual lineages. William C. Chittick, for example, identifies a similar concept in Sufi cosmology:

> A single dreaming subject experiences a multiplicity of forms and things that in fact are nothing but his own single self. Their manyness is but the mode that the one consciousness assumes in displaying various facets of itself. . . . Existence as a whole . . . is a *barzakh*, an intermediary realm between Being and nothingness. Hence existence as a whole can be called "imagination." (Chittick 1989, 15)

3. Speaking in 1985 at the Butoh Festival in Tokyo, just months before his death, Hijikata stated: "I would like to make the dead gestures inside my body die one more time and make the dead themselves dead again. I would like to have a person who has already died die over and over inside my body. I may not know death, but it knows me" (2000, 77).

4. As Rosemary Candelario states in speaking of the conventional framing and perception of Eiko & Koma's work in the United States, "'Asian' too often slips into an Orientalism that says far more about Asian American racialization and the legal and discursive regulation of Asian bodies in the United States than it does about the dance at hand. Moreover, these perspectives that would have the dancers be either generically American or Asian foreclose consideration of the complex personal, political, and dance historical webs that form the foundation of the work" (2016, 9).

5. A famous butoh-associated dancer, for example, told me that Hijikata himself challenged the notion that Ohno Kazuo was butoh. More explicitly, Mikami Kayo cites dance critic Goda Nario as claiming that Ohno was not a butoh dancer, but rather simply a modern dancer (2016, 144). Such controversies are seemingly endless to me.

6. In August 2009, for example, in my conversation with a butoh dancer who made a living as a rice farmer in Japan, he initially viewed one of my dance solos, which blends street dance movement with more recognizable butoh

style imagery and live electro-acoustic new music, as "entertainment" and not butoh. He then agreed with me, however, that my devising of movement vocabulary from the sundry influences of my urban roots was operating by the same principle as Hijikata did when he developed his Tohoku-styled *butoh-fu* based on his personal narrative.

7. Across Hijikata's oeuvre, I read abjection not simply of performers, but of females and femininity. I think of Ohno Yoshito in both versions of *Kinjiki* (1959), Ohno Kazuo in the second version of *Kinjiki* (1959), and many other works through the 1990s, and Ashikawa Yoko, who bared her gapped teeth to audiences (Stein 1986; Loke 1987). Hijikata's legacy of sexualization and commodification of women's bodies, and butoh's continued masculinization, beg deeper examination. For an introduction to gender performance and apprenticeship in butoh, see Mezur (2018) and Coker (2018).

1. DEVELOPING A PRACTICE

1. Mishima Yukio was one of postwar Japan's most acclaimed novelists and playwrights and an increasingly staunch nationalist during his career. He also wrote short stories, poetry, and librettos and directed a short film in 1966, *Patriotism*, in which he plays a soldier forced by circumstance to commit suicide by *seppuku* (ritual disembowelment). Four years later, Mishima committed *seppuku* in real life after leading a failed coup attempt to exhort the military into returning to an emperor-centered martial government.

2. Much later, after I've spent six years as a young performer in Rachel's theatre company, she has commented to me many times that this whole "butoh thing," which I keep chasing after outside of my work with her, is just a phase I'm going through and that I shouldn't get too carried away with it. "It's not for everyone, and you have more potential as an artist than just being a dancer," she states, matter-of-factly. "Yes," I reply, "but this was all your fault in the first place."

3. This description is based on both my experience as a viewer at the Japan America Theater in Los Angeles as well as descriptive passages from Kazuo Ohno and Yoshito Ohno's book, *Kazuo Ohno's World: From without & within* (2004).

4. Spelling in general usage in academic and professional fields is "theatre" as a discipline and art form, "dance theater" and "physical theater" for those specific genres, and "theater" for venues and physical sites.

5. These appliances came to be known popularly as *sanshu no jingi* (three imperial regalia) and "equated with the symbols of imperial legitimacy in the popular media" of 1950s Japan (Igarashi 2012, 78–79).

6. See, for example, Oe Kenzaburo, *A Personal Matter* (1969), or Abe Kobo, *The Woman in the Dunes* (1991) and *The Face of Another* (2003).

7. In addition to the Hosoe references in this book, see Tomatsu Shomei, *Shomei Tomatsu: Skin of the Nation* (2004); Moriyama Daido, *Nippon Gekijo Shashincho* (Japanese Theatre) (1968) and *1965–1970: Magazine Work* (2009); and Fukase Masahisa, *Masahisa Fukase* (2018).

8. See Imamura Shohei, *Buta to Gunkan* (Pigs and Battleships) (1961); Susumu Hani, *Hatsukoi: Jigoku-hen* (Nanami: The Inferno of First Love) (1968); Teshigahara Hiroshi, *Tanin no Kao* (The Face of Another) (1966); and Oshima Nagisa, *Seshun Zankoku Monogatari* (Cruel Story of Youth) (1960) and *Shinjuku Dorobo Nikki* (Diary of a Shinjuku Thief) (1969).

9. Speaking to Donald Richie, Hani Susumu stated: "I do not admire people, though I admire many persons. But I don't like what society does to persons. It perverts them. Yet, I don't want to attack society. . . . What I would like to do is ignore it" (Richie 2005, 412–13).

10. While my project largely focuses on certain key aspects of Hijikata's early to mid-career ideas and achievements, he was by no means the only dance artist at the time who was pushing the edge of expressive form and social commentary. For a more nuanced and expansive discussion of Hijikata's artistic and intellectual relationship to both dancers and other avant-garde artists and thinkers in Japan, see Bruce Baird's comprehensive monograph on Hijikata's career, *Hijikata Tatsumi and Butoh: Dancing in a Pool of Gray Grits* (2012), especially chapter 2, "Forbidden Eros and Evading Force: Hijikata's Early Years," 15–57.

11. As dance critic Inata Naomi describes, "The main discourse of butoh in Japan is a kind of myth of Hijikata. That discourse doesn't say anything about Hijikata's connection to ballet. Just rejecting or just destroying. But I think to destroy or break ballet technique, before breaking ballet, he must learn ballet. Ballet uses the body very symmetrically with the limbs. Because he can use his body that way, then he could change, or he could destroy that method and the body's image" (2019).

12. While much Western postmodern dance since the early 1960s has also challenged this upward and, especially, authoritarian aesthetic in Western classical dance, Hosoe is implicitly referring to mainstream dance styles in postwar Japan that adopted such forms, which constituted the primary aesthetic and value structure against which Hijikata was working.

13. Inata Naomi points out that, in Hijikata's early days, he eschewed modern dance's primacy on emotion in favor of ballet training's corporeal rigor, which allowed him to experiment clearly and precisely with expressive forms for breaking down the body's formalism onstage (Inata 2019).

14. Conversely, in the West, I am often faced with the inverse mindset, one impressed by a seemingly "exotic" and "mystical" practice. Many Western viewers even assume that butoh is a "traditional" Japanese art form, possibly

centuries old. Audience members have also asked me numerous times after a performance if I had intended to frighten them.

15. For multiple explanations of both *kensho* and koans, see *On Zen Practice: Body, Breath, and Mind*, by Taizan Maezumi and Bernie Glassman (2002).

16. For more detailed analysis of how Hijikata developed his aesthetic, cultural, and choreographic concept around *nikutai*, see Centonze 2017.

2. IMAGINING INNOCENCE LOST

1. I refer to *immanence* as inherence, innateness, or a state of remaining or dwelling within. Other religious definitions notwithstanding, the term also connotes a secular mode of sacredness in imagery that circulates within any number of cultural contexts, including that of photos in the butoh community.

2. In 2009, Aperture Foundation produced a new trade book edition with eight additional photos never before published (Hosoe 2009).

3. See also Hosoe's *Otoko to Onna* (Man and Woman, 1961), *Barakei* (Ordeal by Roses, 1963), and *Kimono* (1964).

4. For Hosoe, the apotheosis of this work was the photo series, *Embrace*, which was completed in 1970, published in 1971, and featured many of Hijikata's dancers.

5. Butoh dancer and scholar Megan Nicely comments that many of the photos look very posed, "as if they are meant to draw the attentions of the watchers in the photo. The element of being watched is very strong, they are about spectatorship. These are not private moments" (2010).

6. Here I refer to indigeneity, not in the more common politico-historical sense of long-standing ethnic populations that steward a specific geographical environment or region through intricate cultural customs and vernaculars developed over centuries, but rather in the social sense of an impression of a cultural or subcultural group that is colloquially identified with such a location.

7. For example, Nakajima Natsu, one of Hijikata's first students, stated, "Hijikata would tell us: 'Make the face of an old devil woman, with the right hand in the shape of a horn, and the left hand holding her long hair.'. . . then comes the light of the sun, and the eyes become smaller; then comes the wind, and the eyelids quiver; then you must feel like a stone." (Viala and Masson-Sekine 1988, 135.)

8. As butoh artist Mizu Desierto comments, "I think the biggest danger is a need that so many people feel that has put butoh in so many boxes already. It's fundoshi. It's white body paint. It's grotesque. It's a man. You know, whatever these things are culturally, and those shows are the most boring fucking repetitive pieces of shit out there as far as I'm concerned" (Desierto 2011).

9. While *Otoko to Onna* (Man and Woman) in 1961 was Hosoe and Hijikata's first major collaboration and did take place after Hijikata began staging his early

butoh performances, the project represents a more basic and experimental stage in both artists' developments, as opposed to the mature opus of *Kamaitachi,* which was developed over years and expressed a larger cultural mythos.

10. "Let two mirrors reflect each other; then Satan plays his favorite trick and opens here in his way (as his partner does in lovers' gazes) the perspective on infinity. Be it now divine, now Satanic; Paris has a passion for mirror-like infinities." (Benjamin 1999, 538)

11. Hosoe has stated about his participation in Ohno's choreographic process, "My photographing is part of his dance" (Naggar 2001, 64).

12. Or as a Puerto Rican musician colleague once told me when I asked him why he pronounced his Spanish name with an American English accent, "What's the difference? They're both slave languages."

13. I often speak to audiences and students of my genetic abnormality of having an extra joint connecting my bottom lumbar vertebra to my sacrum as a "seed," or primary motivational force of the asymmetrical, arrhythmic movement that characterizes my dance style.

3. AN EMPTY ROOM

1. Dogme 95: The Vow of Chastity (abridged):

> *I swear to the following set of rules drawn up and confirmed by Dogme 95:*
>
> *1. Shooting must be done on location. Props and sets must not be brought in.*
>
> *2. The sound must never be produced apart from the image or vice-versa.*
>
> *3. The camera must be handheld. Any movement or mobility attainable in the hand is permitted.*
>
> *4. The film must be in colour. Special lighting is not acceptable.*
>
> *5. Optical work and filters are forbidden.*
>
> *6. The film must not contain superficial action.*
>
> *7. Temporal and geographical alienation are forbidden.*
>
> *8. Genre movies are not acceptable.*
>
> *9. The film format must be Academy 35mm.*
>
> *10. The director must not be credited.*
>
> *Furthermore I swear as a director to refrain from personal taste. I am no longer an artist. I swear to refrain from creating a 'work,' as I regard the instant as more important than the whole. My supreme goal is to force the truth out of my characters and settings. I swear to do so by all the means available and at the cost of any good taste and any aesthetic considerations.* (Trischak 1999)

2. For basic analysis of a more recent example, see Belen Fernandez, "Notre Dame and the Case of Misplaced Empathy" in Aljazeera.com, http://www.aljazeera.com. Accessed 1/15/2021.

3. For detailed description, see Kazuo Ohno and Yoshito Ohno, "Workshop Words," in *Kazuo Ohno's World: from without & within* (2004), 189–302.

4. Madonna, "Nothing Really Matters," 1998. Music video. Butoh artist SU-EN coached the dancers. http://www.suenbutohcompany.net. Accessed 1/15/2021.

5. In his book, *Simulacra and Simulation* (1994), Jean Baudrillard conflates the "real" and its projection into the "hyperreal" of the *simulacrum*, which he contends then becomes the only reality, but he also admits between the lines that this is an intentional process. The evisceration of the landscape that the map replaces is, so to speak, a controlled burn.

6. From the "Between Heaven and Earth" section of *Admiring La Argentina*, 160; *Kazuo Ohno's World: from without & within*; and recollection by author from performance viewing in Los Angeles, October 1993.

7. From the "Procession of Foolish King," "Bride," and "Penis" sections of *Hijikata Tatsumi to Nihonjin: Nikutai no Hanran*, description in *Hijikata Tatsumi's* Rebellion of the Body*: Imagery and Documents of Butoh 1968* (2009), by Research Center for the Arts and Arts Administration, Keio University.

8. From video excerpt of *Kinkan Shonen* (1982), by Sankai Juku, choreography by Amagatsu Ushio, https://www.youtube.com/watch?v=uguhzP2BHl4.

9. From the premiere performance of *Empty Boat*, an ensemble work by Kasai Akira at the Aka-Renga Theatre, Yokohama, Japan, October 15, 2011, attended by the author and translated in part by Ishimoto Kae.

10. "What I like to see in the future is to be anonymous. Instead of saying 'my dance,' I am dreaming of becoming Mr. Nobody. I am trying to change the style of my activities so that it will be unnecessary to declare I am Min Tanaka, a dancer. If your point is about how original I am as a dancer, compared to such predecessors as Nijinsky, Martha Graham, Merce Cunningham, I don't care. As long as I can dance, even if what I do is not genuinely true dance, I am satisfied." (Tanaka 2006)

4. DESIRE

1. When Susan Sontag stated, "Photographing is essentially an act of non-intervention" (1978, 11), she was speaking of photography as a solipsistic and socially passive act—the *acquisition* of images—as opposed to the *production* of knowledge and awareness.

2. This is different than the early American postmodern dance artists of the Judson Church era, who resisted any mode of coding and commodification that might lead to easy emotion or pure pleasure.

3. Lawrence Douglas argues that video, such as the secret footage of the "spectacle of vengeance" of the chaotic execution of Saddam Hussein, retains a visceral immediacy capable of even eliciting sympathy for patently immoral individuals:

It achieved the unimaginable: it made a mass murderer appear more dignified than his executioners. . . . Whatever fairness, good faith, and judicial sobriety were evinced . . . has been entirely eclipsed by the execution itself. In our global culture, the battle between word and image is no battle at all. Three hundred pages of legal argument cannot answer two minutes of grainy cell-phone video. (2007)

4. Li was a young photojournalist when the Cultural Revolution began and was granted access to document many of the most visceral and oftentimes violent events of the first few months. He later lost his position and was sent to a labor re-education camp. Many of Li's photos from the period are collected in the book, *Red-Color News Soldier* (2003).

5. For a detailed analysis of the maturing of Hijikata's butoh-fu developments in the 1970s, see chapter 5, "My Mother Tied Me on Her Back: *Story of Smallpox*," 137-58, and chapter 6, "The Possibility Body: Embodying the Other, Negotiating the World," 159-84, in Bruce Baird's *Hijikata Tatsumi and Butoh: Dancing in a Pool of Gray Grits* (2012).

6. Despite Hijikata and Amagatsu's differences in form and concept, they may lie along the same continuum of, after Edward Said, a "reverse Orientalism" that started with Hijikata's essentialized, anti-Western, "Japanese" body and manifested transnationally with Sankai Juku's essentialized, Europeanized, "Asian" body. Ueno Chizuko speaks of such maneuvers as having followed in the footsteps of "European Orientalists who imposed particularity and uniqueness on the Orient in the first place" (2005, 235). She asserts that "reverse Orientalists accepted Europeans' ethnocentric logic, reversed their discourse, and created a counter-discourse following the same logic" in which "nationalist discourses lie within the Orientalist perspective and are no more than by-products of Orientalism, despite their self-conscious particularism" (235).

5. TRICKSTER

1. Trickster figures are often characterized as thieves, so differentiating among them may seem arbitrary. In separating trickster and thief, however, I distinguish between the former, whose stealing expressly instigates new possibilities, and the latter, whose actions divide and destroy. Hermes's pilfering remakes the pantheon and the interaction of Heaven and Earth, whereas a biotech corporation patenting non-genetically modified seed forms steals and encloses natural resources and the productive fruits of other people's labor as

its own "private" property. I mean to emphasize trickster's effects within a set of values that frames as a benevolent act any transformation acknowledging reality.

2. Fans don't necessarily appreciate or desire such messages from beyond. Bob Dylan may have had "Judas!" shouted at him only in Manchester, England, but he and the Hawks (later The Band) endured plenty of jeering onstage from Los Angeles to London over months of touring his new electrified sound in 1966. In the same year, Brian Wilson experienced a near-revolt from the other Beach Boys when he introduced his wildly versatile and dynamic arrangements for *Pet Sounds* (1966). Even a polyglot master musician like Prince, less than three years after becoming a worldwide superstar with the film and album *Purple Rain* (1984), declined to bring his *Sign o' the Times* tour to the United States, perhaps knowing that its massive success in Europe might not be repeated in a Reagan-era United States where interracial eroticism, urban social commentary, evangelical Christianity, and androgynous corporeality weren't generally welcome into the same pop culture brainwave.

3. Trickster as an academic concept may also be considered as a form of *prosopoeia*, a rhetorical device in which a writer or speaker communicates from the position or perspective of another person or entity in order to convey the essence of a more abstract theme or issue or to further clarify an action.

4. James Clifford credits Stephen Greenblatt with making this fundamental point about the nature of ethnography: "The fashioned, fictional self is always located with reference to its *culture* and coded modes of expression, its *language*" (Clifford 1988, 94). At every given moment, expression is always bounded by the socio-cultural conditions in an author's life, which then change, making ethnography almost necessarily a fictional amalgam constructed from the accumulated and disparate temporal-spatial elements of one's research: a construct which may or may not have anything to do with one's actual lived "field" experience, making it inherently subjective. Clifford and Greenblatt share Rimbaud's observation that one "thinks" one's self into existence through the act of self-reflection (see chapter 3).

5. Even toward the end of his life, Douglass agreed to serve in the inherently subordinate role as Haiti's representative to the 1893 Columbian Exposition and World's Fair, where the rebellious Afro-American nation was relegated to third-class status as a "living culture" exhibitor. For more historical details and the controversy of Douglass's role, see Reed (1999).

6. In D. A. Pennebaker's seminal documentary *Don't Look Back* (1967), Dylan famously evades a *Time* magazine reporter's attempt to bait him into acceding to his heroic counterculture image: "Are you gonna see the concert tonight? Are you gonna hear it? It's gonna happen fast. Okay, you'll hear it and see it. It's gonna happen fast, and you're not gonna get it all. And you might

even hear the wrong words, y'know. And afterwards, you see, I won't be able to talk to you afterwards. I got nothing to say 'bout these things I write. I mean I just write 'em. I got nothing to say about 'em. I don't write 'em for any reason. There's no great message. I mean if you wanna tell these people that, go ahead and tell 'em. But I'm not gonna have to answer to it."

7. Little Richard himself "took" from countless and perhaps untraceable sources in rhythm and blues via a reflexive and fairly expected intracultural practice that musicians and audiences to this day communally understand as the primary mode in which many African American vernacular expressive forms circulate and sustain.

8. When Harris's dancers incessantly collapsed to the floor at every mention of the N word in The Last Poets' "Die Nigga," then "rows of people would pile out. And I would be like, yeah, now you missing the glory, because at the end, we're gonna take you to that space. At the end, boom, we go. People just want pleasure without pain, and it can't be. There has to be pain, and then pleasure comes. That's the only way to progress, physically and spiritually" (Harris 2008).

9. Dylan had shocked the Newport crowd without even playing a note, appearing onstage toting a leather jacket and four-piece, electric blues rock band, including blazing guitarist Mike Bloomfield, whose virtuosic, screaming chord-play often set even rock fans at the time scrambling for barely coherent descriptions. Folk music festivals were "an invitation, a gathering, a celebration of values. . . . No one in front, no one in back, no privilege, no shame" (Marcus 2005, 17–18). What they were not were rock concerts, or rather the audience that night didn't yet know that they could be.

10. Isaac is tracing the projects of social theorists to imagine and organize the ideal structures of liberal democracy, including the work of Jürgen Habermas, Seyla Benhabib, Jean Cohen, and Andrew Arato (1998, 10–13).

6. IN THE SOIL

1. Parts of this chapter appeared originally in an article published in *Performance Research* 21 (3), 2016, Taylor and Francis, available online: http://www.tandfonline.com.

2. Casey speaks of the artist's body as the connective tissue that embodies "land" as a metonymic signifier between larger "-scapes"—bounded views seen by viewing bodies—and "works"—constructed entities that encapsulate our perception and imagination of the former (2004, 263-67). Hijikata and Hosoe's *Kamaitachi* and Hijkata's Tohoku imaginary also posit Hijikata's body in as a metonym and metaphor for the artists' root landscape in this manner.

Moreover, Casey argues for the relevance of locally focused, land-conscious art to greater social awareness of environmental and other issues:

This has political and social consequences which we cannot afford to overlook in an age of global capitalism, rampant internationalism, and equally rampant terrorirsm. In this age we need to find, and to valorize, a delimited middle region where place and space, the singular and the universal, earth and world meet and conjoin not only in the specificity of artworks and mapworks . . . but in public actions and social works that are equally sensitive to the specificity of land. (2004, 269)

3. Lawrence Lessig asserts that "nonrivalrous" and its concomitant inverse, "rivalrous," are overly simplistic criteria for comprehending competitive use of common resources (2002). Rather, "what has determined the commons is the character of the resource and how it relates to a community" (2002, 21).

4. Mary Douglas explains the relationship between order and disorder as one of mutuality:

Order implies restriction; from all possible materials, a limited selection has been made and from all possible relations a limited set has been used. So disorder by implication is unlimited, no pattern has been realised in it, but its potential for patterning is indefinite. This is why, though we seek to create order, we do not simply condemn disorder. We recognise that it is destructive to existing patterns; also that it has potentiality. It symbolises both danger and power. (2001, 95)

5. Horton Stallings analyzes "pulp" writer Donald Goines's novels, conversely, as an example of a hip-hop-based, neo-slave narrative form that inherently troubles such distinctions: "Literacy, writing words on paper, simply becomes a means to an end to replace those other unavailable outlets in which the oppressed can express his bondage. In the hip-hop neo-slave narrative, literacy is not simply about learning how to read and write belles lettres, it is about maintaining, rather than coming into, consciousness despite the absence of body" (2003, 189).

6. As Shiva states: "The commodification of biodiversity through patents on life is offered as a solution to the crisis of species extinction driven by the monocultures in which global markets are based. The disease is thus offered as the cure" (2005, 50).

7. I do not mean to assert or imply that Hijikata consciously dedicated himself to the concept of the cultural commons, nor do I assume that he would necessarily publicly support it as such. Again, I am most concerned not with what butoh practice has been but rather what it can be or inspire practitioners and others to become.

8. The cultural commons that is my mind:

Like most early Gen-Xers, I admired Bruce Lee as my first childhood hero of Asian descent.

Fred Astaire, whose films my mother and I watched religiously when I was young, and who was my same height and weight, was my first dance inspiration.

Boogaloo Shrimp moonwalking with a broomstick in the first hip-hop street dance movie, *Breakin'* (1983), and channeling Astaire's coat rack dance from *Royal Wedding* (1950) was my second popping inspiration after Popping Pete in the Talking Heads video, "Crosseyed and Painless" (1981), the first music video to fully incorporate contemporary street dance.

Jimi Hendrix fully reinserting the blues back into rock and roll.

The Kid = Prince in *Purple Rain* (1984), the first R-rated movie I got myself into.

Glenn Gould humming, singing, doing everything when he's not supposed to.

Eric Dolphy. Off-kilter staccato, exactitude, and grace epitomized. Postmodern soul before it existed.

Eihei Dogen, master of the empty room.

9. See William Marotti's book *Money, Trains, and Guillotines: Art and Revolution in 1960s Japan* (2013) for further detail on the connection between this historical moment and key elements of postwar Japanese art history, especially chapter 4, "*The Yomiuri Indépendant*: Making and Displacing History." Marotti also suggests that Hijikata was heavily influenced by *Yomiuri*-centered art experiments (389–90n32).

10. For exploration into historical and popular iterations of this concept, see Alex Kerr, *Finding the Heart Sutra: Guided by a Magician, Art Collector, and Buddhist Sages from Tibet to Japan* (2020).

11. In "Kazedaruma" (1985), Hijikata states: "It's no longer enough simply to be born from the womb. I am reborn again and again. I make such experiments anywhere at all. In the past everyone had a water jar filled with water. I used to slice at the water in the jar with a sickle. 'Stop there, slice!' I would order. How I try somehow to stifle time" (2000, 75).

12. "Although it is Tohoku kabuki, there is a Tohoku in England. The utter darkness exists throughout the world, doesn't it? To think is the dark" (Cited in Kurihara 2000, 21).

13. Similarly, in citing the dangers of an overdefined "collective memory" by Americans after 9/11, Edward Casey argues for wider consideration of the personal in the local—citing the flexibility of Deleuze and Guattari's "local absolute" and "non-limited locality" (1987, 382–83)—in order to foster a "public memory" that is, instead of reactionary, static, and oppositional, rather "never fully and finally made" but "always in the making, giving us to the care and vigilance so often lacking at the site of the initial trauma" (2007, 86).

BIBLIOGRAPHY

PUBLICATIONS

Abe, Kobo. 1962. *Suna no Onna* (Woman in the Dunes). Tokyo: Shinchosha.

———. 1991. *The Woman in the Dunes*. Translated by E. Dale Saunders. New York: Vintage Books.

———. 2003. *The Face of Another*. Translated by E. Dale Saunders. New York: Vintage Books.

Abu-Lughod, Lila. 1991. "Writing Against Culture," in *Recapturing Anthropology: Working in the Present*. Edited by Richard G. Fox. 137–62. Santa Fe: School of American Research Press.

Amagatsu, Ushio, and Watanabe Tamotsu. 2013. "Dialogue between Sankai Juku Artistic Director Ushio Amagatsu and Theatre Critic Tamotsu Watanabe: From Japanese Dance," in *Wochi Kochi Magazine*. 11/15/2013. http://www.wochikochi.jp. Accessed 1/16/2021.

Appadurai, Arjun. 1996. *Modernity at Large: Cultural Dimensions of Globalization*. Minneapolis: University of Minnesota Press.

Arnove, Robert F., and Carlos Alberto Torres. 2003. *Comparative Education: The Dialectic of the Global and Local*. Lanham: Rowman and Littlefield.

Artaud, Antonin. 1958. *The Theatre and its Double*. Translated by Mary Caroline Richards. New York: Grove Press.

Asch, Michael. 2007. "Governmentality, State Culture, and Indigenous Rights," in *Anthropologica* 49 (2): 281–84.

Bachelard, Gaston. 1994. *The Poetics of Space*. Translated by Maria Jolas. Boston: Beacon Press.

Baird, Bruce. 2005. *Buto and the Burden of History: Hijikata Tatsumi and* Nihonjin (Ph.D. dissertation). Philadelphia: University of Pennsylvania, Department of East Asian Languages and Civilizations.

———. 2012. *Hijkata Tatsumi and Butoh: Dancing in a Pool of Gray Grits*. New York: Palgrave Macmillan.

Bakhtin, Mikhail. 1984. *Rabelais and His World*. Translated by Helene Iswolsky. Bloomington: Indiana University Press.

Barthes, Roland. 1972. *Mythologies*. Translated by Annette Lavers. New York: Hill & Wang.

———. 1977. *Roland Barthes by Roland Barthes* (Roland Barthes par Roland Barthes). Translated by Richard Howard. New York: Hill & Wang.
———. 1981. *Camera Lucida*. Translated by Richard Howard. New York: Hill and Wang.
Bataille, Georges. 1962. *Death and Sensuality: A Study of Eroticism and the Taboo*. New York: Walker and Company.
Batchen, Geoffrey. 2009. "Palinode: An Introduction to *Photography Degree Zero*," in *Photography Degree Zero: Reflections on Roland Barthes's* Camera Lucida. Edited by Geoffrey Batchen. 3–30. Cambridge, MA: MIT Press.
Bateson, Gregory. 1972. *Steps to an Ecology of Mind: Collected Essays in Anthropology, Psychiatry, Evolution, and Epistemology*. Northvale and London: Jason Aronson Inc.
Baudrillard, Jean. 1994. *Simulacra and Simulation*. Translated by Sheila Faria Glaser. Ann Arbor: University of Michigan Press.
Bell, Jeffrey A. 2011. "Undoing the Subject: Deleuze and the Making of a Sustainable Life," in *New Directions in Sustainable Design*. Edited by Adrian Parr and Michael Zaretsky. 229–41. London and New York: Routledge.
Benjamin, Walter. 1999. *The Arcades Project*. Edited by Rolf Tiedemann. Translated by Howard Eiland and Kevin McLaughlin. Cambridge and London: The Belknap Press of Harvard University Press.
———. 2019. "The Work of Art in the Age of Mechanical Reproduction," in *Illuminations*. Edited by Hannah Arendt. Translated by Harry Zohn. 166–95. Boston/New York: Mariner Books/Houghton Mifflin Harcourt.
Benkler, Joachim. 2003. "Freedom in the Commons: Towards a Political Economy of Information," in *Duke Law Journal* 52 (6): 1245–76.
Berger, John, and Jean Mohr. 1982. *Another Way of Telling*. New York: Pantheon Books.
Bharucha, Rustom. 1990. *Theatre and the World: Performance and the politics of culture*. New Delhi: Manohar Publications.
Blackwood, Michael, director. 1990. *Butoh: Body on the Edge of Crisis*. Documentary film. Blackwood Productions.
Bogart, Anne. 2001. *A Director Prepares: Seven Essays on Art and Theatre*. New York: Routledge.
Bowers, C. A. 2006. *Revitalizing the Commons: Cultural and Educational Sites of Resistance and Affirmation*. Lanham: Lexington Books.
Bracey, Heyward. 2010. Interview with the author. Los Angeles, CA. 2/1/2010.
Bratspies, Rebecca M. 2006/2007. "The New Discovery Doctrine: Some Thoughts on Property Rights and Traditional Knowledge," in *American Indian Law Review* 31 (2): 315–40.

Brown, Carol. 2010. "Making Spaces, Speaking Spaces," in *The Routledge Dance Studies Reader*, second edition. Edited by Alexandra Carter and Janet O'Shea. 58–72. London and New York: Routledge.

Burns, Lucy Mae San Pablo. 2008. "'Splendid Dancing': Filipino 'Exceptionalism' in Taxi Dance Halls," in *Dance Research Journal* 40 (2): 23–40 (Winter).

Candelario, Rosemary. 2009. Interview with the author. Los Angeles, CA. 10/23/2009.

———. 2016. *Flowers Cracking Concrete: Eiko & Koma's Asian/American Choreographies*. Middletown, CT: Wesleyan University Press.

———. 2019. "'Now we have a passport': Global and Local Butoh" in *The Routledge Companion to Butoh Performance*. Edited by Bruce Baird and Rosemary Candelario. 245–53. London and New York: Routledge.

Cardone, Alissa. 2011. Interview with the author, Los Angeles, CA. 3/14/2011.

Casey, Edward. 2004. "Mapping the Earth in Works of Art," in *Rethinking Nature: Essays in Environmental Philosophy*. Edited by Bruce Foltz and Robert Frodeman. 260–69. Bloomington: Indiana University Press.

———. 2007. "Public Memory in the Making: Ethics and Place in the Wake of 9/11," in *Architecture, Ethics, and the Personhood of Place*. Edited by Gregory Caicco. 69–90. Hanover, NH: University Press of New England.

Centonze, Katja. 2017. "Hijikata Tatsumi's Sabotage of Movement and the Desire to Kill the Ideology of Death," in *Death and Desire in Contemporary Japan: Representing, Practicing, Performing*. Edited by Andrea de Antoni and Massimo Raveri. 203–32. Venezia: Edizioni Ca'Foscari.

Chatterjea, Ananya. 2016. Public workshop at National Performance Network Annual Meeting, Austin, TX. 12/3/2016.

Chang, Jeff. 2005. *Can't Stop Won't Stop: A History of the Hip-Hop Generation*. New York: Picador/St. Martin's Press.

Chey, Chankethya. 2012. Conversation with the author. Los Angeles, CA. 5/1/2012.

Chittick, William C. 1989. *The Sufi Path of Knowledge: Ibn Al-'Arabi's Metaphysics of Imagination*. Albany: State University of New York Press.

Christen, Kimberly. 2005. "Gone Digital: Aboriginal Remix and the Cultural Commons," in *International Journal of Cultural Property* 12: 315–45.

Clifford, James. 1988. *The Predicament of Culture: Twentieth-Century Ethnography, Literature, and Art*. Cambridge and London: Harvard University Press.

Coombe, Rosemary J., and Andrew Herman. 2004. "Rhetorical Virtues: Property, Speech, and the Commons on the World Wide Web," in *Anthropological Quarterly* 77 (3): 559–74 (Summer).

Cosentino, Donald. 2009. Lecture. University of California, Los Angeles. 4/15/2009.

———. 2011. Lecture. University of California, Los Angeles. 1/26/2011.

Cresap, Kelly M. 2004. *Pop Trickster Fool: Warhol Performs Naivete*. Urbana and Chicago: University of Illinois Press.

Cummings, Joe. 2006. *Lanna Rennaisance*. Chiang Mai, Thailand: Dhara Devi Hotel.

De Certeau, Michel. 1984. *The Practice of Everyday Life*. Berkeley: University of California Press.

Debord, Guy. 1970. *Society of the Spectacle*. Translated by Black and Red. Madison, WI, and Detroit: Radical America and Black & Red.

DeKoven, Marianne, ed. 2001. *Feminist Locations: Global and Local, Theory and Practice*. Newark, NJ: Rutgers University Press.

Deleuze, Gilles. 1997. *Critique et Clinique*. Translated by Daniel W. Smith and Michael A. Greco. Minneapolis: University of Minnesota Press.

——— and Félix Guattari. 1987. *A Thousand Plateaus: Capitalism and Schizophrenia*. Translated by Brian Massumi. Minneapolis: University of Minnesota Press.

Derrida, Jacques. 1982. *Positions*. Translated by Alan Bass. Chicago: University of Chicago Press/Phoenix Edition.

———. 1997. *Of Grammatology*. Translated by Gayatri Chakravorty Spivak. Baltimore: Johns Hopkins University Press.

———. 2001. "The Deaths of Roland Barthes," in *The Work of Mourning*. Edited and translated by Pascale-Anna Brault and Michael Naas. 34–67. Chicago and London: University of Chicago Press.

Desierto, Mizu. 2011. Interview with the author via Skype. 3/1/2011.

Dogen, Eihei. 2005. "Longya's 'Thief in an Empty Room,'" in John Daido Loori, *The True Dharma Eye: Zen Master Dogen's Three Hundred Koans*. 265–66. Translated by Kazuaki Tanahashi and John Daido Loori. Boston and London: Shambhala Publications.

Doi, Takeo. 2001. *The Anatomy of Self: The Individual Versus Society*. Oxford: Oxford University Press.

Domon, Ken. 2006. "Photographic Realism and the Salon Picture," in *Setting Sun: Writings by Japanese Photographers*. Edited by Ivan Vartanian, Akihiro Hatanaka, and Yutaka Kambayashi. 22–27. New York: Aperture Foundation.

Dorsey, James. 2001. "Culture, Nationalism, and Sakaguchi Ango," in *Journal of Japanese Studies* 27 (2): 347–79. Seattle: University of Washington.

Douglas, Lawrence. 2007. "The Saddam Hussein Hanging: A Spectacle of

Vengeance," in *Jurist: Legal News and Research*. 1/4/2007. Pittsburgh: University of Pittsburgh Press. http://www.jurist.org. Accessed 1/14/2021.
Douglas, Mary. 2001. *Purity and Danger: An Analysis of the Concepts of Pollution and Taboo*. New York: Routledge.
Dower, John W. 1999. *Embracing Defeat: Japan in the Wake of World War II*. New York: W. W. Norton & Co./The New Press.
Du Bois, W. E. Burghardt. 1903. *The Souls of Black Folk*. Chicago: A. C. McClurg & Co.
Faber, Roland. 2011. "Cultural Symbolizations of a Sustainable Future," in *New Directions in Sustainable Design*. Edited by Adrian Parr and Michael Zaretsky. 242–55. London and New York: Routledge.
Farrell, James Austin. 2009. "The Lanna deception: Interview with Vithi Panichpant," in *Citylife Chiang Mai* 18 (12): pages unknown. http://www.chiangmaicitylife.com. Accessed 1/20/2021.
Fiorentino, Paolo, and Martha Friel, Massimo Marelli, and Walter Santagata. 2010. *Cultural Commons and Cultural Communities: The Case Studies of Milan Designers and Italian Futurists Artists*. Working Paper New Series 2. Torino: Universita di Torino, Dipartimiento di Economia "S. Cognetti de Martiis," International Center for Research on the Economics of Culture, Institutions, and Creativity, Centro Studi Silvia Santagata.
Fisher, C. Tabor. 2008. "Repositioning the Theorist in the Lower Ninth Ward," in *What Is a City?: Rethinking the Urban After Hurricane Katrina*. Edited by Phil Steinberg and Rob Shields. 159–71. Athens: University of Georgia Press.
Fujiwara, Denise. 2018. Email communication with the author. 2/19/2018.
Gallop, Jane, and Dick Blau. 2003. *Living with His Camera*. Durham, NC, and London: Duke University Press.
Garafola, Lynn. 1997. Review of "Yuragi: In a Space of Perpetual Motion," in *Dance Magazine* 71 (3): (March): pages unknown. http://www.thefreelibrary.com. Accessed 1/17/2021.
Genet, Jean. 1949. *Journal du Voleur* (The Thief's Journal). Paris: Éditions Gallimard.
Gluckman, Max. 1963. *Order and Rebellion in Tribal Africa*. London: Cohen and West.
Goldin, Nan. 1995. "Naked City: An Interview with Nobuyoshi Araki by Nan Goldin." *ArtForum* 33 (5) (January): pages unknown. http://www.photobookclub.org. Accessed 3/31/2018.
Goldberg, Greg. 2010. "Rethinking the Public/Virtual Sphere: The problem with participation," in *New Media and Society* 13 (5): 739–54.

Goldman, Michael. Editor. 1998. *Privatizing Nature: Political Struggles for the Global Commons*. London: Pluto Press.

———2006. *Imperial Nature: The World Bank and Struggles for Social Justice in the Age of Globalization*. New Haven, CT: Yale University Press.

Gomez-Peña, Guillermo. 2011. "Theatricalizations of Postcolonial Theory: An Interview with Eduardo Mendieta," in *Conversations Across Borders: A Performance Artist Converses with Theorists, Curators, Activists and Fellow Artists*. Edited by Laura Levin. 107–21. London/New York/Calcutta: Seagull Books.

Grossberg, Lawrence. 1996. "History, Politics and Postmodernism: Stuart Hall and Cultural Studies," in *Stuart Hall: Critical Dialogues in Cultural Studies*. Edited by David Morley and Kuan-Hsing Chen. 151–73. London and New York: Routledge.

Hale, Catherine. 2003. Review of "Kagemi," in *ballet.com* magazine. 6/10/2003.

Harney, Stefano, and Fred Moten. 2013. *The Undercommons: Fugitive Planning and Black Study*. Wivenhoe/New York/Port Watson: Minor Compositions.

Harris, Clare. 2004. "The Photograph Reincarnate," in *Photographs, Objects, Histories: On the Materiality of Images*. Edited by Elizabeth Edwards and Janice Hart, 132–47. New York: Routledge.

Harris, Rennie. 2008. Interview with the author. Los Angeles, CA. 5/21/2008.

———. 2009. Conversation with the author. Los Angeles, CA. 5/15/2009.

Havens, Thomas R. H. 1982. *Artist and Patron in Postwar Japan: Dance, Music, Theater, and the Visual Arts, 1955–1980*. Princeton, NJ: Princeton University Press.

Herron, Elizabeth Carothers. 2009. "Feeling, Art, and Sustainable Civil Society," in *Jung Journal: Culture & Psyche* 3 (4): 112–22.

Hijikata, Tatsumi. 1993. *Hijikata Tatsumi: Three Decades of Butoh Experiment*. Tokyo: Hijikata Tatsumi Memorial Archive, Asbestos-Kan.

———. 2000. "Inner Material/Material," in *The Drama Review* 44 (1): 36–42 (Spring). Translated by Nanako Kurihara.

———. 2000. "To Prison," in *The Drama Review* 44 (1): 43–48 (Spring). Translated by Nanako Kurihara.

———. 2000. "From Being Jealous of a Dog's Vein," in *The Drama Review* 44 (1): 56–59 (Spring). Translated by Nanako Kurihara.

———. 2000. "Wind Daruma," in *The Drama Review* 44 (1): 71–79 (Spring). Translated by Nanako Kurihara.

Hijikata, Tatsumi, Suzuki Tadashi, and Senda Akihiko. 2000. "Fragments of Glass: A Conversation Between Hijikata Tatsumi and Suzuki Tadashi," in *The Drama Review* 44 (1): 62–70 (Spring). Senda Akihiko, moderator. Translated by Nanako Kurihara.

Hirabayashi, Jay. 2010. Interview with the author. Vancouver, Canada. 3/21/2010.

Hoffman, Ethan, and Mark Holborn. 1987. *Buto: Dance of the Dark Soul.* New York: Aperture.

Hollier, Denis. 1992. *Against Architecture.* Translated by Betsy Wing. Cambridge, MA: MIT Press.

Horton Fraleigh, Sondra. 1999. *Dancing into Darkness: Butoh, Zen, and Japan.* Pittsburgh: University of Pittsburgh Press.

Horton Stallings, LaMonda. 2003. "'I'm Goin' Pimp Whores!': The Goines Factor and the Theory of a Hip-Hop Neo-Slave Narrative," in *The New Centennial Review* 3 (3): 175–203 (Fall).

———. 2007. *Mutha' is Half a Word: Intersections of Folklore, Vernacular, Myth, and Queerness in Black Female Culture.* Columbus: Ohio State University Press.

Hosoe, Eikoh. 2010. Interview with the author. Tokyo, Japan, 7/27/2010.

———. 1991. Interview in *Butoh: Piercing the Mask,* film documentary, Richard Moore, director.

———. 2007. "Eikoh Hosoe: Subject Matter," in PEN America #3: Tribes. PEN American Center. https://pen.org/subject-matter. Accessed 1/14/2021.

Hultkrantz, Åke. 1997. "Theories on the North American Trickster," in *ACTA Americana* 5 (2): 5–24.

Hyde, Lewis. 1998. *Trickster Makes This World.* New York: North Point Press.

———. 2010. *Common As Air.* New York: Farrar, Strauss, and Giroux.

Inata, Naomi. 2019. Interview with the author. Tokyo, Japan. 5/6/2019.

Iova-Koga, Shinichi. 2011. Interview with the author via Skype. 2/27/2011.

Igarashi, Yoshikuni. 2012. *Bodies of Memory: Narratives of War in Postwar Japanese Culture, 1945-1970.* Princeton, NJ: Princeton University Press.

Isaac, Jeffrey C. 1998. *Democracy in Dark Times.* Ithaca, NY: Cornell University Press.

Ishii, Tatsuro. 2011. Interview with the author. Tokyo, Japan. 10/10/2011.

Ishimoto, Kae. 2019. Interview with the author via Skype. 3/29/2019.

Itoh, Kim. 2010. Interview with the author. Tokyo, Japan. 7/25/2010.

Ivey, Bill. 2009. "Expressive life and the public interest," in *Expressive Lives,* Demos Collection 27. Edited by Samuel Jones. 23–33. London: Demos.

Kahn, Paul Genki. 2007. Lecture at Zen Center of Los Angeles, CA. July 2007.

Kaminer, Tahl. 2011. *Architecture, Crisis, and Resuscitation: The Reproduction of Post-Fordism in Late-Twentieth-Century Architecture.* Milton Park, UK: Routledge.

Kan, Katsura. 2009. Interview with the author. Los Angeles, CA. 11/15/2009.

Kaneko, Ryuichi, and Ivan Vartanian. 2009. *Japanese Photobooks of the 1960s and '70s*. New York: Aperture.

Kasai, Akira. 2009. Interview with the author. Translator unknown. Tokyo, Japan. 8/5/2009.

Kato, M. T. 2007. *From Kung Fu to Hip-Hop: Globalization, Revolution, and Popular Culture.* Albany: State University of New York Press.

Kay, Jill Boyce, and Helen Wood, eds. 2020. *Cultural Commons*, in *European Journal of Cultural Studies*. https://journals.sagepub.com/page/ecs/collections/covid-19. Accessed 5/24/2021.

Kelley, Robin D. G. 2017. "Coates and West in Jackson," in *Boston Review*, 12/22/2017. http://bostonreview.net. Accessed 1/14/2021.

Kerr, Alex. 2020. *Finding the Heart Sutra: Guided by a Magician, Art Collector, and Buddhist Sages from Tibet to Japan.* London: Random House Penguin/Allen Lane.

Klein, Naomi. 2007. *The Shock Doctrine: The Rise of Disaster Capitalism.* New York: Picador.

Klein, Susan Blakeley. 1988. *Ankoku Buto: The Premodern and Postmodern Influences on the Dance of Utter Darkness*. Ithaca, NY: Cornell University Press.

Koresky, Michael. 2008. "Eclipse Series 13: Kenji Mizoguchi's Fallen Women," in *The Current*. The Criterion Collection. https://www.criterion.com. Accessed 1/14/2021.

Koschmann, J. Victor. 1996. *Revolution and Subjectivity in Postwar Japan.* Chicago: University of Chicago Press.

Kristeva, Julia. 1982. *Powers of Horror: An Essay on Abjection.* Translated by Leon S. Rudiez. New York: Columbia University Press.

Kuppers, Petra. 2001. "The Survival of the Aura," in *Benjamin's Blind Spot: Walter Benjamin and the Premature Death of Aura*. Edited by Lise Patt. 37–41. Los Angeles: Institute of Cultural Inquiry.

Kurihara, Nanako. 1996. *The Most Remote Thing in the Universe: Critical Analysis of Hijikata Tatsumi's Butoh Dance* (Ph.D. dissertation). New York: New York University Department of Performance Studies.

———. 2000. "The Words of Butoh," in *The Drama Review* 44 (1): 12–28 (Spring).

Laage, Joan (Kogut). 2011. Interview with the author. Seattle, WA. 6/7/2011.

Lacan, Jacques. 2004. Écrits*: A Selection*. Translated by Bruce Fink. New York: W. W. Norton & Company.

Leitner, Helga, Jamie Peck, and Eric Sheppard, eds. 2006. *Contesting Neoliberalism: Urban Frontiers*. New York: Guilford Press.

Lessig, Lawrence. 2001. *The Future of Ideas: The Fate of the Commons in a Connected World*. New York: Random House.

Levi-Strauss, Claude. 1955. "The Structural Study of Myth," in *Journal of American Folklore* 68 (270): 428–44 (October–December).

Linfield, Susie. 2010. *The Cruel Radiance: Photography and Political Violence*. Chicago and London: University of Chicago Press.

Lionnet, Francoise, and Shu-Mei Shih, eds. 2005. *Minor Transnationalism*. Durham, NC: Duke University Press.

Lippard, Lucy. 1998. *The Lure of the Local*. New York: The New Press.

Loesch, Alenka. 2011. Interview with the author via Skype. 3/31/2011.

Loori, John Daido. 2005. *The True Dharma Eye: Zen Master Dogen's Three Hundred Koans*. Translated by Kazuaki Tanahashi and John Daido Loori. Boston and London: Shambhala Publications.

Lorde, Audre. 2007. *Sister Outsider*. New York: Crossing Press.

Maeda, Fujio, Watanabe Yohko, Morishita Takashi, and Homma Yu, eds. 2009. *Hijikata Tatsumi's* Rebellion of the Body*: Imagery and Documents of Butoh 1968*. Tokyo: Research Center for the Arts and Art Administration, Keio University.

Maezumi, Taizan, and Bernie Glassman, eds. 2002. *On Zen Practice: Body, Breath, and Mind*. Somerville, MA: Wisdom Publications.

Marchenkov, Vladimir. 2008. "The Dialectic of the Serious and Ludic in Myth and Art," in *Beauty's Appeal: Measure and Excess, Analecta Husserliana: The Yearbook of Phenomenological Research* 97: 173-182. Edited by Anna-Teresa Tymieniecka.

Marcus, Greil. 2001. *The Old, Weird America: The World of Bob Dylan's Basement Tapes.* New York: Picador, 2001.

———. 2005. *Like a Rolling Stone: Bob Dylan at the Crossroads*. New York: Public Affairs.

Marotti, William. 2006. "Political Aesthetics: Activism, Everyday Life, and Art's Object in 1960s' Japan," in *Inter-Asia Cultural Studies* 7 (4): 606–18.

———. 2013. *Money, Trains, and Guillotines: Art and Revolution in 1960s Japan*. Durham, NC, and London: Duke University Press.

Marra, Michele, ed. 2002. *Modern Japanese Aesthetics: A Reader*. Manoa: University of Hawaii Press.

Martinez, D. P., ed. 1998. *The Worlds of Japanese Popular Culture: Gender, Shifting Boundaries, and Global Cultures*. Cambridge: Cambridge University Press.

Mavor, Carol. 2012. *Black and Blue: The Bruising Passion of* Camera Lucida, La Jetée, Sans soleil, *and* Hiroshima Mon Amour. Durham, NC, and London: Duke University Press.

McCann, Anthony. 2001. "All That Is Not Given Is Lost: Irish Traditional Music, Copyright, and Common Property," in *Ethnomusicology* 45 (1): 89–106 (Winter).

McMorrough, John. 2009. "Design for the Apocalypse," in *Bootleg Edition Urban China*. New York: C-Lab/Columbia University. Unpaginated.

Mikami, Kayo. 2016. *The Body as a Vessel: Approaching the Methodology of Hijikata Tatsumi's Ankoku Buotō*. Translated by Rosa van Hensbergen. Birchington, UK: Ozaru Books/BJ Translations.

Miller, Paul D. (aka DJ Spooky, That Subliminal Kid). 2004. *Rhythm Science*. Cambridge, MA: MIT Press.

Mishima, Yukio. 1987. "Kiki no Buyou, Dance of Crisis," in *Buto: Dance of the Dark Soul*. Edited by Michael E. Hoffman and Mark Holborn. New York: Aperture Foundation. Originally published in *Dance Experience*, Hijikata Tatsumi and Hosoe Eikoh (1960).

Mitchell, W. J. T., and Sheng Anfang. 2010. "Reading the Image World? Playing with Pictures? Looking beyond words and pictures? An Interview with Professor W. J. T. Mitchell by Sheng Anfang." Beijing: Tsinghua University. https://lucian.uchicago.edu/blogs/wjtmitchell. Accessed 1/15/2021.

Mitra, Royona. 2015. *Akram Khan: Dancing New Interculturalism*. London: Palgrave Macmillan.

Morgan, David. 1999. *Visual Piety: A Theory and History of Popular Religious Images*. Berkeley: University of California Press.

Morishita, Takashi. 2015. *Hijikata Tatsumi's Notational Butoh: An Innovative Method for Butoh Creation*. Tokyo: Keio University Art Center.

Moten, Fred. 2003. *In the Break: The Aesthetics of the Black Radical Tradition*. Minneapolis and London: University of Minnesota Press.

Mouffe, Chantal. 2000. *The Democratic Paradox*. London and New York: Verso Books.

Muñoz, José Esteban. 2009. *Cruising Utopia: The Then and There of Queer Futurity*. New York and London: New York University Press.

Murobushi, Ko. 2012. Interview with the author. Los Angeles, CA. 4/28/2012.

Naggar, Carole. 2001. "The Costume of the Soul: Eikoh Hosoe's Photographs of Butoh Dancer Kazuo Ohno," in *Aperture* 165: 54–64 (Winter).

Nakajima, Natsu. 2011. Interview with the author. Tokyo, Japan. 10/10/2011.

Nguyên, Nguyễn. 2012. Conversation with the author, Los Angeles, CA. 8/1/2012.

Nicely, Megan. 2010. Email correspondence with the author. 2/1/2010.

Nora, Pierre. 1989. "Between Memory and History: *Les Lieux de Memoire*." Translated by Marc Roudebush. *Representations* 26: 7–24 (Spring).

Oe, Kenzaburo. 1969. *A Personal Matter*. Translated by John Nathan. New York: Grove Press.

Oguri, Naoyuki. 2010. Interview with the author. Los Angeles, CA. 2/21/2010.

Ohno, Kazuo, and Yoshito Ohno. 2004. *Kazuo Ohno's World: from without & within*. Translated by John Barrett. Middletown, CT: Wesleyan University Press.

Ohno, Yoshito. 2010. Interview with the author. Translated by Kae Ishimoto. Yokohama, Japan. 8/14/2010.

Okada, Takahiko. 2009. "Hijikata Tatsumi Butoh Performance," in *Hijikata Tatsumi's* Rebellion of the Body*: Imagery and Documents of Butoh 1968*. Edited by Maeda Fujio, Watanabe Yohko, Morishita Takashi, and Homma Yu. 57. Tokyo: Research Center for the Arts and Art Administration, Keio University.

Onozuka, Makoto. 2011. Interview with the author. Translated by Izumi Kuribayashi. Tokyo, Japan. 10/20/2011.

Oshima, Nagisa. Undated. "How to Die in the 1970s," essay in the DVD, *Tokyo senso sengo hiwa* (The War of Tokyo: Postwar Confidential).

Owomoyela, Oyekan. 1997. *Yoruba Trickster Tales*. Lincoln: University of Nebraska Press.

Parr, Adrian. 2011. "Art, Politics, and Climate Change," in *New Directions in Sustainable Design*. Edited by Adrian Parr and Michael Zaretsky. 6–12. London and New York: Routledge.

Parr, Adrian and Michael Zaretsky, eds. 2011. *New Directions in Sustainable Design*. London and New York: Routledge.

Plumwood, Val. 2006. "The Concept of a Cultural Landscape: Nature, Culture, and Agency in the Land," in *Ethics and the Environment* 11 (2): 115–50 (Fall–Winter).

Price, Charles, Donald Nonini, and Erich Fox Tree. 2008. "Grounded Utopian Movements: Subjects of Neglect," in *Anthropological Quarterly*, 81 (1): 127–59 (Winter).

Renciére, Jacques. 2006. *The Politics of Aesthetics: The Distribution of the Sensible*. Translated by Gabriel Rockhill. London: Continuum.

Reed, Christopher Robert. 1999. "The Black Presence at 'White City': African and African American Participation at the World's Columbian Exposition, Chicago, May 1, 1893–October 31, 1893." World's Columbian Exposition Website. Paul V. Galvin Library. Illinois Institute of Technology. 3/8/1999.

Richie, Donald. 2005. *The Japan Journals: 1947–2004*. Edited by Leza Lowitz. Berkeley, CA: Stone Bridge Press.

Ridgely, Steven C. 2011. *Japanese Counterculture: The Antiestablishment Art of Terayama Shuji*. Minneapolis: University of Minnesota Press.

Roberts, Allen F., and Mary Nooter Roberts. 2003. *A Saint in the City: Sufi Arts and Urban Senegal*. Los Angeles: UCLA Fowler Museum of Cultural History.

Saghafi, Kas. 2010. *Apparitions—Of Derrida's Other*. New York: Fordham University Press.

Sakabe, Megumi. 2002. "Mask and Shadow in Japanese Culture: Implicit Ontology in Japanese Thought," in *Modern Japanese Aesthetics: A Reader*. Edited by Michelle Marra. 242–50. Manoa: University of Hawaii Press.

Sakaguchi, Ango. 2011. "A Personal View of Japanese Culture (Nihon Buka Shikan)," in *The Columbia Anthology of Modern Japanese Literature*. Translated by James Dorsey and edited by J. Thomas Rimer. 434–46. New York: Columbia University Press.

Sakamoto, Michael. 2016. "Soil: Crisis, the cultural commons and performing South-east Asia in America," in *Performance Research* 21 (3): 103–14. Reprinted by permission of the publisher, Taylor & Francis.

Sakurai, Keisuke. 1998. "Butoh—The Dance as Body: An Introduction to the Study of Butoh-ology," in *Butoh-Kaden* (DVD). Yukio Waguri & Kohzensha/JUSTSYSTEM.

Samuels, Shayna. 1999. Review of "Hiyomeki," in *Dance Magazine* (November): pages unknown. http://www.thefreelibrary.com. Accessed 5/16/2021.

Santos, Alessandra. 2009. Email correspondence with the author. 10/23/2009.

Sas, Miryam. 2011. *Experimental Arts in Postwar Japan: Moments of Encounter, Engagement, and Imagined Return*. Cambridge, MA, and London: Harvard University Press.

Schechner, Richard. 1982. *Between Theater and Anthropology*. Philadelphia: University of Pennsylvania Press.

———. 2006. "Towards a Poetics of Performance," in *Performance Theory*. Edited by Richard Schechner. 170–210. New York: Routledge.

Schleitwiler, Vince. 2017. *Strange Fruit of the Black Pacific*. New York: New York University Press.

Shiva, Vandana. 2005. *Earth Democracy*. Cambridge, MA: South End Press.

Silverberg, Miriam. 2009. *Erotic Grotesque Nonsense: The Mass Culture of Japanese Modern Times*. Berkeley: University of California Press.

Sirisook, Waewdao. 2012. Interview with the author, Los Angeles, CA. 7/12/2012.

Sontag, Susan. 1978. *On Photography*. Toronto: McGraw-Hill Ryerson.

———. 2003. *Regarding the Pain of Others*. New York: Picador.

Sorgenfrei, Carol Fisher. 2005. *Unspeakable Acts*. Manoa: University of Hawaii Press.

Spivak, Gayatri. 1999. *A Critique of Postcolonial Reason: Toward a History of the Vanishing.* Cambridge, MA: Harvard University Press.

———. 2012. "Development," in *Political Concepts* 1 (4.1). http://www.politicalconcepts.org. Accessed 1/18/2021.

Takiguchi, Shuzo. 2009. "Kamaitachi: Toward a Vacuum's Nest," in *Kamaitachi.* Translated by Connie Prener. Unpaginated. New York: Aperture Foundation.

Tamano, Hiroko. 2010. Interview with the author. San Francisco, CA. 6/21/2010.

Tanaka, Min. 2006. Interview in *THEME Magazine* 7 (Fall). http://www.min-tanaka.com. Accessed 1/15/2021.

———. 2009. Interview with the author. Hakushu, Japan. 8/16/2009.

Tanigawa Atsushi, and Waguri Yukio. 1998. "Around Butoh-Fu," in *Butoh-Kaden* (DVD). Yukio Waguri & Kohzensha/JUSTSYSTEM.

Tanizaki, Junichiro. 1977. *In Praise of Shadows.* Translated by Thomas J. Harper and Edward G. Seidensticker. Stony Creek, CT: Leete's Island Books.

Thoms, Victoria. 2008. "Martha Graham's Haunting Body: Autobiography at the Intersection of Writing and Dancing," in *Dance Research Journal* 40 (1): 3–16 (Summer).

Tomatsu, Shomei. 2006. "Toward a Chaotic Sea," in *Setting Sun: Writings by Japanese Photographers.* Edited by Ivan Vartanian, Akihiro Hatanaka, and Yutaka Kanbayashi. 30–33. New York: Aperture.

Tomé, Lester. 2017. "Swans in Sugarcane Fields: Proletarian Ballet Dancers and the Cuban Revolution's Industrious New Man," in *Dance Research Journal* 49 (2): 4–20 (August).

Tone, Yasunao. 2009. "The Balloon that Ate the Wind and Went Away," in *Hijikata Tatsumi's* Rebellion of the Body*: Imagery and Documents of Butoh 1968.* Edited by Maeda Fujio, Watanabe Yohko, Morishita Takashi, and Homma Yu. 56. Tokyo: Research Center for the Arts and Art Administration, Keio University.

Trischak, Evamaria. 1999. ". . . dogme 95," in *cinetext: film and philosophy.* Edited by Robert Blanchet and Horst Tellioğlu. Vienna: Department of Philosophy, University of Vienna.

Trucco, Terry. 1984. "Dancers Who Probe the Dark Corners of the Mind," in *New York Times,* 10/28/1984.

Tuan, Yi-Fu. 2001. *Space and Place: The Perspective of Experience.* Minneapolis: University of Minnesota Press.

Turner, Victor W. 1980. "Social Dramas and Stories about Them," in *Critical Inquiry* 7 (1): 141–68 (Autumn).

———. 1982. *From Ritual to Theater*. New York: Performing Arts Journal Press.
———. 1985. On *the Edge of the Bush: Anthropology as Experience*. Edited by Edith L. B. Turner. Tucson: University of Arizona Press.
Ueno, Chizuko. 2005. "In the Feminine Guise: A Trap of Reverse Orientalism," in *Contemporary Japanese Thought*. Edited by Richard Calichman, 225–62. New York: Columbia University Press.
Van Gennep, Arnold. 2004. *The Rites of Passage*. Translated by Monika B. Vizedom and Gabrielle L. Caffee. New York: Psychology Press.
Vartanian, Ivan, Akihiro Hatanaka, and Yutaka Kanbayashi, eds. 2006. *Setting Sun: Writings by Japanese Photographers*. New York: Aperture.
Viala, Jean, and Nourit Masson-Sekine. 1988. *Butoh: Shades of Darkness*. Tokyo: Shufunomoto Co.
Waguri, Yukio. 1998. *Butoh-Kaden* (DVD). Tokyo: Yukio Waguri & Kohzensha/JUSTSYSTEM.
Weber, Max. 1991. *From Max Weber: Essays in Sociology*. Translated and edited by Hans Heinrich Gerth and Charles Wright Mills. New York: Psychology Press.
West, Cornel. 2004. *Democracy Matters*. New York: Penguin Books.
White, Bob W. 1999. "Modernity's Trickster: 'Dipping' and 'Throwing' in Congolese Popular Dance Music," in *Research in African Literatures* 30 (4): 156–75 (Winter).
Wigley, Mark. 1993. *The Architecture of Deconstruction: Derrida's Haunt*. Cambridge, MA: MIT Press.
———. 2009. "Space in Crisis," in *Bootleg Edition Urban China*. Unpaginated. New York: C-Lab/Columbia University.
Yoshida, Kyoko. 2006. "A Conversation with Ushio Amagatsu, Artistic Director of Sankai Juku," in *Fourth Wall*. Translated by Kyoko Yoshida. http://www.walker.org. Accessed 1/16/2021.
Yoshioka, Yumiko. 2019. Interview with the author via Skype. 4/4/2019.
Zizek, Slavoj. 1997. "Desire: Drive=Truth: Knowledge." http://www.lacan.com/zizek-desire.htm. Accessed 1/14/2021.

FILMS

Dunn, Cheryl, director. 2013. *Everybody Street*. 83 min. Los Angeles/New York/Portland: Alldayeveryday.
Imamura, Shohei, director. 1961. *Buta to Gunkan* (Pigs and Battleships). 108 min. Tokyo: Nikkatsu.
Ishii, Teruo. 1968. *Edogawa Rampo Zenshū: Kyoufu Kikei Ningen* (Horrors of Malformed Men). 1968. Tokyo: Toei Studios.

Mizoguchi, Kenzo, director. 1948. *Yoru no Onnatachi* (Women of the Night). 74 min. Tokyo: Shochiku.

Oppenheimer, Joshua, director. 2012. *The Act of Killing*. 117 min. Copenhagen: Final Cut for Real DK.

Oshima, Nagisa. Director. 1960. *Seshun Zankoku Monogatari* (Cruel Story of Youth). 96 min. Tokyo: Shochiku.

———. Director. 1969. *Shinjuku Dorobo Nikki* (Diary of a Shinjuku Thief). 94 min. Tokyo: Sozo-Sha.

———. Director. 1970. Tokyo *Senso Sengo Hiwa* (The War of Tokyo: Postwar Confidential; additional English title: The Man Who Left His Will on Film). 94 min. Tokyo: Sozosha and Japan Art Theater Guild.

Pennebaker, D. A., director. 1967. *Don't Look Back*. 96 min. Leacock-Pennebaker Co.

Scorsese, Martin, director. 2005. *No Direction Home*. DVD. 2005; Paramount Home Entertainment.

Susumu, Hani. 1968. *Hatsukoi: Jigoku-hen* (Nanami: The Inferno of First Love). 108 min. Tokyo: Hani Productions.

Terayama, Shuji, director. 1974. *Death in the Country*. 104 min.

Teshigahara, Hiroshi, director. 1966. *Tanin no Kao* (The Face of Another). 124 min. Tokyo: Toho Eiga Co.

Velez, Edin, director. 1989. *Dance of Darkness*. 58 min. New York and Paris: WNET and La Sept.

Workman, Chuck, director. 1998. *The Life and Times of Andy Warhol: Superstar*. DVD. Shout Factory Theater.

PHOTOGRAPHY

Araki, Nobuyoshi. 1971. *Sentimental Journey*. Tokyo: Self-published.

———. 1991. *Sentimental Journey/Winter Journey*. Tokyo: Shinchosha Company.

Fukase, Masahisa. 2009. *Masahisa Fukase*. Paris: Éditions Xavier Barral.

Hosoe, Eikoh. 1961. *Otoko to Onna* (Man and Woman). Tokyo: Camerart.

———. 1963. *Barakei* (Ordeal by Roses). Tokyo: Shueisha.

———. 1971. *Embrace*. Tokyo: Shashin Hyoron-Sha.

———. 2009. *Kamaitachi*. New York: Aperture Foundation.

Li, Zhensheng. 2003. *Red-Color News Soldier*. London: Phaidon.

Moriyama, Daido. 1968. *Nippon Gekijo Shashincho* (Japanese Theatre). Tokyo: Muromachi-Shobo.

———. 2009. *1965–1970: Magazine Work*. Tokyo: Getsuyosha.

Rudoff, John. 2008. "Baez—Dylan 1963 Aug 3rd 3," on artist website.

Uploaded 12/23/2008. https://www.flickr.com/photos/johnrudoff/sets/72157611490418013. Accessed 1/14/2021.
Tomatsu, Shomei. 2004. *Shomei Tomatsu: Skin of the Nation*. New Haven, CT, and London: San Francisco Museum of Modern Art in Association with Yale University Press.

PERFORMANCES

Amagatsu, Ushio, choreographer, performer. 1980. *Kinkan Shonen*. Tokyo/Paris: Sankai Juku. Excerpt: https://www.youtube.com/watch?v=uguhzP2BHl4. Accessed 1/15/2021.
Brook, Peter, director. 1985. *The Mahabharata*. Written by Jean-Claude Carrière. Premiered at Festival d'Avignon, Avignon, France, 7/7/1985.
Hijikata, Tatsumi. Choreographer, performer. 1959. *Kinjiki* (Forbidden Colors). Premiered at Daiichi Seimei Hall, Tokyo, Japan, 5/24/1959.
———. Choreographer, performer. 1968. *Hijikata Tatsumi to Nihonjin: Nikutai no Hanran* (Hijikata Tatsumi and the Japanese: Revolt of the Flesh). Premiered at Nippon Seinenkan, Tokyo, Japan, 10/9/1968.
Ohno, Kazuo. Performer. 1977. *Admiring La Argentina*. Choreographed by Hijikata Tatsumi. Premiered at Daiichi Seimei Hall, Tokyo, Japan, 11/1/1977.
———. Choreographer, performer. 1981. *My Mother*. Premiered at Daiichi Seimei Hall, Tokyo, Japan, 1/23/1981.
Sakamoto, Michael. Choreographer, performer. 2011. *Tsuchi* (orig. *Soil*). Premiered at the Seattle Butoh Festival, 6/4/2011.
———. Choreographer, performer. 2011. *Flash Mixtape*. Premiered at the Nyoba Kan Butoh Fest, Kuala Lumpur, Malaysia, 12/2/2011.
———. Co-writer, co-choreographer, co-director, video artist. 2015. *Flash*. Premiered at Colorado College, Colorado Springs, CO, 9/12/2015.
———. Writer, director, choreographer, filmmaker, performer. 2014. *blind spot*. Work-in-progress performance at Bangkok Art and Culture Center, Bangkok, Thailand, 10/11/2014.
———. Director, filmmaker, co-writer, co-choreographer. 2017. *Soil*. Premiered at Hancher Performances, Iowa City, IA, 2/2017.
Terayama, Shuji. 1969. *Inugami* (The Dog-God). Premiered at Theater am Turm, Frankfurt, Germany, 6/3/1969.
———. Writer, director. 1967. *Aomori-ken no Semushi Otoko* (The Hunchback of Aomori). Premiere location and date unknown.

SOUND RECORDINGS

Smith, Harry. Producer. 1952. *Anthology of American Folk Music*. Six-disc LP set. Washington D.C.: Folkways.

INDEX

ABOUT THE AUTHOR

Michael Sakamoto is an artist, scholar, educator, and curator active in dance theater, photography, media, and culture. His work has been presented in fifteen countries throughout Asia, Europe, and North America. His scholarship has appeared in journals and anthologies from Routledge, Taylor and Francis, Palgrave Macmillan, and other publishers. He is former Assistant Professor in Dance at the University of Iowa and former Co-Program Director of the MFA in Interdisciplinary Arts Program at Goddard College. He currently serves as Performing Arts Curator and Director of the Asian and Asian American Arts and Culture Program at the University of Massachusetts-Amherst Fine Arts Center.